The De Stijl Environment

The MIT Press   Cambridge, Massachusetts, and London, England

The De Stijl Environment

Nancy J. Troy

Color plates provided through a grant from
the Graham Foundation for Advanced
Studies in the Fine Arts.

This book was set in Futura
by The MIT Press Computergraphics
Department
and printed and bound by Halliday Lithograph in the United States of America.

Library of Congress Cataloging in
Publication Data

Troy, Nancy J.
   The De Stijl environment.

   Includes bibliography and index.
   1. Neoplasticism. 2. *Stijl* (periodical)—
Influence. 3. Art, Modern—20th century—
Netherlands. I. Title.
N6948.5.S8T7   1983
709'.492   82-12517
ISBN 0-262-20046-5

Contents

Acknowledgments

This book is the culmination of an interest in De Stijl that began when I worked for several summers at the Solomon R. Guggenheim Museum under the guidance of three inspiring curators and scholars: Margit Rowell, Angelica Rudenstine, and Louise Averill Svendsen. Subsequently, under the direction of John Paoletti, I wrote an undergraduate thesis on Mondrian and a number of his American followers. I am grateful to those who encouraged my early efforts and to Alan Shestack, director of the Yale University Art Gallery, who later entrusted me with the organization of an exhibition devoted to Mondrian and Neo-Plasticism in America. But without doubt I owe the greatest debt of gratitude to my graduate advisor and friend at Yale, Robert L. Herbert, whose concern for every aspect of my research and writing manifested itself time and again.

Many scholars of De Stijl were especially generous in sharing knowledge, experience, and the fruits of their own research. In particular, Robert P. Welsh gave much time and careful attention to reviewing a series of manuscript drafts; the book has benefited immeasurably from his comments and suggestions. I am also tremendously thankful to Joop Joosten and Herbert Henkels, not only for their continued assistance with matters of research but also for their enthusiastic support in countless discussions of the material that forms the subject of this book. Others in Holland, including Hans L. C. Jaffé, Fons Asselbergs, Carel Blotkamp, Manfred Bock, Kees Broos, Wim van Dam, Jean Leering, Frank den Oudsten, Joop Smid, and Evert van Straaten, assisted me in various essential ways while graciously tolerating my less-than-perfect Dutch. I am similarly grateful to Luellin Bienert, Max Bill, Lucy Del Marle-Leyden, Cesar Domela, Cornelis van Eesteren, G. A. van de Groenekan, Harry Holtzman, André Kertesz, Mrs. Annie Oud-Dinaux, Mrs. Truus Schröder, and Michel Seuphor as well as the many other artists and collectors, and their friends and families, who gave time and energy to reminiscences of people and events long past. Without their insights and recollections it would not have been possible to trace the history of the De Stijl environment. And were it not for a Fulbright-Hays Fellowship and additional support from The Johns Hopkins University, I could not have spent sufficient time in Holland to carry this project out.

I express my deep appreciation to the directors and staffs of the Fondation Custodia, Institut Néerlandais, Paris; the Nederlands Documentatiecentrum voor de Bouwkunst, Amsterdam; and the Dienst Verspreide Rijkskollekties and the Rijksbureau voor Kunsthistorische Documentatie, The Hague. They not only permitted access to important archival resources but also gave freely of their time.

I am particularly grateful to the Graham Foundation for Advanced Studies in the Fine Arts for providing a subvention that made it possible to include color reproductions in this volume.

Numerous colleagues and friends offered invaluable advice and support at crucial stages in the progress of this study. Brenda Richardson, Victoria Kahn, and Michael Fried contributed substantial editorial help, which was supplemented in important ways by the staff of The MIT Press. Elizabeth Carroll typed several versions of the manuscript. Yve-Alain Bois, whose enthusiasm for De Stijl has been a constant inspiration, gave generously of his profound knowledge of De Stijl and related subjects. To Mildred Friedman, Anne van der Jagt, Rosalind Krauss, Clark Poling, Danielle Rice, Helen Searing, David Solkin, and many others I have failed to mention I extend my heartfelt thanks.

Finally, I shall always be grateful to my family for their constant understanding—perhaps best manifested by the foresight of my parents in choosing a reproduction of a painting by Mondrian with which to embellish my childhood surroundings. To Wim de Wit I express very special thanks for the concrete assistance, support, and encouragement that gave direction to my wanderings through what might otherwise have been an extremely abstract environment.

The De Stijl Environment

Introduction: Contextual Considerations

■ 2

The date of birth of De Stijl *has been established exactly. The introduction to the first number of the periodical, written by van Doesburg, bears the date June 16th, 1917. And with the first number of this small, unobtrusive monthly, "De Stijl" presents itself to the world as a closed whole, a dynamic and revolutionary movement.*
Hans L. C. Jaffé[1]

Although Theo van Doesburg tried always to present De Stijl as a homogeneous entity, the artists who contributed to the periodical *De Stijl*, founded by van Doesburg in Holland in 1917, consistently maintained their individual and often divergent interests. They neither formed an official De Stijl organization nor ceased to develop their own distinctive attitudes and artistic modes of expression. The term "De Stijl," first of all the title of a journal, was chosen for its allusion to what the contributors hoped to set out in the pages of the review: a single stylistic credo to which they all could subscribe. Only later did the name become attached to the group of artists responsible for the material published in the magazine.

It may have been inevitable that De Stijl would become inextricably connected in the public mind with the work of its most important theorist and painter, Piet Mondrian. Mondrian's paintings have rightly been considered paradigmatic of the style of De Stijl, and it may therefore seem surprising that he chose a different, far more awkward name—Neo-Plasticism—for his aesthetic philosophy. Although *plastic* in the sense of formative or shaping appears frequently in the writings of several De Stijl artists,[2] Mondrian was the only one for whom it may be said to have retained a consistent meaning, though in his case too it was defined in relation to a constantly evolving style. Although Mondrian's Neo-Plastic paintings had a profound influence on every De Stijl painter, and on several architects as well, the way in which other artists modified his style—sometimes to the point of denying basic tenets of Neo-Plasticism—were critically important in the evolution of De Stijl from the moment of its inception.

The retrospective view of J. J. P. Oud's early projects and Gerrit Rietveld's Schröder House as characteristic examples of De Stijl architecture has had similar consequences. The tendency to see De Stijl in terms of the nascent International Style often leads to neglect of the facts that Oud's most advanced work of the late teens and early twenties was never carried out and that Rietveld's exceptional design was not executed until 1924. A number of important structures that were built in the early period by De Stijl architects, Oud included, bear scant resemblance to the generally held conception of the stylistic characteristics of De Stijl. This again points up an urgent need to reexamine the assumption that De Stijl consistuted a homogeneous entity, a coherent movement.

In fact, De Stijl can be understood as a movement only insofar as it was loosely based upon the working together of architects, painters, sculptors, and other artists who shared a common set of ethical and aesthetic principles at one time or another between 1917 and 1932, when the last issue of *De Stijl* was published. The dynamic character of De Stijl is most clearly reflected in the products of collaborative relationships, especially those between painters and architects, rather than in the pioneering abstract paintings or the architecture alone.

While many scholars have explored the isolated spheres of De Stijl painting and architecture, little attention has been directed to an equally characteristic product of De Stijl creative activity: the painted abstract environment, in which pure color, free of all figurative associations, was merged with modern architecture to form an encompassing, total work of art. From 1916 on, artists associated with De Stijl participated jointly in the design and execution of dozens of environmental projects, particularly interiors, which had as their aim the union of the arts in a constructive harmony that would herald a radically new postwar society.

De Stijl artists designed a great variety of abstract environments. Their work included coloristic projects destined not only for private houses but also for public spaces such as cafés and a university hall. Furthermore, their ateliers often functioned simultaneously as private dwellings and quasi-public exhibition spaces. Formal exhibitions also provided a locus for design activity, as did the theatrical stage. In such situations it was possible to realize a temporary setting that could serve as a microcosm of the larger environment—the city, in particular. It was especially the modern urban environment that the De Stijl artists hoped would one day be transformed into an abstract, aesthetically balanced composition reflecting the new social era they envisioned.

Dutch artists were not alone in exploring the possibility of merging the arts to form an abstract environment. This was the goal toward which the German Expressionist Bruno Taut directed his executed works and his writings during and after the First World War. Although different in many crucial respects, the De Stijl artists were like Taut in viewing their most abstract designs as proposals for the future, when a new kind of harmonious environment would be needed to reflect a reintegrated social structure.[3] El Lissitzky's concept of Proun (an acronym for the Russian *Pro Unovis*—projects for the affirmation of the new) as a station or point on a continuum that begins with painting and ends with the construction of a new form of utopian architecture has much in common with the ideas of the De Stijl artists, and many exchanges of influence are reflected in their work. Similarly, Kurt Schwitters's Merzbau, which appears to have been conceived in a Dada spirit that monumentalized chaotic confusion and which on its surface seems so different from the products of De Stijl sensibility, was in fact a manifestation of a desire to join art and life that was fundamental to almost every ambitious mode of artistic expression in the early 1920s. Both Schwitters and Lissitzky were active participants in certain aspects of De Stijl. Lissitzky published in the magazine, while Schwitters was joined by van Doesburg, and on occasion by another De Stijl artist, Vilmos Huszar, in a Dada tour of Holland in 1923. Schwitters also devoted the first issue of his own journal, *Merz*, to the subject of Dada in Holland.

It is not always easy to understand how De Stijl could have forged strong links with Dada and Constructivism. That it did so, however, is crucial to an appreciation of the central role played by De Stijl in the early 1920s. Traditional considerations of De Stijl in terms of Mondrian's Neo-Plastic painting or the roots of International Style architecture have too often prevented us from recognizing the need, for instance, to incorporate van Doesburg's Dada activities in a broad perspective that acknowledges his attempts to replace the early expressionist orientation of the Bauhaus with a greater regard for the principles of Constructivism. In fact, De Stijl can be seen as just one forum among many in which van Doesburg sought to promote his conception of the total work of art, the work embracing all of modern life. Even the fact that De Stijl defined itself in the pages of what might be

called a propaganda organ suggests its inherently expansive nature, its aspiration to extend far beyond both aesthetic limitations and national boundaries in order to join the disparate arts and to unite artists throughout Europe, Russia, the United States, and eventually the entire world.

In addition to assuming this international perspective, it is necessary to place the coloristic architecture of De Stijl, and the abstract interior in particular, in their proper historical context as the culmination of late-nineteenth-century aspirations for a synthetic environment. Despite the obvious stylistic differences, De Stijl environments shared at least one fundamental characteristic with those produced by Arts and Crafts and Art Nouveau designers several decades earlier: Like William Morris and Henry van de Velde, for example, the De Stijl artists considered that the harmonious environment reflected the process of its creation—that the working together of architects, painters, and craftsmen implied the reintegration of their roles in society as a whole. The environment was thus endowed not only with aesthetic value but also with moral integrity, because the means of achieving it—the collaborative effort itself—was understood to be a reflection of sound social and working conditions.

There were, however, detractors who warned against the domination such a totally harmonious environment might exercise over its inhabitants. In 1900 Adolf Loos satirized "the poor rich man" whose house is built as a work of art by an architect who has designed every detail, leaving no room for individual expression, growth, or change on the part of the occupant, who consequently finds himself imprisoned in an unlivable museum.[4] Similarly, Hermann Muthesius complained that what was being done at the Darmstadt Artists'

Colony was "just as much an artist's art as painting." Muthesius explained his objections: "Just as one buys pictures or sculpture, one buys . . . furnished rooms. . . . These interiors cannot be that felt arrangement of our personal environment they ought to be. They are foreign intrusions to which the occupant has to adapt instead of their adapting to him."[5]

Muthesius's criticism of the total design concept was later to be leveled against several De Stijl environments. The attitude of the De Stijl artists differed from that of Muthesius, who stressed the functional aspect of design and who eventually identified this as the link between an outmoded handicraft tradition and the principles of modern industrial design. He saw in exactness, simplicity, and regularity the fundamentals of form that mediated between the artistic demands of handicraft and the functional demands of industrial production. By placing primary emphasis on design types rather than hand execution, Muthesius initiated a trend toward rational functionalism that called into question the aesthetic bias that, while no longer associated with handicraft, continued to be essential to the De Stijl enterprise. Although the notion of designing for industrial production was often invoked by De Stijl artists, it was rarely allowed to determine the basic character of their work. Formal considerations almost invariably took precedence, and industry was exhorted to find a means of carrying out the results.

The importance attached to formal issues weighted the De Stijl scale of values in a manner significantly different from that of the Bauhaus, for example, but De Stijl environmental designs need to be distinguished as well from the basically superficial stylization characteristic of the Maison Cubiste, a *projet d'hôtel* designed by a group of French artists for the Paris Salon d'Automne in 1912. The Cubist artists involved in that project wanted to combine their efforts in order to create a modern style of architectural and interior design that, far from being revolutionary, would be adaptable to the traditional French mode of living—hence the evocation of earlier French stylistic forms in the facade and the arrangement of a *salon bourgeois* as the principal room exhibited in the *hôtel*, itself a bourgeois type of dwelling.[6]

The attitude of the De Stijl artists was in many ways antithetical to the attitude that had inspired the Maison Cubiste, and the roots of their abstract environments lay elsewhere: in the emphasis on modern design as an avant-garde means of social change. Their refusal to adapt to national traditions or the demands of an existing social structure was a posture similar to the one assumed by the first generation of Italian Futurists. However, by insisting on an uncompromisingly severe stylistic purity, the De Stijl artists sought to preserve the primacy of aesthetic principles, which they considered to be morally justifiable as agents of social reform in their own right. Thus the formal purity of De Stijl architectural and interior designs demanded adjustment on the part of the occupant and, in an environmental context, change in society as a whole.

The colored abstract environments of De Stijl must be viewed with these considerations in mind. Each individual project should be seen not only as a product of the particular situation that gave rise to it but also as an expression of a goal that virtually every advanced artist active in the period after the First World War held dear: to work through the arts to achieve an ideal future when all the walls that separate men would be broken down and when society would be truly integrated and capable of constructing a utopian urban environment of abstract forms. That this goal was indeed almost universal again points up the importance of De Stijl's environmental concerns, especially within their historical context. Thus, not only are the projects that are the focus of this volume crucial to any comprehensive assessment of De Stijl itself; they also shed light on the attitudes and activities of a wide range of contemporary artists who pursued aims analogous, if not in every case identical, to those of De Stijl.

This study is not intended to offer an exhaustive examination of every environmental project produced in the late teens and the twenties. However, while focusing attention on De Stijl projects, it may also provide insights into the work of artists, architects, and designers who were not intimately associated with De Stijl. It should, for example, enable the reader to recognize those characteristics that made De Stijl environments different in a fundamental sense not only from the abstract interiors of Lissitzky and Schwitters but also from the functionally oriented designs of the Bauhaus or those of Le Corbusier. Furthermore, it is my hope that this study, because it minimizes the distinctions between media that are all too often made to play a determining role in the history of art, will be seen to have certain methodological implications for the consideration of the art of the post–World War I period. The painting and the architecture of the late teens and early twenties have too often been treated separately rather than as dual aspects of a synthetic approach to formal creation. The same might be said of film and typography, and indeed of literature, music, and dance. De Stijl

artists were active in all these areas, and the broad scope of their interests was common among their contemporaries. Moreover, monographs on the work of individual artists and studies devoted to isolated collaborative projects are by nature circumscribed and so cannot provide a fully integrated examination of widespread environmental concerns. Thus the literature that deals specifically with the topic of the abstract environment has remained fragmentary and diffuse.

It is the special object of this book to demonstrate that the De Stijl artists' achievement of a coloristic architecture was the result of a process of collaboration that was constantly in flux, changing over time in a manner that reflected the different backgrounds as well as the changing interests and relationships of the artists involved. I will argue that the history of De Stijl as a whole can best be understood through a study of the collaborative efforts that produced so many of the environmental designs I shall be examining. From this perspective the shapes of individual projects become explicable in terms of the ways in which like-minded painters and architects sought to combine their respective arts. I will show that an evolution occurred from environments in which color played a discrete and architecturally predetermined role to ones in which color and architecture had equally expressive spatial values that were merged in abstract harmony. I will suggest that this evolution not only indicates an ever closer relationship between the arts but also signifies a change in the working relationships among De Stijl artists.

In light of these considerations, the history of De Stijl abstract environments, and by extension that of De Stijl itself, can be divided into three roughly defined periods. The first period, from 1916–17 until about 1921, is characterized by collaborations in which architect and painter played essentially different roles; the painter was subordinate, in practice if not in theory, to the architect. The second phase, which lasted until the mid-1920s, began after many attempts at collaboration according to these premises had broken down; it is marked by the increasingly assertive role of the painter, who personally or through the form of his contribution demanded authority equal to or even exceeding that of the architect in determining spatial design. Although the collaborative ideal was never absolutely repudiated, this evolution eventually ended in the disavowal of the efficacy of collaborative work. In this third and final phase (if one can call it that), architects and painters became alienated from one another; the architects emphasized the purely functional value of their work and often prohibited color altogether, while the painters used color almost exclusively, disregarding physical structure, to arrive at an abstract conception of space divorced from just those kinds of realities upon which architects were insisting.

For painters, the environment came to assume an abstract character not simply because its forms lacked reference to historical styles or figurative content, but also because it embodied a revolt against—an abstraction from—existing conditions that architects felt duty-bound to confront. Unwilling to collaborate and unable to agree upon a means of achieving the many aims they still had in common, painters and architects were able to join only in a more generalized call for collectivity, in the shared hope that their social and aesthetic goals would one day be realized on an environmental scale.

1 Early Collaborations: Their Premises and Results

Intensive collaboration can have a profound effect on many different kinds of undertakings, even when it has not been a conscious goal of the people involved. The character of a magazine, for example, always depends in part upon the working relationship established between the editor and the contributors. The publication *De Stijl* represents a special phenomenon because it was intended to express an aesthetic point of view—visually proclaimed through the typography on its cover—that was shared by artists working in a variety of media. The potential for collaboration among painters, sculptors, architects, and designers was implicit in the task of promulgating a common artistic credo, and was discussed in the pages of the magazine from the start.

Of the artists who joined Theo van Doesburg in founding *De Stijl* in 1917,[1] Bart van der Leck was the first to articulate a well-defined concept of collaborative work, one based upon his experience during the 1890s in several stained-glass ateliers where he was trained in applied art. In 1893 van der Leck met P. J. C. Klaarhamer, a furniture maker and architect influenced by the ideas of William Morris and Walter Crane. Klaarhamer was to have a profound influence not only on van der Leck but also on Gerrit Rietveld and several others who eventually became contributors to *De Stijl*. Often overlooked, Klaarhamer's presence in the background of De Stijl is important because it establishes a firm link between De Stijl and the English Arts and Crafts tradition. That this tradition gained momentum in The Netherlands during the 1890s is demonstrated by the establishment in 1898 of an atelier-showroom in The Hague called—in English—Arts and Crafts. From its inception, Arts and Crafts was heavily influenced by Henry van de Velde, whose Belgian interpretation of the English movement thus became conspicuous in The Hague. As a result The Hague functioned as a center in Holland for the development of what has come to be known as the Art Nouveau style. In Amsterdam, however, other forces were at work, particularly in the person of H. P. Berlage. Berlage was vehemently opposed to the Art Nouveau orientation of Arts and Crafts on the grounds that it placed excessive emphasis on superficial ornament at the expense of material and constructive integrity. But he too was inspired by some of Morris's ideas, and in 1900 he was instrumental in establishing a rival workshop and showroom, 't Binnenhuis (the interior). Within only a few years 't Binnenhuis began to supersede Arts and Crafts as the focal point of Dutch activity and interest in the applied arts, particularly as they related to one another in the interior as a whole.[2]

In certain respects 't Binnenhuis was similar to Klaarhamer's office in Utrecht. Because of Klaarhamer's relatively advanced thinking, it was at first difficult for him to obtain commissions as an architect, and he therefore concentrated on furniture design. In his capacity as a designer, however, Klaarhamer was in a position to help van der Leck by commissioning him to devise color schemes and fabrics for furniture.[3] As a result of this activity, in 1904 van der Leck published an article on Klaarhamer's furniture in which he had an opportunity to discuss his own ideas about design and applied art. Echoing the Morris-derived attitude of his mentor, van der Leck called for "a striving motivated by forthright honesty, prudently expressed, well conceived, without affectation or rhetoric—in a word, inspired." "The result," he said, would "have an element of eternal beauty in it."[4]

Although van der Leck's artistic horizons broadened considerably after 1905, he maintained close ties with Klaarhamer, whose Utrecht studio he shared between 1911 and 1915. It was during those years that Gerrit Rietveld, already an independent furniture maker with his own workshop in Utrecht, attended evening courses taught by Klaarhamer, who introduced him to van der Leck. In 1915 Rietveld built several pieces of furniture that Klaarhamer had designed. About the same time, Klaarhamer and van der Leck met Rob van 't Hoff, a young Dutch architect who had studied in England from 1906 to 1914. Having read about the work of Frank Lloyd Wright, van 't Hoff became fascinated by the American architect, whom he was able to meet while traveling in the United States in 1914. When he returned to Holland the next year, van 't Hoff designed two houses in Huis ter Heide, near Utrecht, that strongly resembled the architecture of Wright. The houses were completed in 1916, and two years later the owners of one of them asked Rietveld to copy some of Wright's furniture for the interior. When the imitations were shown to van 't Hoff, he asked who had made them and subsequently introduced himself to Rietveld.[5]

These events demonstrate that the work of Frank Lloyd Wright was well known and much respected by the architects and designers who came into contact with one another through Klaarhamer in the mid-teens. Morever, in November–December 1911, three years before van 't Hoff, Berlage had already been to the United States, where he too was impressed by Wright's work. Berlage must have transmitted his admiration to J. J. P. Oud and Jan Wils, two De Stijl architects with whom he was closely associated in the teens. However, that virtually all the De Stijl architects acknowledged Wright in this period as an important kindred spirit, and occasionally even copied his work, does not mean that Wright played a dominant role in the evolution of De Stijl architecture in general. As Auke van der Woud has pointed out, the architecture of De Stijl developed within a rich and complex European cultural context, and although Wright's example helped certain young architects to find a form for their ideas, his importance for De Stijl should not be emphasized to the exclusion of other influences—not only painters, but also architects, including Josef Hoffmann, J. L. Mathieu Lauweriks, Adolf Loos, Joseph Maria Olbrich, Charles F. A. Voysey, and, in particular, H. P. Berlage.[6] Similarly, although Wright's treatment of interior design was obviously appreciated, it served as only one of many precedents for the totally unified approach to the subject that developed in The Netherlands. To the extent that Wright's designs for furniture, stained glass windows, lighting fixtures, and other objects of applied art embodied an attempt to make a given interior into an environment that harmonized with his architecture as a whole, he was no different from most of his advanced contemporaries at the turn of the century. Moreover, like that of Charles Rennie Mackintosh, much of Wright's applied design work, particularly his early stained glass windows, involved a repetition of geometric motifs that constituted a decorative arrangement of forms—something the De Stijl artists were especially anxious to avoid. Although geometric and abstract, the windows later designed by De Stijl artists bear only a superficial similarity to Wright's. The stained glass work of Theo van Doesburg and Vilmos Huszar, as well as that of van der Leck,

must be understood in the context of their easel paintings, in which these artists were attempting to achieve a monumental style suited for architecture and yet divorced from the decorative solutions characteristic of Wright's work. This is demonstrated by van der Leck, who, while still closely associated with Klaarhamer, began to develop a monumental easel-painting style and at the same time to establish new contacts that led to commissions from large commercial firms in Holland.

As early as 1912, van der Leck made paintings in which a simplified, almost primitive figurative image was placed against a stark white background that suggested a direct relationship between the work of art and the wall surface on which it hung. In the following year he began to experiment with materials, such as casein and asbestos cement, that made the connection between his easel paintings and the wall surface more explicit. While mixing his pigments with architectural materials, he also continued to simplify and flatten his painterly style in order to conform to the planar character of the wall. Thus van der Leck was producing art suitable for placement within an architectural context even before he began work on an important mural commission from an insurance company in 1913. Van der Leck's sketches were eventually rejected, and his two mural designs were never carried out, but he wrote to the art critic and pedagogue H. P. Bremmer (who had helped him secure the commission) that he enjoyed working on the project. He liked the fact that it involved dealing with a specific space provided by an architect. In such commissions van der Leck saw a kind of nobility that he associated with collaborative work.[7]

1 Bart van der Leck, *Window with Mine Scenes*, 1916, stained glass, 370 × 210 cm. Rijksmuseum Kröller-Müller, Otterlo.

Bremmer, who was aware of van der Leck's desire to collaborate with other artists (or at least to define his painterly style in the context of architecture), was in a position to promote his work. In 1913 he arranged for van der Leck's first one-man show. Shortly thereafter he introduced the artist to the Kröller family, and as a result van der Leck was asked to design and execute a large stained glass window (figure 1) for a staircase in the main office of the family's mining and shipping firm, Wm. H. Müller & Co., in The Hague. As part of his preparation for this task, van der Leck traveled through Algeria and Spain, inspecting the activities of the company and making numerous sketches upon which he would base the figural stained glass window as well as other designs and easel paintings he was to produce during the next few years. After the window was completed, van der Leck was hired as a color consultant to the building department of Müller & Co. In this capacity he came into almost daily contact with Berlage, who had also been hired under an exclusive contract to work for the Müller firm and the Kröller family. Van der Leck contributed color schemes for glazed-brick walls and a mosaic ceiling to Holland House, the London office of Müller & Co. designed by Berlage, as well as color schemes for rooms in several family houses with which Berlage was also involved. It was through his working relationship with Berlage that van der Leck's concepts of the role of color in architecture and of the collaboration between painter and architect matured.

Van der Leck's connections with Berlage extended at least as far back as 1905, when he dedicated a twenty-three-page essay on glass painting to the architect, who was well known and highly respected in advanced circles for his Amsterdam Stock Exchange of 1898–1903. Van der Leck's article was never published, but he sent a copy of it along with several drawings to Berlage, whose criticism he took very seriously even then. Berlage found van der Leck's work retardataire, too much in imitation of Romanesque and Gothic art, noting also that in the article on glass painting van der Leck himself had called for a break with the styles of earlier periods.[8] Thus, from the beginning, van der Leck's relationship with Berlage was not an easy one. Nevertheless, Berlage had been in a position to support the nomination of van der Leck for the mural commission of 1913, and he was also present when van der Leck first went to The Hague to discuss plans for the Müller & Co. stained glass window. In 1916 the two were asked to work together on renovations in the home of the director of Müller & Co., Anthony Kröller, whose wife Helene was in the process of assembling an important collection of modern art.

Because it sheds light on van der Leck's collaboration with Berlage, it is worthwhile to outline the prehistory of this commission, starting in 1910, when the Kröllers had planned to build a home in Wassenaar. At that time Bremmer, acting as Mrs. Kröller's art advisor, suggested that the couple engage an "artist-architect" who would be able to carry out Mrs. Kröller's desire not only for a well-constructed and aesthetically pleasing structure but also for "a philosophy of life to be expressed in the building."[9] The commission was initially given to Peter Behrens in 1911, but neither his designs nor those of his associate Ludwig Mies van der Rohe were accepted by the Kröllers, who in the interim had decided to build a much larger house where Mrs. Kröller could display her growing art collection. When plans made by Berlage in

1913 were also rejected, the parcel of land was sold.[10] The Kröllers decided instead to remain in Huize ten Vijfer, their home at that time, which they began to redecorate along modern lines with the help of van der Leck in 1914.

At Huize ten Vijfer, van der Leck was responsible for making new color schemes for everything from walls and floors to tablecloths and even a heater. From his correspondence with Mrs. Kröller it is known that he used strong, bright colors, not exclusively primary but limited to an only slightly broader scale. As R. W. D. Oxenaar has remarked, the colors "must have played a striking and spatially determining role in the interior. . . . Loose planes of color were not yet applied to the walls of Huize ten Vijfer, but the effect of what van der Leck did actually do there quickly brought [such] ideas to mind."[11] This work prepared van der Leck to design color schemes for Berlage's renovation of Groot Haesebroek, another home in Wassenaar that the Kröllers purchased in 1916. According to Oxenaar,

It was van der Leck's task to apply color to virtually everything that needs to be repainted when new inhabitants move into an old house, and he very soon found this to be excessive. It was work that he no longer found satisfying. He wrote to Mrs. Kröller, "—and now I would like to suggest, if you permit, that I no longer do this kind of work, i.e., paint old houses. If it involved a modern work, or a room in which something specfic needs doing, then I would be glad to do it, but to be this kind of master house painter—I have absolutely no desire for it."[12]

Nonetheless, Mrs. Kröller was able to prevail upon van der Leck to produce a color scheme for her Art Room at Groot Haesebroek, an interior specially designed for art courses conducted by Bremmer in the Kröller home. Berlage was responsible for the architectural details as well as the furniture of the room, including three high vitrine cabinets and a large oval table and accompanying chairs (Rijksmuseum Kröller-Müller, Otterlo). This was precisely the kind of commission van der Leck had always hoped to obtain, but the collaboration with Berlage proved to be far more difficult than he anticipated.

The design of the Art Room required the incorporation of van der Leck's notion of modern monumental painting in an interior to which it was not easily adapted. The architectural details and furniture designed by Berlage left hardly any room for van der Leck to apply colors in an appropriately free manner—which he was developing simultaneously in mural-size pictures such as *Mine Triptych* (Gemeentemuseum, The Hague) and *Work at the Docks* (Rijksmuseum Kröller-Müller, Otterlo), both of 1916, and in the *Donkey Riders* series,[13] completed in 1917. Nonetheless, Oxenaar finds van der Leck's design ''not decoratively ornamenting but spatially activating.''[14]

Van der Leck's gouache drawing (figure 2), an exploded-box plan dated [19]16–17, provides an idea of his intended color scheme for the large, rectangular Art Room. The walls of the interior were to be mostly white, with a band of red running around the top, close to the ceiling, and underneath that a thinner strip of blue. A white wall-to-wall carpet covered the floor, in the center of which van der Leck placed a smaller rug consisting of a black rectangle surrounded by red and blue bands. Bright blue fabric covered the chairs, and for the table van der Leck sketched in the upper right a white cloth accented with bars of red, blue, brown, and black. As Oxenaar notes,

. . . the carpet, the small accents of color in the white table-cloth, and the blue chair coverings made the table into a true center of attention for the courses [Bremmer was to conduct in the room]. It would have been a light, cheerful interior, not simply with painted walls, but with a total consideration of color in space; as envisioned, it was forceful but also functional and liveable. The conception was still somewhat static and symmetrical, but for just that reason it functioned well in the given architecture.[15]

Van der Leck's color applications respected the structural divisions inherent in Berlage's remodeling of the interior architecture. Color was restricted to surfaces defined by architectonic considerations of ceiling, floor, door, individual wall surfaces, and so on. For example, the white portion of each wall plane was separated from those adjacent to it by a thin line of black. The band of red near the ceiling was broken in such a way that the divisions echoed the placement of the cabinets below, and the height of the black plinth was also determined by the structure of the vitrines Berlage had designed.

Van der Leck's notion of color in architecture was based on the premise that the painter and the architect perform essentially different functions in creating a harmonious interior and that their respective contributions should not infringe on each other. He saw his role as that of a monumental painter and color designer applying color to interiors in which structural details should be neutral. This neutrality would provide a broad field for the painter, who in turn would contribute color schemes that would accent the constructive elements of a given architectural space. The collaborative effort he envisioned demanded restraint in the working relationship between painter and architect. In the in-

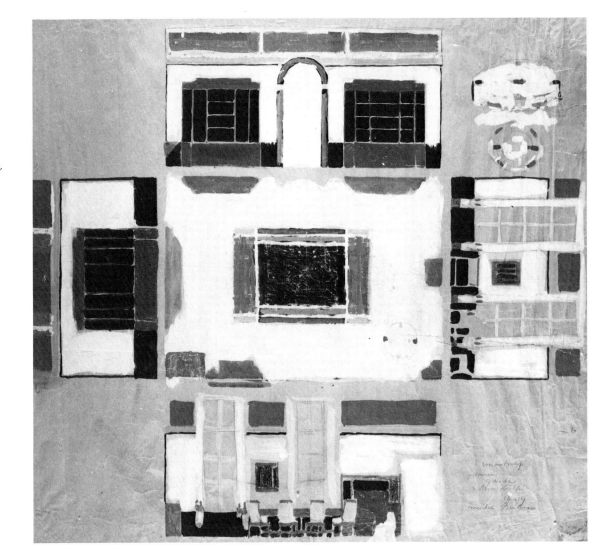

2 Bart van der Leck, *Color Study for Art Room, Groot Haesebroek, Wassenaar*, 1916–17, gouache on paper, 70 × 77 cm. Rijksmuseum Kröller-Müller, Otterlo.

terior for Mrs. Kröller, however, Berlage's contribution seemed far too imposing. Thus the collaboration presented van der Leck with what he felt was an insurmountable problem: the obstinate determination of the architect to control every aspect of any space he designed. In a letter to Mrs. Kröller, van der Leck complained bitterly:

As long as the architect holds fast to his high priesthood, and his parochial leadership is not superseded by a broader vision—and because of this situation the opposition of architecture and painting knows no bounds—the architect will endeavor to work in all areas of the arts, which seems dilettantish with respect to his architectural concerns. But he will naturally be very content with whatever it is because it remains subordinate to his architecture. Not until a more modern view has developed, in which all the arts have equal value, can the consequences of this principle have an influence on the position of the arts in architecture. Only then will a unity come about, not through subordination of one art to another, but through equal independence.[16]

It was principally as a result of his collaboration with Berlage, and in reaction against Berlage's view of architecture as the supreme art to which all the others must submit, that van der Leck developed and refined his own attitude toward the relationship between painting and architecture. He spelled out his rejection of the painter-colorist's subordinate role in two closely related articles published in *De Stijl*, the first in October 1917 and the second in February 1918.[17] In his view, architecture, as distinguished from building, was nothing more or less than the joining together of all the separate, independent arts, each expressed purely according to its elementary means. Van der Leck believed that the essence of architecture was its collaborative nature, which Ber-

lage had threatened by overstepping the solely constructive domain of the builder, supplying furniture so imposing in scale that it impinged upon other aspects of spatial design, such as the application of color, which belonged in the painter's sphere. Although he recognized that "painting always needs a flat surface and it will always remain its ultimate ambition to make use of the necessary, practical plane created by architecture," van der Leck also felt that painting had its own history, its own laws and definitions, and that insofar as it had "developed independently, apart from architecture" it required an expertise that only the painter and not the architect could provide:

Regarding painting, we must say to the architects and engineers: become and remain architects and give up your attempts at painting. . . . If the architect does this, a great deal will devolve from him, but opportunities for work and development will, on the other hand, accrue to various related arts. The applied arts concerned will then develop out of modern plastic painting. Modern plastic painting has not been created by architectural concepts, not as an extension of building and construction. On the contrary, it has arrived at its simplified creation of space via free painting from the life.

Van der Leck was eager to demonstrate that, although modern painting was concerned with constructive principles and dependent upon the wall surface for its literal support, historically and formally it was fundamentally different from architecture. To reinforce his argument that the painter and architect must sustain one another, each providing essentially different contributions to the unified work of art, he listed five characteristics that distinguish painting from architecture:

1. Modern painting is destruction of the plasticism of nature, as opposed to the plastic, natural, constructional character of architecture.
2. Modern painting is open, as opposed to the connective, closed character of architecture.
3. Modern painting provides color and space, as opposed to the lack of color and the flatness of the planes of architecture.
4. Modern painting is plastic expression in spatial flatness: extension as opposed to the limitation architecture imposes on space with its planes.
5. Modern painting is plastic equilibrium, as opposed to the constructional equilibrium (load and support) of architecture.

In these definitive points van der Leck suggested that painting and architecture are intrinsically opposite means of expression, and on this basis he concluded that neither architect nor painter ought to attempt to practice the other's trade. Instead each should confine his work to his own sphere and collaborate to produce the complete work of art: " . . . architecture is created through the growing together and interlocking of various independent arts which do not go beyond their own domains." Modern painting, van der Leck felt, had already reached the level of elemental purity at which it was prepared to be subsumed in the architectural whole; the task of the architect, whose product was formally less advanced, was "to carry his work through to that degree of purity whereby it of itself becomes capable of accepting one of the arts that are distinct from it."

The two texts from which the above quotations have been cited provide abundant evidence of van der Leck's negative attitude toward the architectural practice of his time. His experience with Berlage led him to conclude that, at least insofar as Berlage was representative of the profession, most

architects had not yet reached a level of stylistic purity equal to that already achieved by painters. Van der Leck saw the domination of the architect over the painter as a direct result of this formal inequality. He therefore wanted to guard against the potential threat involved when a painter would be asked to contribute a color scheme to an interior being designed at the same time by an architect who, like Berlage, saw himself as master of the space he created. Van der Leck's aversion to architects in general became so strong that in 1917, as soon as he discovered that several were involved with the newly established De Stijl, he immediately broke all ties with the magazine. As he related to Michel Seuphor,

After a long discussion [with Theo van Doesburg in 1916–17], we agreed on the usefulness of founding an art review without any architects on it. It was to be edited solely by painters, and be directed against the architects, that is, against their meddling with color, which should be the business of the painter. This would at last put things in the right place: to each his own skill. We were entirely in agreement on that score. But when the first issue appeared, there were several architects among the contributors. This was precisely the opposite of what we had agreed to. No one had tipped me off. I was just shown the "fait accompli," like that. That couldn't go on: I immediately resigned.[18]

Van der Leck's remarks are interesting not only because they shed light on his motives for leaving De Stijl almost immediately after its inception but also because they suggest that Theo van Doesburg, editor of the magazine and foremost propagandist for its principles, shared at least some of van der Leck's opinions about the part color ought to play in architecture and the respective roles of the painter and the architect. The concurrence of their ideas is not surprising in view of the fact that in his easel paintings of this period van Doesburg was directly indebted to van der Leck's style of late 1916.[19] Furthermore, both artists had been conditioned by their activities within the realm of applied art, where the role of the artist involved the treatment of individual objects or surfaces destined for a specific location within a larger context. Indeed, the influence of van der Leck's interior color schemes can be seen in those produced by van Doesburg slightly later, in 1917–18.

Van Doesburg's color designs were not made in collaboration with Berlage, but they did involve two architects closely associated with him: Jan Wils and J. J. P. Oud. Wils worked in Berlage's office between 1914 and 1916, and Oud, who had already established himself as an independent architect by 1913, was friendly with Berlage. It was through Berlage that Wils and Oud first met, and in their architectural designs, at least until 1917, they were both strongly influenced by the older architect. In 1917, when Berlage was in the employ of Müller & Co. and therefore unable to accept a commission to build a Sunday and holiday retreat for the Leiden Volkshuis (community center), he arranged for it to be passed along to his younger protégé, Oud.

The Leiden Volkshuis, a social center for working people, particularly young women employed in local factories, was established in 1899 on the model of London's Toynbee Hall. The driving force behind the Volkshuis was Emilie C. Knappert, a friend of Berlage who, like him, came from a wealthy bourgeois family and also had developed liberal social ideas. She was an activist involved in a variety of causes similar to those espoused by Jane Addams, who had established Hull House in Chicago ten years earlier. As the membership of the Volkshuis grew after the turn of the century, the scope of its activities broadened beyond those of a clubhouse to include trips to the countryside on the outskirts of Leiden, where working women were encouraged to enjoy fresh air and exercise. In 1911 an association was established to solicit funds for a permanent vacation house, but not until the war was nearly over was a site for this purpose purchased, near the shore in Noordwijkerhout. Oud's designs date from 1917, but the house, called De Vonk (the spark), was not officially opened until February 8, 1919.[20]

The exterior of De Vonk (figure 3), with its simple brickwork and strict symmetry, attests to Berlage's continuing influence on Oud. In 1920 Jan Gratama faulted the exterior for "not drawing attention" and for seeming "completely ordinary."[21] However, Gunther Stamm has recently noted in it a "striving for equilibrium between vertical and horizontal." According to Stamm, "the horizontal lines in plinth, balcony, and parts of the roof, indeed even in the window arrangement, form an opposition to the unbroken vertical lines in the wings."[22] In these elements Stamm finds evidence of Oud's first attempts at incorporating De Stijl aesthetics into architecture. Three glazed brick mosaics above and on either side of the front door are also evidence of Oud's link to De Stijl. The mosaics, as well as the tile floors and the colors of the doors in the interior, were designed by Theo van Doesburg, whom Oud had met in Leiden in the spring of 1916. During that year Oud had designed a house for W. de Geus, the mayor of Broek in Waterland, a small town just north of Amsterdam; van Doesburg contributed a stained

3 J. J. P. Oud, *De Vonk, Noordwijkerhout,*
1917–18. Illustrated in *Klei* 12 (1920): 16.

glass window depicting a swan, the town's emblem. De Vonk, however, represents the first large-scale collaborative effort between Oud and van Doesburg to create an environment in which color and architecture worked harmoniously. As early as June 1, 1916, in a letter to Oud, van Doesburg had expressed his eagerness to participate in such a project:

For the pure revelation of painting, what is necessary in the first place is an atmosphere. And who is in a better position to bring this atmosphere into being than the architect? . . .

. . . we are in need of a new interior. And who brings the new interior about? The Architect. Therefore we must do business with the architect and fight with him to achieve a spiritual equilibrium. . . . Thus it should not surprise you that I very much desire a collaboration with you. Around our realized emotions you can create a space, an atmosphere, which shall do justice to our artistic expression, we can bring your emotion, realized in space and atmosphere, to its full independence precisely through our coloristic and formal projects.[23]

In relation to De Vonk, Hans Jaffé has stated, ''This collaboration succeeded in realizing a counterpoint composition, indicating the way for a logical and independent collaboration of the two branches of art on the same basis and according to the same principles, that is to say, toward a new style.''[24] But it is important to understand that the collaboration between Oud and van Doesburg was based on certain premises that limited the placement of color to architecturally defined surfaces. The painter's contribution, however stylistically advanced for its time, was once again subordinate to the architect's prerogatives in determining the character of the spaces involved.

Van Doesburg's mosaics around the entrance to De Vonk (figure 4) were each composed of blue, green, yellow, black, and white glazed bricks arranged in a nonfigurative design corresponding to the style of his easel paintings of about the same period. The three designs function much like separate paintings, but they are framed by and themselves help to frame the architectural elements of the facade. It is clear that in using brick in nearly symmetrical arrangements—the two lateral designs are almost mirror images of one another—van Doesburg intended to integrate the mosaics with the materials and with the symmetrical design of the architecture, thus contributing to the monumental effect of the central entrance area. Each mosaic was composed according to a modular system derived from the materials; the length of the largest brick was three times that of the smallest. In the interior, the muted-yellow, white, and black floor tiles were also composed on a grid pattern, which van Doesburg introduced in his easel paintings in 1918 and 1919.

Van Doesburg's treatment of color in the interior of De Vonk was similarly related directly to elements of construction, not only in the tile floors but also in the doors. Here the structural components were highlighted by giving each a different tone. In the hall on the first floor above ground level (figure 5), the ten doors were treated in this manner. Each was painted in a different sequence of black, white, and gray, with the exception of the doors to the rooms of the directress. Van Doesburg indicated the special significance of these doors, which opened into centrally located rooms with a balcony over the front entrance, by painting them in opposite arrangements of black and white only.

4 Theo van Doesburg, *Three Glazed-Brick Mo-saics, De Vonk, Noordwijkerhout*, 1917–18. Il-lustrated in *Klei* 12 (1920): 17.

5 Theo van Doesburg, *Color Applications, First Floor Hall, De Vonk*, 1918. Photograph: Nederlands Documentatiecentrum voor de Bouwkunst, Amsterdam.

In "Aanteekeningen over monumentale kunst" (notes on monumental art), published in *De Stijl* in November 1918 as a commentary on the interior design of De Vonk, van Doesburg discussed his current view of the cooperative relationship between the arts. Like van der Leck, who had by then severed his connections with *De Stijl* as a result of his more vehement attitude in this regard, van Doesburg believed that a collaborative effort involved a division of labor among professionals. Each artist must limit himself to his own field of technical competence, contributing designs composed only with means appropriate to that field: "Each art, architecture, painting or sculpture, requires the whole man. Only when this is again realized, as in antiquity, will a development towards a monumental architecture, towards style, be possible. When that happens, the concept of applied art will also automatically disappear, as will every example of one art being subservient to another."[25] Van Doesburg expressed much the same idea in *Drie voordrachten over de nieuwe beeldende kunst* (three discourses on the new plastic art), a collection of notes and essays published in 1919. Referring to the interior designs of De Vonk, he wrote: "For the time being it is clear that no style can arise when an equal division of work between the various arts does not exist. In other words, there can be no development of style when renowned architects do not practice the theories they themselves propound, and the architect does everything himself as far as color and form (by which I mean sculpture) are concerned."[26]

Van Doesburg and van der Leck also subscribed to the same concept of the essentially opposite natures of painting and architecture. In "Aanteekeningen over monumentale kunst" van Doesburg contrasted the open, unbinding, extending functions of painting with the enclosed, joining, confining aspects of architecture, noting that in their opposing characteristics of movement and stability lay the potential for their harmonious combination in what would thus become a monumental work: "Through the consistent carrying forward of this complementary combination of architecture and painting, it will be possible to achieve in the future on a purely modern basis the aim of monumental art: to place man within (instead of opposite) the plastic arts and thereby enable him to participate in them."[27]

Van der Leck's and van Doesburg's ideas as of 1917–18 concerning the role of color in architecture are clear. Those of Oud are somewhat more difficult to ascertain because he did not write about this particular issue until several years later. However, Oud did profess to be in agreement with the collaborative principle, seeing it as a means of arriving at both ethical and aesthetic ends: "In order to achieve style, only the universal is of importance. Acting through purity of means, a monumental style will be able to arise through the cooperation of the different art forms, because cooperation is possible only where each art form moves within its own field and admits no impure elements. The characteristic feature of each art form then becomes apparent and the need for cooperation is clearly felt."[28] Although he may have assimilated the stylistic influence of the De Stijl painters, whom he credited with inspiring the first results of his De Stijl architecture, Oud continued to be indebted to relatively conservative attitudes professed by Berlage. This is demonstrated not only by the style of buildings such as De Vonk but also by the limitations he implicitly placed on van

Doesburg's coloristic contributions to that structure. Because the color scheme of De Vonk was contained within architecturally defined surfaces, in an important sense Oud retained ultimate control over the spatial design. Though this kind of aesthetic domination would later lead to difficulties between van Doesburg and Oud, at the time van Doesburg apparently believed he had sufficient freedom in his color applications. He did not feel that the restriction of them to surfaces provided by the architect conflicted with his own aspirations as a colorist. Indeed, in his previously cited letter of June 1916 to Oud, van Doesburg had conceded to the architect the major role in creating the new atmosphere around designs that painter and architect would realize together.

The comments van Doesburg made in "Aanteekeningen over monumentale kunst" about the colored interior of De Vonk provide further evidence of his regard for architectural elements and the way he thought color could interact with them, contributing an aesthetic, abstract character to what would otherwise be a simple, functional space:

Both in the composition of the tiled floor and in the painting of the doors, etc., an aesthetic spatial effect through destruction has been achieved by other means, i.e., by means of painting-in-architecture. It is true that the floor is the most closed surface of the house and therefore demands, from an aesthetic point of view, a counter-gravitational effect by means of flat color and open spatial relationships. It has been carried through consistently here from the entrance through the whole of the lower and upper halls and passages.[29]

Van Doesburg's only criticism was directed against the window in the stairwell, designed by H. H. Kamerlingh Onnes. Because of its darkness, he said, "the [insufficient amount of] light, one of the chief factors of the art of monumental space, cancels out much of the effect" of van Doesburg's color design. This large, five-part window, which Kamerlingh Onnes had intended to execute in stained glass, was instead painted by hand because of a lack of stained-glass materials during the war years. The window disrupted van Doesburg's interior composition not only because it inhibited the passage of light, but also because its design, with scenes of young girls at play in each of the four seasons, was in a primitivizing figurative style that did not correspond to van Doesburg's more architectonic color applications. Furthermore, van Doesburg himself was becoming an accomplished designer of stained glass windows at this time. According to Oud, by 1918 van Doesburg had already made a thorough study of the requirements of stained glass design and realized that the composition of a window must be based on the amount of light required for the interior while also being responsive to "the need to withstand wind pressure, rain, snow, sagging and bending, from which follows the construction using more or less translucent glass, wide or narrow lead strips, and horizontal or vertical fortifying elements."[30] Thus van Doesburg's criticism of Kamerlingh Onnes's De Vonk window may also have been generated in part by his frustration at not having been asked to contribute the design himself. The green color of the rooms themselves, for which Kamerlingh Onnes was also responsible, provided yet another reason for his disappointment. Had his own commission included these elements, van Doesburg would have been in a position to ensure the complete harmony of his coloristic design.

In 1917, the same year that he began work on De Vonk, Oud gave van Doesburg an opportunity to design a window for a seaside villa he was helping to renovate not far from Noordwijkerhout, in the neighboring town of Katwijk aan Zee. The house was called Allegonda, after the wife of its owner, J. E. R. Trousselot, a coffee and tea merchant from Rotterdam.[31] It stood opposite the home of the painter Menso Kamerlingh Onnes, the father of Oud's friend who had been responsible for parts of the De Vonk color scheme. The elder Kamerlingh Onnes had recently made a trip to Tunisia, where he had been impressed by the simplicity of the cubic white architecture he saw, and upon his return he had convinced Trousselot to modernize his house in that style. Menso Kamerlingh Onnes contributed the basic designs, and Oud oversaw their technical application.

Oud asked the younger Kamerlingh Onnes to design a mosaic tile nameplate, which was made by the ceramicist Willem Brouwer and placed on the facade of Allegonda. He commissioned van Doesburg to design the stained glass window, which was placed in a stairwell that joined a new tower to the previously existing part of the house. The window, *Composition II* (figure 6), involved the theme of the rising surf, and its abstract treatment accorded well with the sober whitewashed architecture (which, Oud wrote in an article he dated January 1918, "harmonized outstandingly with the white dune landscape"[32]). In another article, dealing with van Doesburg's stained glass oeuvre, Oud wrote of *Composition II* that "the motif is transformed and also worked out in the space, that is, in the white light, so that the aesthetic idea which forms the basis of the piece—'the rhythmic, upward-rising movement of sea surf'—is imaged

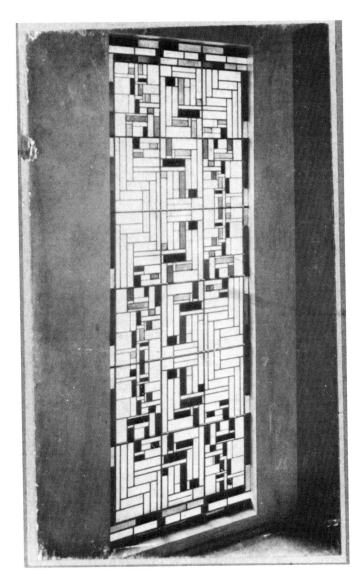

6 Theo van Doesburg, *Composition II*, 1917, stained glass. Photograph: Van Doesburg Archive, Dienst Verspreide Rijkskollekties, The Hague.

only through relationship, without impinging upon the concept of the window as a light-permeating barrier."[33] The pattern of *Composition II* was set within a frame and designed in such a way that the upper portion formed a reversed mirror image of the pattern in the lower half. The red, yellow, blue, and clear pieces of glass[34] were here again arranged on a modular grid. Van Doesburg used a grid in his stained-glass and tile-floor compositions—where it was a logical result of the materials employed—before introducing it in his easel paintings. In paintings van Doesburg used grid structures as a means of obliterating the distinction between figure and ground. This enabled him to achieve a composition of pure relationships similar to his rendering of the rising-surf motif in *Composition II*. Mondrian, in his "checkerboard" paintings of early 1918, also employed grids to this end, but in his case they must be seen as a strictly pictorial solution to the figure-ground problem. Unlike van Doesburg's use of the grid, Mondrian's evolved in the context of painting rather than in the realm of applied art, where material considerations gave the grid practical as well as aesthetic purpose.[35]

Oud permitted van Doesburg to contribute only portions of the interior color schemes for De Vonk and Allegonda, but in 1917 Jan Wils gave him an opportunity to make a more thoroughly integrated design for the interior of a town house he was building for the de Lange family at Wilhelminalaan 2 in Alkmaar. Wils, who had been born in Alkmaar and had begun his architectural studies with the municipal architect of that town, had met van Doesburg through Oud in 1916. In May of that year the three had founded an art club in Leiden called De Sphinx, which included drawings by

Oud, Kamerlingh Onnes, van Doesburg, and Wils in its first exhibition, held in January 1917. At about the same time, having left the office of Berlage, Wils established his own architectural practice in Voorburg, a small town near The Hague. One of his first independent commissions was the de Lange Town House, the plans for which were completed in February 1917. Van Doesburg contributed color designs, which were applied throughout this house. He not only treated the doors in a manner similar to those at De Vonk (figure 7), but also designed a painted wall pattern for the dining room and, for the stairwell, a bannister post and a large, tripartite stained glass window, *Composition IV* (figure 8). In a letter to the poet Anthony Kok he described some of his contributions to the interior design: "The whole [window] stands out against the air. The color composition is completely free in space. . . . I have also designed colors for the entire building. . . . In order to give you an idea of my conception, I would say that I started out with the notion that all the planes had to be made free-floating by means of an opposing light color. The deep blue door panels, for example, are freed by means of white."[36] The window, each of whose three parts is almost three meters high and more than half a meter wide, was composed as a triptych in a manner that van Doesburg likened to a fugal theme by Bach, whose music he appreciated for what he felt was its scientific, mathematically precise mode of expression.[37] Van Doesburg hoped to assimilate those qualities in his own work, and like many of his contemporaries he proceeded from a belief that in formal purity music had progressed further than painting. He therefore sought inspiration in what he believed to be the more elemental, abstract art. As he

7 Theo van Doesburg, *Color Applications, Ground Floor, de Lange Town House, Alkmaar,* 1917. Illustrated in *Levende Kunst* 1 (1918): 132.

8 Theo van Doesburg, *Composition IV* (in three parts), 1917, stained glass, each panel 286.5 × 56.6 cm. Inv. nos. R5533–R5535, Dienst Verspreide Rijkskollekties, The Hague. Shown in color on page 87.

wrote in *Klassiek–Barok–Modern*, an essay dated December 1918 but not published until 1920,

In means of expression music is more advanced than painting. In music—e.g., that of Bach—the idea of unity or harmony is directly transposed into musically tuned sound and measure relationships, thus into musical means of expression only.

If there is anything else in the music, e.g., repeating melody or imitation of a natural element by means of an instrument, then it is no longer absolute music.

Exactly the same is true for all the arts. Also for absolute painting, although with this difference: The plastic means are different, because the one art reveals beauty by means of audition and the other by means of vision.[38]

The two outer sections of *Composition IV* are made of black, clear, yellow, red, and blue translucent glass rectangles. These primary-color sections frame the middle portion, in which the colors employed are the secondaries—green, orange, and purple—derived by mixing the primaries that constitute their opposites on the color chart. The respective compositions of the two primary-color panels are mirror images of one another, and, much as in *Composition II*, the top half of each repeats the configuration of the bottom section. Van Doesburg related the central panel to the two outer ones by incorporating the theme of contrasts, not only in the use of secondary colors for this portion as opposed to the primaries employed in the lateral areas but also in an inverted variation of the basic pattern employed throughout. Here the two sections forming the middle of the window were inserted upside down in relation to the same sections of the two outer panels, and, rather than the mirror image,

each half is the reverse of the other. By means of this kind of asymmetrical but balanced repetition, the design creates a stable sense of symmetry where absolute symmetry does not exist while providing enough thematic and coloristic variation and contrast to suggest the measured rhythmic movement of a fugue.

In the pattern for the white wall of the dining room (which has since been painted over), van Doesburg once again employed primary colors plus black, now in a horizontal design whose two sides formed inverse mirror images of one another (figure 9). Compositionally, the configuration of forms was similar to the Allegonda window with the rising-surf motif and to the brick mosaics on the exterior of De Vonk, but van Doesburg did not treat it exactly like a painting or window composition applied directly to the wall surface. Although the composition for the dining room was confined within a rectangular area, it was not limited by an enclosing frame. Instead it was organized to suggest a flow of space around the individual elements that was continuous with the space outside the bounds of the composition as a whole. The colored forms seemed to hover as if in a magnetic field holding them in a dynamic tension between centrifugal and centripetal forces. The composition signaled an important breakthrough in van Doesburg's coloristic designs for architecture that was related to his attitude toward individual easel painting and his understanding of the problem of the frame in particular.

In an article entitled "Lijstenaesthetiek" (the aesthetic of the frame), published in *De Stijl* in 1920, van Doesburg criticized the use of frames in a manner that sheds light on the wall design he had made three years earlier for the de

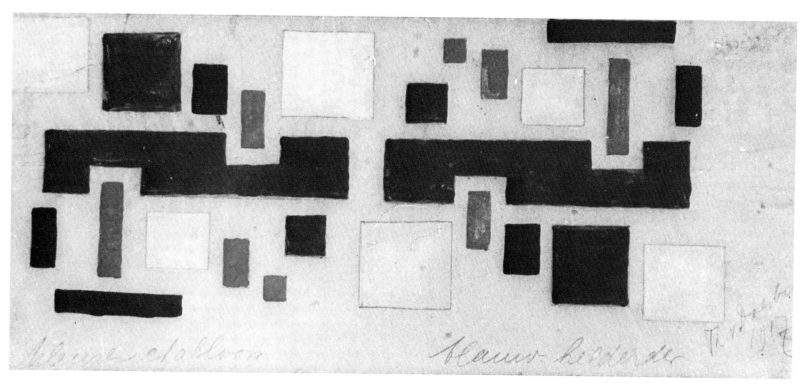

9 Theo van Doesburg, *Arazzo (Color Design for the Dining Room Wall, de Lange Town House, Alkmaar)*, 1917, gouache on paper, 13.5 × 30.5 cm. Dienst Verspreide Rijkskollekties, The Hague, Schenking van Moorsel.

Lange Town House. He explained that frames tend to emphasize the separate, individual character of easel paintings, reinforcing the viewer's sense of standing before a single object rather than in the extended space of the painted composition. To stress the point that he strove for an unbounded spatial composition of color, van Doesburg made the identification of abstract art and spatially unrestricted painting explicit, stating that he favored the development of "an abstract, that is to say, *frame-less* art of painting."[39]

To a certain degree, van Doesburg's wall design of 1917 recalls Piet Mondrian's *Composition with Color Planes* series,[40] painted during the same year. But whereas Mondrian employed an apparently random arrangement of rectangles, allowing the forms to reach the edges of the canvas (where the frame prevented their implied extension beyond its boundaries into real space), van Doesburg removed the literal frame and painted directly on the wall surface in the dining room of the de Lange Town House. He thus manifested the connection between painting and the environment in an explicit, material sense, through the application of color to the architectural plane itself.[41]

In the essay "De Stijl der toekomst" (the style of the future), written in November 1917, van Doesburg described the efforts of contemporary artists, such as himself in the de Lange Town House, to arrive at monumental, "architectonic painting":

[It is that] painting whose abstract nature makes it fit to form a rhythmical unity with architecture. The independent painting, the "tableau de chevalet," was not suited to this because, in its chiaroscuro and perspectival elements, it was contrary to the architectonic idea. For this reason no monumental painting could evolve from Impressionism. Impressionism could not work with architecture and therefore it remained easel painting [kamerschilderkunst].

The perspectival landscape does break the architectural plane, but in the wrong way, i.e., *in depth*. A modern flat painting applied *in* an architectural plane breaks the plane rhythmically according to the architecture in *height* and *breadth*. It follows that, if we want to understand the significance of modern planar painting, we must see it in immediate connection with modern architecture, that is: in its intended place. . . . Imagine . . . [that a] wall is filled with a flat, nonrepresentational painting and that this painting is made in such a way that it dissolves the closed nature of the constructive plane, or breaks it in height and breadth, then the architectonic quality of the wall is retained. The painting works rhythmically with the architecture and there is a balanced relationship between painting and architecture.[42]

Van Doesburg's repeated use of mirror and inverse pattern imagery can, in light of this passage, be explained by his express intention to avoid strictly symmetrical compositions, which he identified with traditional perspective and the destruction of the integrity of the architectural surface. He employed a rhythmic, geometric pattern as an alternative solution to the problem of organizing abstract forms across the wall. This approach to composition enabled him to arrive at what he believed to be the essence of monumental, frameless painting, which was justified by its placement "*in* and *on* the modern neutral architecture, as the counterpart of the pure constructive nature of architecture."[43]

Here again van Doesburg's remarks reveal an affinity with the attitude expressed at about the same time by Bart van der Leck. Both artists were applying their experience in designing stained glass toward the development of their architectural painting styles. For van Doesburg the result was the kind of rhythmic pattern he used in the de Lange Town House, not only in the window but also in the wall painting for the dining room. In van der Leck's case, the simplification of form necessary for window compositions involved the same process of abstraction evident in his *Donkey Riders* series, for which two sketches appear to have been stained glass window designs (figure 10). The abstract compositional style developed in that series of paintings, which combined horizontal, vertical, and diagonal arrangements of rectangular planes of primary colors, was then applied to color designs freely incorporated in architecture.

This can be seen in a design van der Leck produced in 1918 in which, in accordance with van Doesburg's requirements for successful monumental painting, the flat, nonrepresentational use of primary color dissolved the closed nature of the constructive wall plane without sacrificing its architectonic qualities. The design (figure 11) was for a room in De Leeuwerik (the skylark), the home of J. de Leeuw, a neighbor of the artist in Laren.[44] This interior was much smaller than the Art Room in the Kröller home, but the effect of van der Leck's color scheme was far more open and expansive, so that the later interior would seem spacious in spite of its actual dimensions. The walls and the rug on the floor were treated as white ground planes; even the window and the door were covered with white curtains so that no apertures pierced the wall surfaces or allowed extraneous elements to affect the overall unity van der Leck was striving for. All the surfaces could thus be organized in a similar manner as coloristic compositions, each with one central diamond[45]

flanked by rectangles and squares. The furniture had a similar, simplified geometric character, and therefore harmonized with the color designs. The compositions were echoed on a smaller scale in the designs van der Leck applied to several pillows, to the curtain over the doorway, and to the fabrics covering the two tables in the room.

The way van der Leck drew the De Leeuwerik design differs slightly but significantly from the Kröller Art Room gouache, in which he had made more of a distinction between the sides of the room. In order to distinguish between the top and the bottom of the design for the Art Room, one wall was rendered upside down in relation to its position in the actual space. In contrast, the De Leeuwerik drawing is a full-fledged exploded-box plan (albeit without ceiling), and its correct orientation is determined only by reference to the artist's signature and the positioning of the tables sketched in the corners, just outside the bounds of the design itself. The result is a drawing whose free orientation corresponds to the openness of the color design.

Van der Leck's concept of color in architecture as manifested in De Leeuwerik involved the activation of space by means of decentralized color accents rather than enclosed patterns repeated across a single surface, as had sometimes been van Doesburg's practice. Although van der Leck did apply almost identical compositions to each of the four walls, the colors (red, yellow, blue, and black) were used slightly differently in each case. Furthermore, van der Leck adapted the pattern to the shape of the surfaces, stretching it out horizontally to accommodate the two longer walls, and he considered the placement of the furniture as well. The limitation of his color design is only barely suggested in

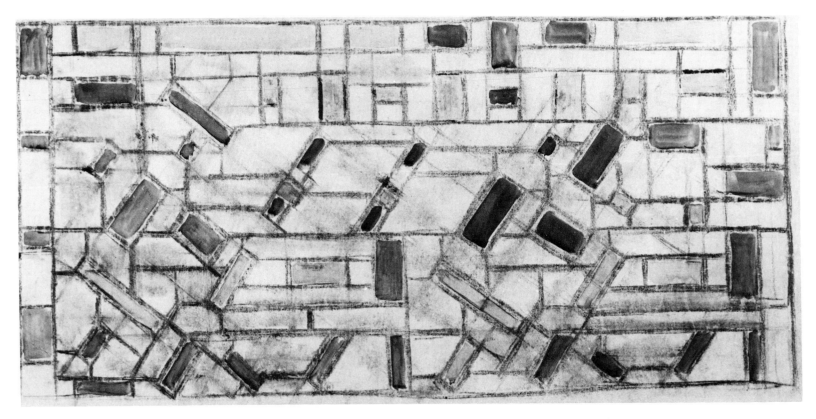

10 Bart van der Leck, *Study for Composition 1917 No. 5 (Donkey Riders)*, 1917, charcoal and gouache on paper, 62.5 × 121 cm. Collection of J. P. Smid, Kunsthandel Monet, Amsterdam.

11 Bart van der Leck, *Design for Interior, De Leeuwerik, Laren*, 1918, pencil and watercolor on paper, 70.5 × 76 cm. Graphische Kunstsammlung, Staatsgalerie, Stuttgart. Shown in color on page 87.

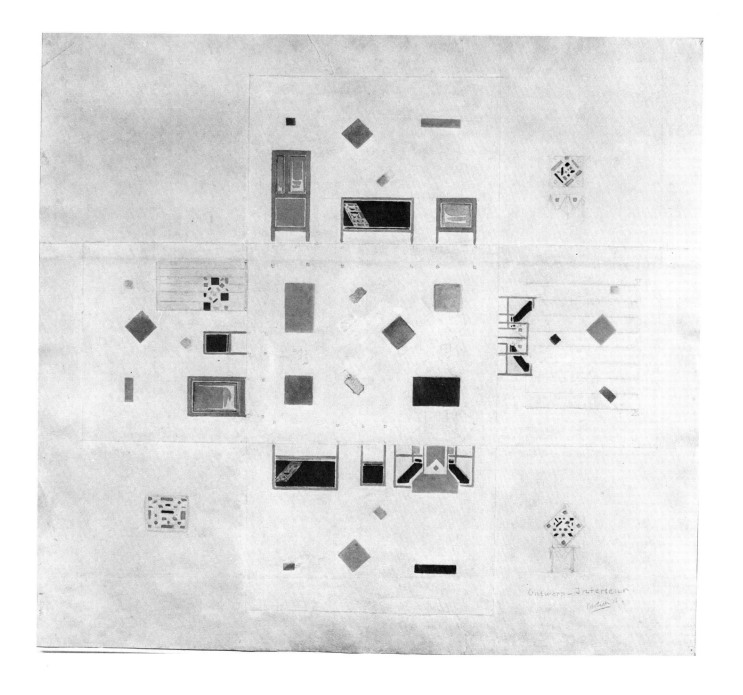

Ontwerp—Interieur

the rug, whose border is accentuated by the outer edges of large colored rectangles near each corner; it is somewhat more evident in the cushions and tablecloths, to which van der Leck's easel paintings of the same period are closely related. Indeed, at least three of these objects can be identified with paintings or drawings van der Leck executed in 1918.[46] The direct correspondence between van der Leck's applied designs and his easel paintings again demonstrates the synthetic nature of his solutions to painterly problems, whether worked out on a single, flat, delimited surface or applied within a larger architectural context.

The development of a free, nonfigurative style in van der Leck's easel paintings of 1918 should certainly be considered in accounting for the similar form of his contemporaneous design for De Leeuwerik, although the conditions under which this interior was designed must also have played a significant part in determining its ultimate form. Unlike the Kröller Art Room commission, the one for de Leeuw gave van der Leck freedom to apply color within a neutral architectural setting limited only by the location of the windows and door (which he was able to control by placing white curtains over them) and by the inclusion of furniture—which, in contrast with the furniture Berlage had provided for the Kröller Art Room, accorded well with the character of his own coloristic contribution. It seems likely that in this instance van der Leck was not working directly with an architect, at least not with one as imposing as Berlage had been, and consequently he was able to achieve a successful interior color scheme on his own terms.

After leaving De Stijl, van der Leck evidently remained faithful to its collaborative ideal. For example, he contributed an interior color scheme to a display stand designed by his friend Klaarhamer for an industrial exhibition in 1919. But van der Leck obviously found the collaborative relationship a difficult one. He preferred situations where he could be assured of aesthetic independence, which he felt he could not exercise within the context of De Stijl. In one sense, van der Leck's reaction to collaborative work brought him into conflict with the rest of the De Stijl group, but his position did not differ significantly from that taken by other De Stijl artists in the following years. Even in the way he expressed his objections—by leaving De Stijl and working only under conditions he controlled to a significant degree—he was later joined by many of those with whom he had found himself in disagreement around 1917–18. It is important to keep in mind that at any given moment the De Stijl circle was composed of individuals who considered themselves independent of one another, although they might work together and although they all contributed to the magazine De Stijl. Van der Leck was only the first of several early contributors, including van 't Hoff, Wils, Oud, and Mondrian, who eventually detached themselves from the group.

Vilmos Huszar's interest in the applied arts, particularly stained glass windows, led him, like van der Leck and van Doesburg, to an involvement with interior design and collaborative work. Huszar was born in 1884 in Budapest, where, beginning in 1901, he studied for two years in the department of decorative art at the School of Applied Art, training to be a wall painter. After leaving school he began to work in the fine arts, concentrating particularly on portraiture. In 1904 he entered the studio of Simon Hollosy in Munich. In Holland, toward the end of 1905, he was influenced by Josef Israels and then by the work of Vincent van Gogh. Only later, well after a trip to Paris in 1907–08, did he begin to paint in a Cubist-oriented style.

Paralleling that of van Doesburg around 1917, Huszar's easel painting style was strongly influenced by van der Leck's work. Huszar would also have been familiar with van der Leck's theories about the role of color in architecture, at least once they were published in *De Stijl*, and he must have known their practical applications as well—through Klaarhamer, if not directly. Both Huszar and van der Leck collaborated with Klaarhamer during this period, producing color schemes for his architecture and furniture designs commissioned by the Bruynzeel family. Van der Leck provided the color scheme for the Utrecht Annual Industrial Fair stand (actually a rather large interior) that Klaarhamer designed for the Bruynzeel wood products and paneling firm in 1919 (figure 27). Huszar collaborated with Klaarhamer—whom he probably met through van der Leck—applying color to an interior in the house of Cornelis Bruynzeel, Jr., for which Klaarhamer designed the furniture.

Huszar was a neighbor of Bruynzeel in Voorburg, and in addition to a bedroom for Bruynzeel's two sons he contributed color designs for other interiors in the Bruynzeel house, De Arendshoeve, at Oosteinde 34, as well as the design for the firm's 1918 industrial fair stand. Bruynzeel himself apparently maintained an active interest in the aesthetic as well as the practical aspects of the family business,[47] and Huszar undoubtedly found him a sympathetic patron, unusual in his willingness to experiment with advanced design concepts not only in his own home but also in his business concerns.

In Huszar's view, the patron or commission giver was also involved in the collaborative effort to realize a total work of art. He played an important but strictly defined role: The patron "must only express his practical needs," and the others involved in a given commission, architect-builder, interior designer, and painter, each contributed similarly, according to his professionally determined means:

The builder must only create the spaces plastically. If he does this well in all respects, so that the technical and constructive elements are resolved in the whole, then the builder has enough to take care of. His own profession demands a fundamental study. If he carries this out, then he himself will see that he must allow the other professions opportunity for expression. . . .

The interior-architect must consider the *colors* determined by the painter when choosing his material in relation to the rest of the building, thus he only creates *form* in space.

The painter, who is the most free of all, must exercise discretion in relation to the form-creating artist, so that his color composition does not compromise the formal arrangement. . . .

All this will take on a social significance which will work both ethically and aesthetically on the masses. Thus shall art come to be *in* life.[48]

Huszar was a firm believer in the collaborative nature of the arts, and he clearly extended that view to include those who commission or make use of objects produced by artists. He felt, furthermore, that it was the modern artist's task to learn as much as possible about the materials at his disposal. For the painter, that meant the scientific study of color. Huszar's own efforts in this field provided the impetus for his article on Wilhelm Ostwald's book *Die Farbenfibel*, published in *De Stijl* in August 1918. In it he described Ostwald's book as an "a.b.c.-color-book in which there is an attempt to make everything about color as scientific and exact as possible." Huszar called on artists to use the practical and technical knowledge of color made available by Ostwald as a means of understanding the relationships among colors and, through them, of creating "form-spaces" in art. With an exact, scientifically grounded knowledge of color, he argued, the artist can control his intuition and transform his subjective instincts into objective expression.[49] It was largely with this goal in mind that van der Leck and Mondrian had already begun to restrict their palettes to the primary colors and "noncolors," which, by virtue of their purity, were thought to be more objective than the colors derived by mixing the primaries and thus better suited to the elemental, universally applicable values these artists wanted to express. In his article Huszar intimated that he viewed the scientific rationalization of color in direct relation to architecture. Moreover, he saw his own role as a painter in terms of the objective, scientific application of color to individual objects, including furniture, as well as to interiors as a whole. It was therefore his task to collaborate with other artists in the design of the total aesthetic interior, such as the one he and Klaarhamer produced for the Bruynzeel family in 1918.

The following year, a critic named Ro van Oven wrote that one of Huszar's primary concerns was to distinguish between decorative and plastic art. According to Huszar, van Oven related, "the decorative is subordinated to the whole in which it is applied, whereas plastic art wants to create a self-sufficient image, something that is a whole in itself." Huszar was concerned with the problem of applying color within an architectural context in a manner that harmonized with that context (and could, therefore, be called decorative) but at the same time maintained the independence of color as a formal or spatial value. It was his aim to merge color and space in such a way that color would be more than "merely" decorative, in that it would fulfill internal principles established through the study of color as a medium of plastic expression. Van Oven paraphrased Huszar's ideas as follows:

The decorative element is included in modern plastic art because it is linked with architecture, but products of plastic art also have value in themselves. All the elements of the interior work plastically together and therefore furniture, windows, doors, etc., are all plastic forms which must work well together, with respect to each other, while also maintaining their own integrity.

Therefore the painter must have the same essential attitude as the architect in order to achieve a complete, harmonious whole.[50]

Of several designs Huszar produced in collaboration with Klaarhamer for the Bruynzeel house, the first was for a stained glass skylight window over the main stairwell. Apparently the design was made in 1916 and the window executed the following year. It was probably in order to create an appropriate setting for the skylight that Huszar later designed a *Ruimte-Kleurcompositie Trappenhuis* (spatial color composition for a stairwell) (figure 12) in a style corresponding to the Bruynzeel bedroom he designed in 1918.[51]

The bedroom of the Bruynzeel house was an irregularly shaped space in which there was an alcove with a lowered ceiling where two beds were placed on either side of a

12 Vilmos Huszar, *Spatial Color Composition for
a Stairwell*, 1918. Illustrated in *Levende Kunst* 2
(1919): 60.

13 P. J. C. Klaarhamer and Vilmos Huszar,
Chair for Bedroom, Bruynzeel House, Voorburg,
1918, painted wood with fabric cushion, 90.2
× 40.6 × 41.9 cm. Gemeentemuseum, The
Hague.

■ *38*

closet door. Another alcove containing two sinks was opposite the beds. The large windows along one wall were surmounted by three smaller stained glass windows, also designed by Huszar; these faced a dresser next to the entrance of the room. Klaarhamer designed several small, low chairs for the boys, which Huszar painted wine-red and black, adding a hand-stitched blue cushion with black bands to the seat (figure 13). In comparison with Gerrit Rietveld's Red-Blue Chair (figure 14), which was designed at about the same time (although it may not have been colored until several years later), Klaarhamer's and Huszar's furniture seems old-fashioned, in spite of its basically plain, rectangular form. The thick wooden members look heavy beside the thin, almost weightless appearance of Rietveld's design. As Rietveld later recounted: "The so-called red-blue chair, the chair made of two boards and a number of laths, that chair was made to the end of showing that a thing of beauty, e.g. a spatial object, could be made of nothing but straight, machined materials. So I had the plank sawn into strips and laths; the center part I sawed in two halves, so I had a seat and back and then, with the laths of various lengths I constructed the chair."[52] The furniture in the Bruynzeel bedroom, on the other hand, possessed relatively little sense of simplified, machine-oriented construction, and although Huszar's color scheme for the room included yellow as well as the blue, red, and black he chose for the furniture, he used muted colors rather than the bright, primary tones that Rietveld eventually employed.

Although the individual elements in the Bruynzeel bedroom are certainly less striking than Rietveld's Red-Blue Chair, the overall coloristic treatment of the interior, to which those ele-

14 Gerrit Rietveld, *Red-Blue Chair*, ca. 1918,
painted wood, 60 × 84 × 86 cm. Museum of
Modern Art, New York; gift of Philip Johnson.

ments were intentionally subordinated, was tremendously important in the evolution of De Stijl's abstract, environmental concerns. Several photographs of the completed interior were published in *Bouwkundig Weekblad* in 1922 alongside Huszar's article "Over de moderne toegepaste kunsten" (on the modern applied arts). In this essay Huszar stated that he and Klaarhamer had endeavored to plasticize the interior space (plasticizing meant "arranging the spaces and the functions rhythmically and at the same time practically") according to the means appropriate to their respective professions. Huszar discussed the photographs of the room (here cited by their numbers in the present book) as follows:

Figure [15]. . . . The closet door separates the two beds, and I attempted to find a connection in the middle, via the door between the two beds, by painting the wall above one bed white and that over the other gray, and the planes on the walls the reverse.

This was continued on the left side wall, where the blue and yellow planes against the white ground form a composition with the red and black bed. . . .

Figure [16]. In another photograph one can see more clearly how the interchanges and reconciliations between the ground itself and the applied color planes work, and how the bed is assimilated into the whole. The left side plane is the same color, blue, as the lowest plane and the ceiling above the bed.

The yellow in the smaller planes is complementary with the other colors.

Figure [17]. Similarly, the carpet is included in the composition. Color is divided *light*, and if it is balanced the total impression should be one of light.

What the pointillists saw in nature, I have here attempted to do with planes, which are logically deduced from the plastic forms. Thus light can be plasticized in the interior.

In this room, the planes could be so combined with the furniture that they complement each other; the deliberate placement of the beds, etc., makes this mutual fulfillment possible.

If the furniture in a room is placed in an appropriate position, then it is accounted for. Each interior demands its own space-color solution and its own complementary color combination.

As a result there is always a new composition.

Some artists mistakenly apply a decorative rather than a plastic solution; repetition occurs and empty mannerism ensues.[53]

Huszar's color scheme represents a significant advance over the earlier interiors designed by van Doesburg because, although still strictly predetermined by the architectural setting and placement of furniture, his color applications were not framed or enclosed like easel paintings, nor did they form an internal pattern in the spatially defined manner of van Doesburg's Town House dining room design of the previous year. Instead, Huszar used large planes, each composed of a single color and oriented in such a way that it helped to render visible the extent and shape of the surface to which it had been applied.[54]

Insofar as the colors Huszar painted on each wall of the Bruynzeel bedroom formed compositions that included the furniture, his design is similar to the one van der Leck produced for De Leeuwerik in the same year. Furthermore, in these two interiors both Huszar and van der Leck used coloristic compositions to make associations across space. In the De Leeuwerik interior van der Leck painted nearly identical designs on the two sets of opposite walls, while in the Bruynzeel bedroom Huszar reversed the colors of the rec-

15 Vilmos Huszar, *Color Applications, Bedroom of Bruynzeel House, Voorburg,* 1918–19. Photograph: Nederlands Documentatiecentrum voor de Bouwkunst, Amsterdam.

17 Vilmos Huszar, *Color Applications, Bedroom of Bruynzeel House, Voorburg*, 1918–19. Photograph: Nederlands Documentatiecentrum voor de Bouwkunst, Amsterdam.

16 Vilmos Huszar, *Color Applications, Bedroom of Bruynzeel House, Voorburg*, 1918–19. Photograph: Nederlands Documentatiecentrum voor de Bouwkunst, Amsterdam.

tangular forms he repeated above each of the two beds. Van Doesburg, on the other hand, seems not to have achieved a design of similar sophistication until 1919, when he produced a blue, green, reddish orange, black, and white color scheme for a room, probably in a house belonging to his friend Bart de Ligt, an antiwar socialist and philosopher.[55] Discussing a photograph of that interior published in *De Stijl* in 1920 (figure 18), van Doesburg claimed that, in spite of the ''accidental and materialistic . . . poor, impressionistic'' architecture, he had succeeded in realizing ''a compositional whole out of the five painted planes (ceiling and walls) along with the furniture, designed by Rietveld according to specific dimensions and relations.''[56]

Huszar's attitude toward the activation of space by means of color seems to have been evolving while he was executing the designs for the Bruynzeel bedroom. As an apparently preliminary drawing shows, Huszar originally conceived of each side of the room as an individual unit. He thus drew each wall as it would look to a stationary viewer standing opposite it (figure 19). These four individual views, which included the furniture, were treated together as a flat composition in two rows aligned more or less as a continuous frieze. Each view formed a composition in itself, but by displaying them together in this manner Huszar was able to convey a sense of their interrelation in the actual space. Two photographs of the completed interior published by Huszar in 1922 (figures 16 and 17) accomplished this much more effectively because they focused on corners of the room and so emphasized the compositional relationship among the surfaces that met in these areas.

In earlier drawings Huszar had concentrated on the composition of each side of the bedroom as an individual unit related to the others as images arranged sequentially across a flat surface, but in the photographs of the actual space the corners where the surfaces met assumed much greater importance: They reinforced the continuous nature of the viewer's experience of the interior. Huszar had been able only to suggest such a continuous interlocking in the earlier frieze drawing where each wall still retained its separate character as an individual composition not unlike an easel painting seen from the viewpoint of a stationary observer opposite it. The experience of the actual space conveyed in the photographs emphasized the continuity inherent in the whole. Each surface and the furniture arranged in front of it formed a composition, but each surface also interacted spatially with those adjacent to it, fusing the entire room into a single, harmonious whole. The continuous character of the spatial environment—achieved primarily through the coloristic, compositional relationship of separate architectural surfaces—thus became readily apparent.

This experience of the total space helped to bring about a new attitude toward the role of painting in the interior. Heretofore, as seen in the earlier work of van Doesburg and van der Leck, painting had always been considered strictly in terms of the activation of a neutral architectural plane by means of color applied in discrete areas determined and very often limited by structural considerations (including the placement of furniture, the doors, ceiling, and floor, and the divisions between wall surfaces). Thus color had been understood as a complement to architecture, accenting but not interfering with the perception of its functional or constructional elements. Because the integrity of each colored surface was always preserved, architectural and coloristic contributions to the space maintained their characteristic features within the design as a whole. This was a fundamental premise of the collaborative endeavor. But once the interior was completed, the integration of space could be apprehended as involving something more profound than the simple coordination of various discrete elements in a single decorative scheme; the interlocking fluidity exemplified by Huszar's designs for the Bruynzeel bedroom created a holistic impression in which all the individual elements were far more effectively subsumed, though they still maintained their identities as plastic forms. The holistic effect of interlocking continuity soon developed into a conscious goal of abstract colorists, and, insofar as architects saw it as compromising the integrity of the spaces they designed, it upset the original conception of collaborative work and led to a redefinition of the respective roles of the colorist and the architect in creating an abstract, colored architectural design.

18 Theo van Doesburg, *Example of Coloristic Composition in an Interior*, 1919. Illustrated in *De Stijl* III, 12 (1920), plate XIV.

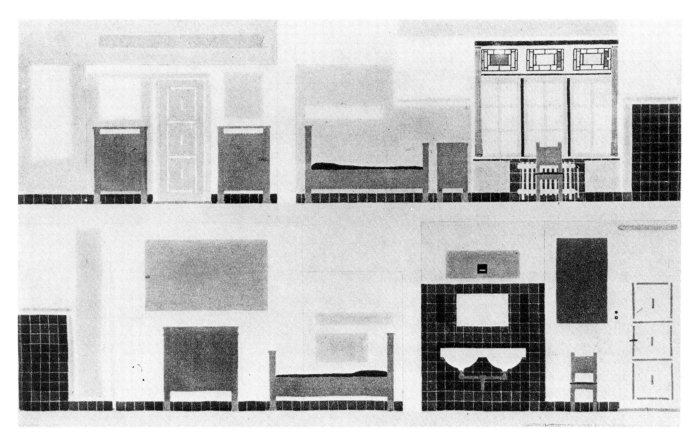

19 Vilmos Huszar, *Spatial Color Composition for
Bedroom of Bruynzeel House, Voorburg*, 1918.
Illustrated in *Levende Kunst* 2 (1919): 59.

2

Transition: The Problem of the Corner

In the evolution of the abstract environment after 1920 from a space defined primarily by architectural considerations to one that was determined more by coloristic design, the treatment of corners played a vital role. This can be seen quite clearly in several interiors where color was manipulated so as to deny the discrete character of individual surfaces in order to allow for a continuous experience of color in space. Although it was not the earliest of these projects, Vilmos Huszar's *Spatial Color Composition in Gray* (figure 20) provides a particularly well-resolved example of how the corner could be handled to promote a sense of interlocking colored planes.

Huszar's *Composition*, probably executed in 1924, was a remodeled music and sitting room in the home of the Dada poet and essayist Til Brugman, in The Hague.[1] The presence of a piano allied the interior to a tradition of music-room design reaching back at least to the turn of the century, when the music room, physically embodying the union of the arts, became the focal point of the aesthetically conceived house. Just as music created an enveloping mood, so the music rooms designed by Peter Behrens, Charles Rennie Mackintosh, and Henry van de Velde were arranged to evoke a similarly sensual, aesthetic experience. The abstract harmony of the interior design was directly associated with the abstract harmony of the music played there, and thus the environment of the music room had not only a practical function but an explicitly aesthetic one as well. The choice and arrangement of objects had to fulfill the requirements of good acoustics in addition to those of good design.[2] Nevertheless, in the turn-of-the-century music room, as in Huszar's interior, functional demands played a subordinate role to the demands of aesthetic design in establishing an environment suitable for the evocative experience of music.

Two photographs of the Brugman interior, one taken before (figure 21) and the other after (figure 20) it was redesigned, convey a sense of the radical transformation Huszar effected. The new room as a whole can best be seen in Huszar's preliminary design (figure 22), a symmetrical perspective view of the rectangular space. One entered through a door on the right, rather than through the double doors behind the piano, which even earlier had been closed off. To one side of the entrance was a daybed facing the hearth. Huszar replaced the original Persian rug with a plain, dark gray carpet, over which hung a lamp of his own design, composed with elegant simplicity of two tinted or frosted glass planes suspended from the ceiling by thin wires. Instead of the high dado surmounted by patterned wallpaper, the walls received a uniform coat of neutral color upon which Huszar painted a composition of large, often overlapping rectangular planes. Just as the lamp created an illusion of floating planes of light, so the areas where the rectangles overlapped were painted in a different tone in order to suggest transparency and yet prevent a spatial reading of one plane in front of another. The effect is reminiscent of paintings by Laszlo Moholy-Nagy that Huszar could have seen in Berlin in 1923.[3] Even more significant is the fact that in one corner of the room (figure 20) a rectangle was made to camouflage a closet door and to extend around the corner onto an adjacent wall, forming a compositional unity of the two surfaces. Furthermore, the rectangles painted here seem to float freely in space, being neither strictly centered on the surfaces to which they were applied nor framed and thus anchored by the furniture placed in front of them as were the colored forms in Huszar's Bruynzeel bedroom design.

Huszar's evocation of transparent planes of light and especially his decision to ignore the structural limits of the wall and door surfaces mark a significant change in his conception of the role of color in architecture. Whereas in the Bruynzeel bedroom the correspondence of colors through and across space became evident only after the individual surfaces were composed separately in relation to furniture placed in front of them, in the Brugman music room Huszar set out from the start to use color—or, rather, gray tones—to suggest connections between discrete surfaces. In contrast to his earlier practice of determining color schemes in deference to the primacy of functional and structural considerations, here color was employed to disguise functional and architectural elements such as the closet door and the corner. Huszar no longer adhered to the neutral surfaces provided by the architecture, but instead used color to obscure them and thus to question if not deny their integrity. Literally and figuratively he crossed the bounds he had set himself in collaborations with Klaarhamer and with Jan Wils. As he aimed for a continuous reading of an integrated interior composition, his intention was to allow color (again, in this case, several tones of gray), rather than architecture, to play the major role in determining the spectator's experience of the spatial environment. It was especially in the corner of the room that Huszar's color scheme proclaimed its independence from architecture. Seemingly detached from structural components, as if floating freely, it lent a sense of openness and buoyancy to the music room, effectively fulfill-

20 Vilmos Huszar, *Spatial Color Composition in Gray, Brugman House, The Hague*, 1924. Photograph: Department of Applied Arts, Stedelijk Museum, Amsterdam.

21 Music/Sitting Room, Brugman House, The Hague, before 1924. Photograph: Department of Applied Arts, Stedelijk Museum, Amsterdam.

22 Vilmos Huszar, *Design for Spatial Color Composition in Gray*, 1924. Photograph: Department of Applied Arts, Stedelijk Museum, Amsterdam.

ing van Doesburg's dictum that in monumental art "not only does painting oppose the loose and open to the constructionally closed, that is, extension to enclosure, it also liberates organically closed relief from its confinement, opposing movement to stability."[4]

Several years before Huszar redesigned the Brugman interior, Piet Zwart had already formulated an analogous solution to what might be characterized generically as "the problem of the corner." Zwart never contributed to the magazine *De Stijl*, but around 1920 he was closely associated with Huszar as well as several other De Stijl artists.[5] Before 1918, when Zwart met Huszar and Wils, his work had been linked to a relatively conservative arts-and-crafts tradition. He had studied applied art several years after van der Leck at the National School for the Applied Arts in Amsterdam, and thereafter had been a teacher of drawing and art history in Leeuwarden. Zwart had designed furniture, interiors, and exhibition installations for the Haagse Kunstkring (Hague art circle), but before 1919 most of his work had employed decorative flower and plant motifs in a style reminiscent of the Wiener Werkstätte (Vienna workshops). It was largely due to his close association—and in some instances direct collaboration—with De Stijl artists that Zwart moved from his handicraft orientation in the direction of a more sober, functional attitude toward design between 1919 and 1921.

Early in 1919, Zwart became a draftsman in Jan Wils's architectural office. Two years later he contributed stained glass windows and interior color schemes to the Dans Instituut Gaillard-Jorissen in The Hague, designed by Wils. Together with Huszar he designed furniture and interiors—

notably for the Bruynzeel family and firm, for which Klaarhamer, van der Leck, and Wils all worked. In spite of these connections, Zwart's initial attitude toward De Stijl had been negative. He stated this openly in an article published in May 1919 in which he discussed van der Leck's color scheme for the interior of the industrial fair stand that Klaarhamer designed for the Bruynzeel company. Van der Leck's contribution consisted of small red and blue rectangles positioned so as to accent the architectural construction. Zwart assessed the design as a whole as "a practical, timely, sober construction of planes, one overtaking another to achieve a rhythmic effect" and noted that it involved "an attempt to manipulate the essential nature of the four walls so as to destroy them and make them work together with the ceiling and floor." However, he saw the "officious presence of 'De Stijl'" in the restriction to primary colors and rectangular forms. He used this as an opportunity to attack the rigidity of De Stijl's aesthetic "formula," which he felt stifled creative intuition and led to "a tragic expression of impotence."[6] In retaliation, van Doesburg labeled Zwart a "representative of the Vienna style" when he commented on Zwart's "reactionary" article in October 1919.[7] For his part, Zwart apparently respected van Doesburg's work while at the same time criticizing his desire "to renew art from an 'overly pictorial point of view' and not from an 'attitude conditioned by technical primacy.'"[8]

Although the influence of De Stijl on Zwart was growing stronger at this time, he did not contribute to van Doesburg's magazine or consider himself a member of the group that had formed around it. Nonetheless, in his simultaneously ethical and aesthetic approach to design Zwart had much in common with the De Stijl artists. His attitude has been paraphrased by Kees Broos: "Out of the old chaos must arise a new unity of all aspects of life; individualism, decoration, handwork—these were the reprehensible characteristics of a bygone era. Their counterparts are the principles upon which a new art shall be based: generality and universality, abstraction and practical formation, mechanical production. From these elements a new world must be shaped."[9] In response to what he perceived to be a lack of respect for aesthetic considerations on the part of almost every firm participating in the 1919 Annual Industrial Fair, Zwart wrote the following:

The law of slowness works nowhere more intensively than in Holland. For years our craftsmen and applied artists have called in vain for collaboration with industrial producers. After more than a decade during which Germany and Austria have recognized the tremendous importance of this collaboration and mobilized artistic power in the struggle to conquer the world market, it is distressing to see that so few Dutch firms take advantage of architects and applied artists in order to raise the commercial value of their wares by means of some special attractive quality, or to create a representative milieu for the products they exhibit.[10]

During the summer of 1921, a commission by a celluloid manufacturing firm to produce a stand for the coming Annual Industrial Fair gave Zwart an opportunity to carry out ideas concerning exhibition design that he had begun to develop several years earlier in response to stands such as the one van der Leck and Klaarhamer had designed in 1919. At that time Zwart had outlined the requirements a successful fair stand must satisfy:

1st is the fact that its temporary nature must be kept clearly in mind.

2nd it must form a background for the articles displayed and cannot have any pretentious purpose in and of itself.

3rd it must adjust to the demands of the elements of the interior architecture.

4th its form must be born out of the modern consciousness (in which all old, antiquated, exotic, and lifeless style reminiscences are prohibited).[11]

The celluloid firm's commission stipulated that, in contrast to the great majority of stands, theirs was not to require large financial expenditures. The task of building an inexpensive stand for a small company that produced goods in a new, experimental material was ideally suited to Zwart's interests. He met the challenge, producing an extraordinary interior for only 350 guilders, including his honorarium.[12]

Three surviving drawings for the stand demonstrate the development of Zwart's ideas in relation to his previous interior-design activities. They also show his novel approach to the activation of space by means of a very original solution to the problem of the corner.

Zwart's first drawing specified a rectangular room with cabinets and shelves built into the walls (figure 23). The colors were pinkish-red, blue, and black. The floor was divided by color in such a way that a black square formed a separate, independent area on one side of the room. A table and two chairs were provided in an adjoining portion of the space, presumably to accommodate the company's representatives. In this area the floor and part of one wall were painted blue, creating a buffer zone between the display area with the cabinets and the remaining uncolored area

23 Piet Zwart, *First Design for Celluloid Manufacturer's Stand, Annual Industrial Fair, Utrecht,*
1921, pencil and watercolor on paper, 23 ×
28.5 cm. Gemeentemuseum, The Hague.

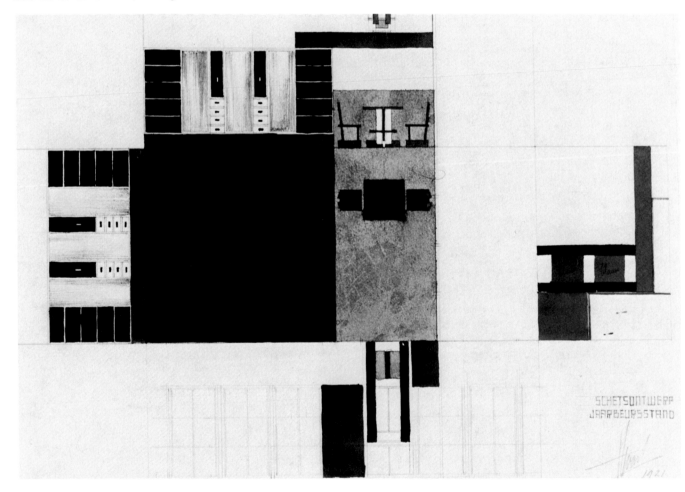

near the entrance, from which visitors would see the display as a whole before entering the room.

The format Zwart chose for this architectural rendering is the same one he used for most of his contemporaneous color designs for Wils's Dans Instituut: an exploded-box plan in which the wall elevations were laid flat and shown together with the floor plan on a single plane. This was a common format used at one time or another by virtually all the De Stijl colorists because it allowed them to avoid the distortion inherent in diminishing perspective views and to suppress any sense of architectural mass. The result is a planar vision of architecture that corresponds closely to De Stijl easel paintings. Furthermore, the colors Zwart used were the same ones Huszar had applied to a chair designed by Zwart (figure 24) that was similar to those suggested for the fair stand. Except for a lighter red, the colors were also reminiscent of the wine-red, blue, and black of Huszar's Bruynzeel bedroom furniture (figure 13). These similarities make it seem likely that Zwart consulted Huszar about the color scheme soon after receiving the fair-stand commission. The two had collaborated on the design of a conversation room in a women's home during the previous year, and in 1921 Huszar provided color schemes for numerous furniture designs by Zwart.

Although the circumstances are not known, for some reason Zwart's first design was not used. He made a second drawing for the stand, dated August 1, 1921 (figure 25). In style and coloristic treatment this design makes a definite break with Zwart's original conception. Here, instead of an exploded box plan, Zwart drew an oblique perspective view focusing on one corner of the interior, including portions of

24 Piet Zwart and Vilmos Huszar, *Design for Chair*, 1920, ink and watercolor on paper, 51.3 × 34 cm. Gemeentemuseum, The Hague.

25 Piet Zwart, *Second Design for Celluloid Manufacturer's Stand, Annual Industrial Fair, Utrecht,*
1921, pencil and crayon on paper, 21.5 ×
33.4 cm. Gemeentemuseum, The Hague.

 54

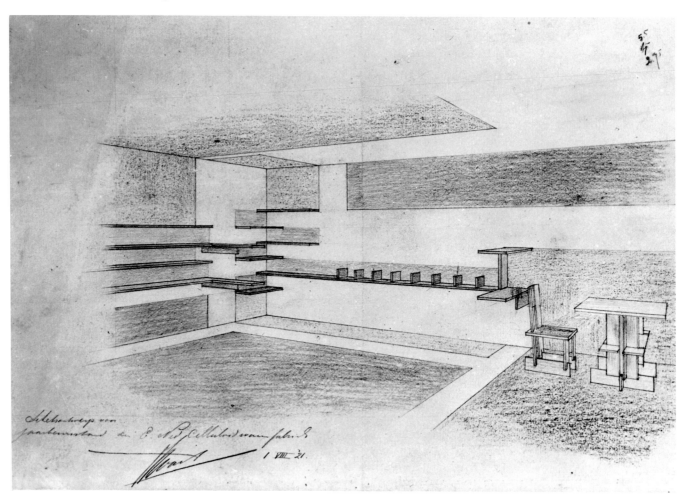

the floor, the ceiling, and two walls. Using pencil and crayon rather than watercolor, he lightly sketched in the colors (blue, muted red, and gray) in bands that crossed over the boundaries between walls, ceiling, and floor. Perhaps the original design would have been too expensive to execute; now, instead of built-in shelves and cabinets, ordinary planks of wood were attached to the walls in asymmetrical arrangements. These formed the shelves on which the celluloid firm's display was to be arranged.

The marked changed between Zwart's first and second design is not easy to account for, but it may have had something to do with the fact that just around the time he made the second design he left Jan Wils's office to enter that of H. P. Berlage as chief draftsman. In making this move, Zwart broke away from his involvement—however tangential—with the De Stijl circle. Thereafter he was associated with an architect whose influence can be detected in the work he had done before his contacts with De Stijl. It may have been Berlage who encouraged Zwart to abandon the intense colors and the planar, exploded-box technique used by De Stijl artists and by Zwart himself when he worked with Huszar and Wils. In their stead Zwart returned to a format he had used much earlier, for example in an interior design of 1913 (figure 26). In that drawing, as in his second fair-stand design, Zwart had used conté crayon to render an oblique perspective view of one corner of a room.

Another, perhaps more compelling reason for Zwart's concentration on the corner was related to the layout of the fair stand. As indicated in the initial design, one wall was almost entirely made up of windows while another would have

26 Piet Zwart, *Design for an Interior*, 1913, ink, watercolor and conté crayon on paper, 31.9 × 30.9 cm. Gemeentemuseum, The Hague.

been situated behind the spectator when he first looked toward the main display area of the exhibition space. As a result of this configuration, it was logical for Zwart to concentrate on only two of the wall surfaces and to focus on the corner where those surfaces met.

Zwart may also have been prompted to switch to an oblique perspective by photographs such as one he reproduced in his article on the Annual Industrial Fair of 1919, which shows a corner of the stand designed by Klaarhamer and van der Leck (figure 27). That photograph and another interior design Zwart produced in 1921 (figure 28) are similar to the second fair-stand design insofar as they all employ oblique perspective views that tend to activate bands of color and form. In each case the resultant diagonals energize the projected interior space in a manner far more radical than that made possible by an exploded-box drawing or even by a symmetrical perspective view such as Zwart had employed in one drawing for Wils's Dans Instituut (figure 29).

It was in this vigorous, dynamic style that Zwart created his third and final proposal for the celluloid manufacturer's stand (figure 30). Here Zwart planned a series of shelves supported by a scaffold of horizontal, vertical, and diagonal planks of wood that reached out into space beyond their points of contact in a manner reminiscent of Rietveld's Red-Blue Chair, produced several years earlier. The black shelves and the red, yellow, and blue scaffolding make the color scheme remarkably close to that of Rietveld's chair, whose horizontal and vertical supporting structure is black, with yellow marking the ends of each piece, and whose diagonally slanted seat and back are respectively blue and red. In Zwart's definitive design, the furniture shown in his two earlier drawings was removed so that the space could be divided and activated by color and the structure of the shelf scaffolding alone. The entire design focused on and emanated from the corner of the room where, on a black area of the ceiling, Zwart placed a white rectangle suggestive of a skylight. The design was similar in its manipulation of perspective and its ambiguous rendition of three-dimensional space to paintings of the same period by El Lissitzky. In its conception it was far bolder and more abstract than anything Zwart had previously produced. Bands of color not only crossed over the boundaries of walls, ceiling, and floor, they also acted to confound the viewer's sense of where those boundaries actually were. By concentrating on the corner Zwart was able to manipulate the oblique perspective in such a way that space was not only activated but made to seem irrational in order to heighten the viewer's experience of what would otherwise have been an ordinary rectangular room.

The definitive drawing is larger than the first two, and its size, together with the use of highly saturated watercolor rather than pencil and crayon, produces a forceful effect. The design conveys a sense of the flexibility and the temporary status of the display area, and the cropping off of colors in irregular shapes at the edges suggests the extension of space beyond the bounds of the drawing to incorporate the spectator. By solving the problem of the corner in a new way, like Huszár, Zwart achieved what van Doesburg had defined in 1918 as the aim of monumental art: "to place man within (instead of opposite) the plastic arts and thereby enable him to participate in them." Indeed, the

27 P. J. C. Klaarhamer and Bart van der Leck, *Bruynzeel Stand, Annual Industrial Fair, Utrecht,* 1919. Illustrated in *Elsevier's Geillustreerd Maandschrift* 29 (1919): 317.

28 Piet Zwart, *Design for Interior, Cramer House, The Hague,* 1921, pencil and colored pencil on paper, 23.2 × 31 cm. Gemeentemuseum, The Hague.

29 Piet Zwart, *Design for Interior, Dans Instituut Gaillard-Jorissen, The Hague*, 1921, pencil and watercolor on paper, 18.5 × 47.2 cm. Nederlands Documentatiecentrum voor de Bouwkunst, Amsterdam.

30 Piet Zwart, *Definitive Design for Celluloid Manufacturer's Stand, Annual Industrial Fair, Utrecht.* 1921, pencil and watercolor on paper, 45.7 × 64.7 cm. Gemeentemuseum, The Hague. Shown in color on page 88.

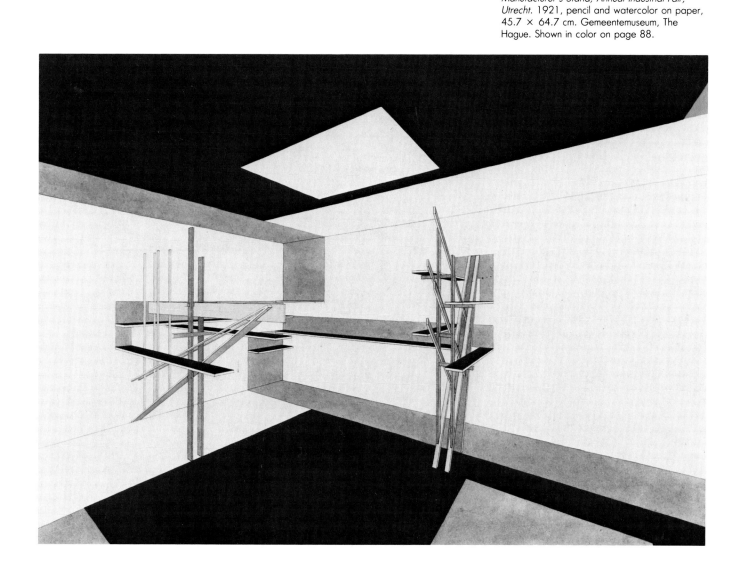

viewer feels pulled into the space of the design, not only by the vigorous use of diagonals, but also by the construction of the shelves and the way they interlock visually with the painted bands of color in the far corner of the room. Furthermore, the shelves, by projecting into the room rather than extending along the walls as in the second design, bring the spectator into more immediate contact with the exhibited objects. To heighten this effect, Zwart did away with the buffer zone of furniture so that the visitor would be attracted by the forms themselves to enter the exhibition space and experience it as a continuous whole. Thus, in his definitive fair-stand design, Zwart fulfilled the requirements he had established for exhibition display two years earlier. And by focusing attention on the corner of the room where several surfaces were fused, he also managed to produce a powerful and effective demonstration of how primary colors and simple constructive elements could be combined to form a totally harmonious abstract interior.

Zwart gave his exhibition environment a radically abstract appearance by making the corner the nucleus of the design. This set a precedent not only for Huszar's music room but also for a design made by van Doesburg in 1924–25. Although van Doesburg had experimented with ways to unite color compositions applied to several exterior surfaces of a single building as early as 1921, he did not focus intensively on the problem of the corner until after he had learned about axonometry, a drafting technique that influenced his development of Elementarism in easel painting and also had a profound effect on the way he rendered color in architecture.[13] The impact of axonometry can be seen in van Doesburg's design for the color scheme of the Flower Room he designed for the Comte and Comtesse de Noailles,[14] even though in it he did not actually make use of any axonometric techniques. In his drawing for the tiny interior, intended for cutting and overnight storage of flowers, van Doesburg rendered the wall and ceiling planes in an exploded-box format (figure 31). However, instead of orienting the design so that its edges would parallel those of the page on which it was drawn he rotated it 45° and placed his signature so as to indicate that the page was to be seen as a somewhat irregular diamond rather than a nearly square rectangle. The colors (red, yellow, blue, black, and gray) were again shifted 45° in relation to the white ground of the design. They formed oblique-angled planes similar to those in van Doesburg's axonometric projections of 1923 (figure 53) and in subsequent paintings whose compositional form was developed on the basis of those projections (figure 76).[15] As in Mondrian's diamond paintings, to which van Doesburg's oblique-angled compositions were surely related, the sliced-off forms in the Flower Room design suggest extension of the composition beyond its literal edges and thus tend to deny the function of the corners as marking the limits of the four wall planes. Indeed, van Doesburg must have intended the broad diagonal bands of color to act as a foil for the narrowness of the closetlike interior space. They contrasted violently with the architecture and created an abstract environment by virtually exploding all sense of confinement in the actual room. Thus the Flower Room represents van Doesburg's own solution to the problem of the corner. Color was not made to cross over from one surface to another, but it nonetheless denied the corner by appearing to extend indefinitely in spite of the corner. In doing so it called into question the limiting and enclosing functions of architecture.

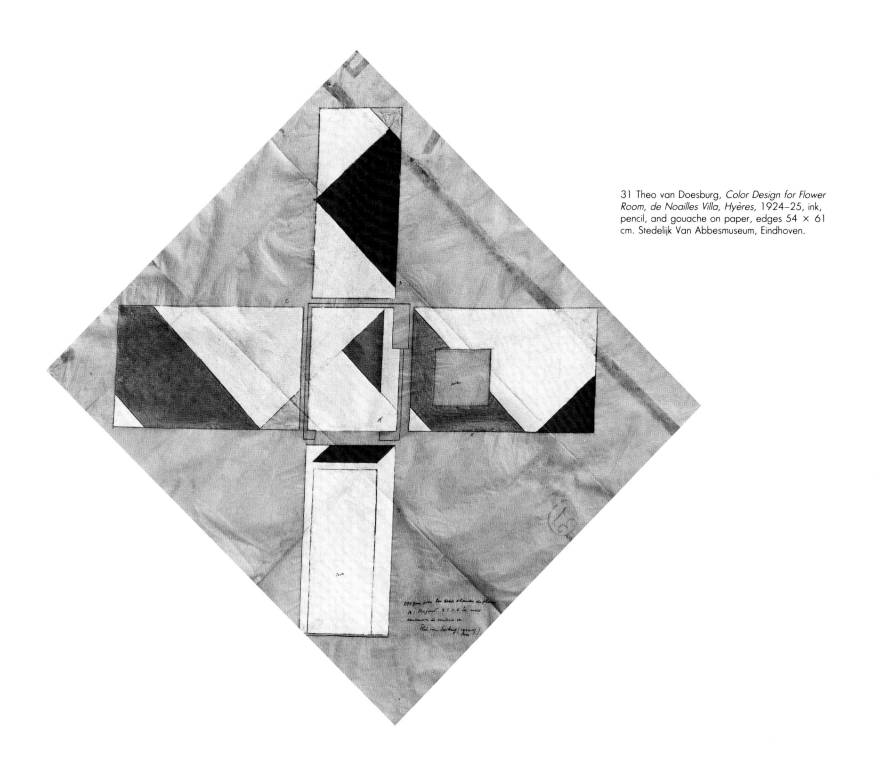

31 Theo van Doesburg, *Color Design for Flower Room, de Noailles Villa, Hyères*, 1924–25, ink, pencil, and gouache on paper, edges 54 × 61 cm. Stedelijk Van Abbesmuseum, Eindhoven.

Although a retrospective view of their designs may suggest that they could not have evolved in any other way, it is significant that Huszar, Zwart, and van Doesburg all formulated their solutions to the problem of the corner in terms of designs for three-dimensional space. Huszar and van Doesburg, as well as van der Leck, were painters with a great deal of experience in applied art, and it is not surprising that this was a determining factor in their approach to interior design. Indeed, these De Stijl artists responded to a wide range of issues (including the use of frames or framing devices and the need to integrate figure and ground) in the context of architecture; that is, in their applied art and their interior designs.

The work of Piet Mondrian did not, however, evolve under these circumstances. Mondrian never made designs for stained glass or other applied art, and he always considered himself to be first and foremost an easel painter, rather than a colorist or interior designer. Although Mondrian did apply color to architecture, and therefore dealt with some of the same aesthetic problems as van der Leck, van Doesburg, and Huszar, his solutions were consistently thought out in terms of individual easel paintings, often well before they were applied in three-dimensional space. As a result his interior designs, like his concept of space in general, were largely concerned with—even dependent upon—issues involved in painting on a single, delimited, flat surface.

Proceeding from his stylistic concerns in individual paintings, Mondrian's attitude to interior design involved strict adherence to planar and orthogonal relationships. Even in his diamond paintings he rejected the overt emphasis on the

oblique that was so important to the development of Zwart's and van Doesburg's abstract interior designs. He understood architecture as "a multiplicity of planes"[16] that relate to one another through space and time in an essentially conceptual rather than a material manner. Thus, unlike Huszar, who did not make use of the oblique but whose colors did cross the boundaries between surfaces, Mondrian confined his applications of color to individual surfaces that visually maintained their validity as such because they were not fused by bands or rectangles of color crossing the boundaries between them. This helps to explain why Mondrian's approach to interior design was so different from that of Huszar, Zwart, and van Doesburg. They took advantage of the problem of the corner by focusing on it, whereas Mondrian's solution amounted to a decision not to deal with it at all.

Mondrian advocated a conception of architecture as a multiplicity of flat planes, in contrast with the traditional attitude based on the manipulation of three-dimensional mass. He identified the latter as an outmoded view of architecture that corresponded to naturalism in painting, in pursuit of which an artist attempts the impossible task of reproducing on canvas the three-dimensional image he sees before him rather than rendering form in terms appropriate to painting: pure colors and flat planes. In "De Realiseering van het Neo-Plasticisme in verre toekomst en in de huidige architectuur" (the realization of Neo-Plasticism in the distant future and in architecture today), an article published in De Stijl in 1922, Mondrian condemned both of these traditional approaches for being linked to "the (perspective) vision of the past." "Neoplasticism," he continued, "does away with that. . . . The new vision—even before Neo-Plasticism—does not proceed from one fixed point of view: it takes its viewpoint *everywhere* and is *nowhere limited. It is not bound by space or time* (in agreement with the theory of relativity). In practice it takes its viewpoint before the plane (the most extreme possibility of plastic intensification).''[17]

Like van Doesburg, who had confronted the issue of perspective in the context of monumental painting in architecture, Mondrian wanted to find a means of rendering form in relation to a new, fluid concept of space. Both van Doesburg and Mondrian avoided traditional perspective because—by its very nature, they believed—it related only to the individual spectator viewing a painted image from a single, fixed point in space. But whereas van Doesburg described his aim in monumental painting as being ''to place man within (instead of opposite) the plastic arts,'' Mondrian accepted the fact that the viewer stands ''before the plane,'' in front of what he sees, and thus comprehends the simultaneity of spatial perception intellectually rather than empathetically, as a multiplicity of planar views. As Mondrian explained in a portion of his dialogue ''Natuurlijke en abstracte realiteit'' (natural reality and abstract reality), published in *De Stijl* in May 1920: ''. . . a room, too, can be seen at a single glance, relatively that is. Remember: our inner vision is different from our sensory perception. We survey the room with our eyes, and afterwards we form an inner image, which causes us to see the various planes as a single plane.''[18]

Mondrian's conceptual attitude toward space as a multiplicity of views brought together in the mind of the spectator was rooted in his understanding of Cubist theory and can

be aligned with the notion of formal apprehension expressed by Albert Gleizes and Jean Metzinger in their 1912 essay *Du ''Cubisme''*: ''To discern a form implies, beside the visual function and the faculty of moving oneself, a certain development of the mind; to the eyes of most people the external world is amorphous.''[19] Although by 1920 Mondrian's work differed significantly from that of the Cubists and his thinking was not identical to theirs, his emphasis on the intellectual assimilation of planar views seems to have been indebted to Gleizes's and Metzinger's belief that the artist discerns a three-dimensional form in terms of a preexisting idea of the form, which enables him to distill it and to render it on the two-dimensional canvas.

Mondrian's emphasis on planes in space also recalls Huszar's approach in designing the color scheme of the Bruynzeel bedroom. Huszar's original conception of the interior as a series of planar compositions was manifested in his drawing of four elevations related to one another sequentially by means of their friezelike placement on the page. In contrast to Huszar, who went on to realize other possibilities for relating surfaces to one another (particularly in the corners of a room), Mondrian continued to insist on the ''plastic of the plane'' as the fundamental constitutive element of the painted interior and indeed of architecture itself. Proceeding from his belief that mass is not necessarily a characteristic intrinsic to architecture, Mondrian stressed that, in spite of its three-dimensionality, architecture, like painting, must be understood in terms of planar composition. In *Le Néo-Plasticisme*, an essay published in Paris in 1920, he wrote: ''Seen as an equilibrated opposition of *expansion and limitation in planar composition*, architectural expression (despite its third dimension) ceases to exist *in corporality and as object*. Its abstract expression appears even more directly than in Painting."[20] Mondrian's emphasis on the flat plane was echoed in an article written in 1926 by a correspondent of a Dutch newspaper who had visited the artist's studio. The writer's description of that space bears the imprint of Mondrian's own ideas: ". . . it would be wrong to speak of [Mondrian's interior design as] spatial art because the abstract artist persistently sees architecture as an intersection of planes, which, through our rapid visual and mental movement, always seem to remain frontal, so that the essential rectangularity is not compromised."[21]

Mondrian's insistence on the discrete, planar architectural surface was not the result of any limitations imposed upon him by architects. In fact, he never worked directly with architects. Although he supported the notion of collaboration, he was by no means thoroughly convinced of its absolute necessity, believing instead that "architect, sculptor and painter find their *essential identity in collaboration* or are all united *in a single person*."[22] Neither was his vision of architecture and interior design conditioned by training or practice in applied art, as was the case with the other De Stijl colorists. Mondrian's ideas were founded primarily upon the development of his easel painting style and his attempts to realize the same Neo-Plastic principles on an environmental scale, particularly in his own atelier.

It is difficult to determine exactly when Mondrian's interest in abstract interior design was first manifested in his atelier. In 1917 he wrote to Theo van Doesburg, "You should remember that my things are still intended to be paintings, that is to say, they are plastic representations, in and by them-

selves, not part of a building."[23] In maintaining the validity of easel paintings independent of architecture, Mondrian may again have been indebted to ideas prevalent among the French Cubists. Gleizes and Metzinger had condemned decorative works of art: "A painting carries within itself its own *raison d'être*. . . . Essentially independent, necessarily complete. . . . It does not harmonize with this or that ensemble, it harmonizes with the meaning of things, with the universe: it is an organism."[24] But although Mondrian continued to believe in the efficacy of individual easel painting throughout his career, he was also convinced that "the abstract-realist [or Neo-Plastic] picture will disappear as soon as we can transfer its plastic beauty to the space around us through the organization of the room into color areas."[25] To this end, probably several months after he moved to Paris in mid-July 1919, he began to treat the interior of his studio as a composition in its own right. This date is confirmed by a letter Mondrian wrote to van Doesburg on December 4, 1919, in which he described how he had arranged his new atelier:

I can't use paint on the wall and have instead affixed some painted cardboard. But I have now clearly seen that it is indeed possible to achieve N[eo]-P[lasticism] in the room. Of course I've also had to paint the furniture. I don't regret the trouble it's taken because it has a favorable effect on my [easel painting] work. I have now begun one thing [a painting] that I like better than all the earlier ones. Of course I don't mean that it's a result of this atelier (I've already been working on it for months).[26]

This letter clearly indicates that the compositional arrangement of Mondrian's studio was intimately related to his central aesthetic concerns, not only in his easel paintings but also in his theoretical writing. As he went on to say to van Doesburg, the studio inspired his treatment of "het decoratieve" (the decorative) in "Natuurlijke en abstracte realiteit," published in *De Stijl* in thirteen installments between June 1919 and August 1920. In this series, a discussion is carried on between three characters: X, a naturalistic painter; Y, an art lover; and Z, an "abstract-realist" painter, who represents Mondrian. The conversation takes place during the course of a walk that begins in the countryside and ends in the city at Z's studio. Mondrian must have written part of the dialogue before leaving Holland for Paris in July 1919. Although it is possible that the atelier he had been using in Laren was also arranged in a manner consistent with his paintings, it is much more likely that the studio of Z described in the dialogue's seventh scene, which was published between March and August 1920, corresponded to the studio he then occupied in Paris, an urban environment like the one portrayed in the last part of the dialogue. Whereas the studio in Laren had been borrowed, the one Mondrian rented on the rue du Coulmiers several months after his arrival in Paris was his own. Although he remained there for only two years, it was an interior that, so long as he did not paint on the walls, Mondrian was free to arrange as he pleased. In the dialogue he described it thus:

Z: The loft, the closet and the built-in fireplace effect an initial division of space and surfaces. The architectonic division is continued by the skylight, by the big studio window, and by the subdivision of the latter into smaller surfaces or panes with, into the bargain, the door in the back under the loft. From this constructive division follows the color division of walls, furnishings and utensils.

Y: Everything contributes to make this division perfect, that I see; for instance, the ivory colored curtains, now drawn.

Z: They form a rectangular plane dividing the planes of the wall next to the window. To continue this partition, I added red, gray, and white planes. And the division of the space is furthered by the white shelves with the gray box and the cylindrical white jar. . . . The gray tool box in the corner also has its importance . . . note the work table in light gray with, on one side, the jug painted in a flat white, and on the other, the bright red box contrasting with the black and white planes of the wall under the windows. And then, next to the work table, note the varnished black bench against the dark red plane of the wall next to the window.[27]

Mondrian had been in Paris for two years just before the First World War, and upon his return he stayed briefly in the studio he had previously occupied on the first floor at 26 rue du Départ, near boulevard Edgar Quinet, behind the Gare Montparnasse. The studio was not his own but belonged to another Dutch artist named Conrad Kikkert, and before long Mondrian was obliged to move. In November 1919 he found the accommodations described above, near the Porte d'Orléans, on the ground floor, reached through the courtyard, at 5 rue du Coulmiers. Nelly van Doesburg later recalled that Mondrian was still at this address early in the spring of 1921, although by that time "he already was making plans to return to the block of artists' studios on the rue du Départ. . . ."[28]

Mondrian was living on the rue du Coulmiers in June 1920 when a Dutch newspaper correspondent visited him.

The correspondent wrote in terms that clearly evoke the studio of Z that was being described in *De Stijl* at the same time. Entering the "austere, sparsely furnished room filled with a clear, cool light," the visitor was overcome by "amazement" at the "ascetic cell reflecting the painting" that Mondrian had placed on an easel in the center of the atelier. He listened while Mondrian explained the principles of his art; then he posed a number of questions:

How does the painter of such work, which itself seems hardly determined [besloten], intend to frame, to limit, to place it in the interior? The easel painting has served its purpose, hasn't it? Mondriaan did not have to answer this question: the atelier speaks for him. The walls of this room, which already have their own pleasing stereometric proportions, are divided spatially by unpainted or primed canvases, so that each wall forms a painting of little blocks, several times enlarged. It is Mondriaan's goal to supplement the work of the architect in this way, by enlivening his single-color planes . . . [and] incorporating the window and door openings in the design as much as possible.[29]

This description and Mondrian's letter to van Doesburg prove that by the end of 1919 Mondrian was already working in a studio to whose white walls he had applied rectangular planes of primary color, plus the black, white, and gray he described in his dialogue. Taking the given structure of the room as his starting point—and thus in essential agreement with the early practice of van der Leck, van Doesburg, and Huszar—Mondrian went on to employ furniture and functional objects further to divide and organize the space. He then added flat colors to the walls and some of the furniture to complete the compositional form of the interior and reinforce the planar character of the surfaces. By incorporating the doors and windows in his design, Mondrian emphasized them as plastic forms with a compositional value equivalent to the colored rectangles he applied to the walls; at the same time, they retained the formal signification of their utilitarian purposes within the architectural setting.

In the arrangement of his studio, Mondrian intended to express the fundamental tenets of his aesthetic philosophy. He felt that "the artist can be fully satisfied only when his conception of the beautiful is reflected in the world around him,"[30] and that an environment that manifested the principles of Neo-Plasticism had a positive effect on the rest of his work—indeed, on his attitude in general: "It is no doubt difficult to conceive the beautiful in our society, for it is difficult to be concerned with balance in the midst of things which lack it."[31]

In 1921 Mondrian returned to 26 rue du Départ. He occupied a studio on the top floor on November 1,[32] and once again he arranged the space according to "the new architectonic plasticism of color."[33] The studio was only one of several rooms in which Mondrian lived and worked until 1936. Located in what were actually two different buildings, his rooms were obliquely connected through a small hallway by a series of steps. The studio, which was on the second floor above street level, over the passage connecting the street and the courtyard (figure 32), was accessible only through the adjoining structure (visible to the right in figure 32), where Mondrian's more private living area was located. In March 1922 a visitor described how Mondrian had arranged the various spaces: "At Mondriaan's everything is self-contained. Here he does his little housekeeping,

32 Courtyard, 26 rue du Départ, Paris. Photograph: Rijksbureau voor Kunsthistorische Documentatie, The Hague.

there he cooks his frugal meals. On the way out, in the hallway where there is another little set of stairs, he parted some curtains. Here is the gas heater, his pots and pans, and also the sleeping area. And in the spacious, light atelier, peaceful although right next to the Gare de Montparnasse, he explains. . . , 'I am happy here. Paris agrees with me, and the atelier pleases me.' ''[34]

In 1959 Mrs. M. van Domselaer-Middelkoop, widow of the Dutch composer Jacob van Domselaer, published some reminiscences of Mondrian. Her description of a visit to the rue du Départ in October 1922 complements and expands upon the one quoted above: "We ate in his bedroom where he set the meal on a chest in front of the only window. We looked out on a gray courtyard with discolored windows on all sides, while hearing the shunting-engine noises from the railyard behind the Gare Montparnasse. At his place everything was extremely trim and orderly. Although not much was in this room—a small iron bed in the corner, a chest in front of the window with chairs around it—nevertheless it had atmosphere."[35]

The most comprehensive description of Mondrian's studio is provided by Michel Seuphor, who first visited Mondrian there in April 1923. In 1956 he recalled that the studio had had a large window facing east, overlooking the rue du Départ, and a much higher, wider window facing southwest, with a view of the railway tracks of the Gare Montparnasse. "The room," Seuphor wrote, "was quite large, very bright, with a very high ceiling." Seuphor described the arrangement of the studio as follows:

Mondrian had divided it irregularly, utilizing for this purpose a large black-painted cupboard, which was partially hidden by an easel long out of service; the latter was covered with big gray and white paste-boards. Another easel rested against the large rear wall whose appearance changed often, for Mondrian applied to it his Neo-Plastic virtuosity. The second easel was completely white, and used only for showing finished canvases. The actual work was done on the table. It stood in front of the large window facing the rue du Départ. . . . He had two large wicker arm-chairs, also painted white, and, on the scrupulously clean floor, two rugs, one red, the other gray.[36]

More recently Seuphor recalled that when he first saw it the studio was white and gray, and that Georges Vantongerloo had done the actual work of painting the walls according to Mondrian's instructions.[37] Although the only large, unbroken wall surface in Mondrian's rue du Départ studio apparently retained a relatively subdued treatment for several years, as can be seen in photographs taken of it in 1926 (figures 62 and 67), rectangular planes of primary color were applied to other surfaces and at times were also attached to parts of the long wall. This is suggested by a badly focused picture, published in *De Stijl* in 1924, showing Mondrian, cigarette in hand, standing in front of a painting set up on an easel (figure 33). Visible behind the easel is a part of the long wall (usually hidden by the cupboard and a second, pasteboard-covered easel) to which planes of color had been applied. It was at a table facing another portion of this wall, and not while looking out over the rue du Départ as may be inferred from Seuphor's description quoted above, that Mondrian worked on his paintings. The long wall, almost directly opposite the entrance area, was the main focus of the studio space and the object of Mondrian's concentrated attention in the following years.

The early date of Mondrian's first studio arrangements seems particularly significant when one considers that he began to organize the space as a Neo-Plastic composition of planes at about the same time that the other artists with whom he was associated through *De Stijl* were moving away from a strictly planar conception of color in the interior. It is of course important to bear in mind that from 1919 on Mondrian was living in Paris, keeping himself at least physically distant from the activities of the De Stijl artists who remained in Holland or traveled elsewhere. Moreover, Mondrian's studio was different from their work insofar as it was not a product of collaboration with an architect and was not developed through preliminary designs on paper. The studio underwent continual transformation alongside the evolution of the artist's easel painting style, for which it served as a background and perhaps as a kind of three-dimensional sketch. The temporary nature of the studio's design at any given moment helps to explain why, with the exception of the subdued use of gray, Mondrian seems not to have employed paint to add color directly to the white walls of his studio. Instead he attached rectangular canvases or, more often, colored pasteboard planes to the walls and some of the furnishings. Apart from the fact that this reliance on either canvas or pasteboard rectangles may have been an additional factor in Mondrian's avoidance of the problem of the corner (it would doubtless never have occurred to him that these materials could be used, like paint, to cross the boundary between one wall and the next), the technique was also important because it allowed for constant alteration and guaranteed that the studio would never become a fixed interior like those designed by the other De Stijl color-

33 Piet Mondrian in his studio, Paris. *De Stijl* VI, 6–7 (1924): 86.

ists.[38] But although Mondrian did not intend his studio to be understood as a finished work of art in the same sense as his easel paintings, he obviously felt that in it he had successfully applied the principles of Neo-Plasticism to interior design. As we have seen, Mondrian himself wrote about his studio, as did several correspondents of Dutch newspapers who visited him in Paris during the 1920s. Furthermore, on several occasions Mondrian provided photographs of the studio to art publications, a fact that also testifies to his consideration of the interior as a representative work.

Mondrian's studios can only be seen as products of his own aesthetic decisions, although he often discussed their arrangement with other artists, as he did with Theo van Doesburg, who visited Mondrian at the rue du Coulmiers in February 1920 and again in the spring of 1921.[39] Several months after his second visit, in a letter written to Oud on September 12, 1921, van Doesburg described his disagreement with Mondrian over the issue of interior design. Van Doesburg stated his belief that painting in an interior is very different from painting on a single plane because in an interior the viewer encounters the compositional design through a simultaneous experience of space and time. According to van Doesburg, by insisting on the "plastic of the plane," Mondrian's spatial design confined itself to a sequential experience of space, one plane after the other, rather than promoting an apprehension of the elements of time and space as a unified entity:

. . . I am now certain that painting in the interior, i.e., in 3 dimensions, brings with it entirely different demands than painting on a plane. The interior again brings the time element to attention, and the earlier ornamentality (continuous ornament, e.g.) was a vague, decorative manner of solving time and space as a unity. Since in his last article Mondriaan completely denies the time moment and wants to banish it from painting, for him 3-dimensional painting (i.e., space-time painting) must be impossible. He remains limited to the 2-dimensional canvas and the attempt to solve a 5-plane space as 1 whole is impossible in terms of 2-dimensional painting. Thus what Mondriaan has made in his atelier with colored cardboard is restricted to one plane (window plane) and is therefore also a painting in 2 dimensions. . . .

Mondriaan as a man is not modern because, in my opinion, although he has developed psychically towards the new, spiritually he belongs to the old. By this I mean that he still sees the spiritual as a conceptual abstraction, thus something like the theosophists. Of life itself as reality he is in fact afraid. He thinks life, but does not live it. He makes his conception, which of course is very good, too much about an ideal image outside of normal life. . . . [40]

In these passages van Doesburg established the criteria that formed the basis for his eventual development of a consistent approach toward the application of color to architecture. Although van Doesburg was already discussing the colored interior in highly abstract terms, the position he took was opposed to Mondrian's insistence that the Neo-Plastic environment could only be realized in the future, so that for the time being attempts at creating a harmonious interior according to the principles of De Stijl had to remain on an essentially conceptual level, within the realm of art. Mondrian wrote to Oud on August 30, 1921: "We can only be pure if we once again regard the art of building as art. Only as art can architecture satisfy the aesthetic demands of Neo-Plasticism."[41] To the same end, in a letter to van Doesburg written two years later he stated: "I do entirely agree when you write that the interior is going to be 'the' important thing. But in the future . . . I am convinced that we are now only capable of doing it on paper, on account of these rotten architects, valets of the public."[42]

Mondrian's derogatory assessment of the architectural profession is important because it corresponds to the increasingly suspect attitude toward collaboration with architects expressed by the other De Stijl colorists, particularly van der Leck as early as 1917. By concentrating his interior-design efforts in the very personal, aesthetic realm of his studio, Mondrian managed to avoid collaborating with architects, even on the few occasions when he made coloristic designs for other spaces. Huszar and Zwart also questioned the ideal of collaboration; however, their conflicts with architecture were expressed not in words but in their work, in the coloristic solution of the problem of the corner. In the early 1920s, van Doesburg too came into sharp conflict with the architect Oud over the role of color in architecture. The problems van Doesburg encountered in relating his work to Oud's architecture exemplify the circumstances that eventually led to the breakdown of De Stijl's collaborative ideal.

3

Collaboration Reexamined: Color versus Architecture

By the early 1920s, the first phase of De Stijl activity in coloristic design had come to an end. Several of the original contributors had already severed connections with the magazine *De Stijl*. Each of the De Stijl painters had realized one or more coloristic designs in architecture, and it seems that as artists they began reassessing not only the role of color in architecture but also the nature of collaborative work. As a result of their greater understanding of the spatial possibilities inherent in the manipulation of color and their desire to create color schemes totally integrated with rather than merely applied to architecture, colorists began to demand concessions from architects. In claiming more responsibility for the affective potential of spatial design, they hoped to ensure that their coloristic contributions would not be subordinated to the prerogatives of architects.

Already in 1920 Theo van Doesburg was attempting to make the abstract consideration of color a more important element in the determination of structural or at least of spatial composition. In a letter to Oud dated January 15, 1920, the ceramicist Willem Brouwer described his difficulties in accepting van Doesburg's newest ideas: "Brick is no longer of any account. Say you design (construct) a house on WHITE paper, THEREFORE . . . that house will also be of white, plastered materials. On purple packing paper, the house becomes a purple house. If windows necessary for the interior utilization of a house appear in the facade, where they are located and how large they are may NOT be determined by the architect. He claims that for 'painters.' If I didn't know the man really means it, then the idea might make me think he'd driven me crazy."[1] Van Doesburg asserted that coloristic considerations should determine the materials used in a given structure, and that the size and placement of functional elements would have to correlate in the first place with the coloristic treatment. Only after fulfilling these requirements could the architect go on to consider practical aspects of a building. As early as 1920 van Doesburg's conception of color in space contained the seeds of his mature architectural credo, which were to bear fruit only several years later, after these radical ideas forced him to break with Oud.

At the time Brouwer wrote his letter to Oud, van Doesburg was completing an interior color scheme for Spangen I and V, two housing blocks Oud had designed in the beginning of 1918, immediately after he was appointed municipal architect of Rotterdam. In an article published September 11, 1920, Oud discussed van Doesburg's handling of a model interior in which the walls were painted yellow to the height of the blue doors, and each wall surface was framed by a band of black that separated the large colored area below from the white one above (figure 34). Oud noted the problems inherent in using wallpaper and proposed paint as the best available alternative:

As a result of difficulties in obtaining good wall linen and wallpaper now, and because we have so often seen how humidity from washing and cooking affects the wallpaper in the living rooms, making it ugly or making it peel off—therefore, as an experiment, the walls have been provided with a painted frame at the height of the top of the door. Beneath this frame the wall is covered with colored plaster, while the upper portion, like the ceiling, is painted white.

. . . wallpaper is made superfluous by the treatment of the walls in strong contrasting colors (yellow, gray, blue, black) in the artistic solution of the interior by Theo van Doesburg. Just how the above-described handling of the walls will work out in actual apartments cannnot be said in advance; in different cities people have had different experiences. Bear in mind that the upkeep is more difficult than with wallpaper because in general it is easier to put up paper than it is to repair plaster. Furthermore, the flat color of the walls will soil more easily than variegated wallpaper, whose decorative ornamentation absorbs and thus conceals any blemishes. The ideal here would be a hard, smooth, colored surface that is washable.[2]

Oud's article demonstrates his appreciation of van Doesburg's contribution for its practicality in terms of cost and durability, the same considerations that led him to ask Rietveld to provide furniture for the model Spangen interior Oud illustrated alongside his article.

Oud's attitude toward painted architecture was bound up with his concern, as municipal architect, for utility more than for the aesthetic solution of the interior composition. As a designer of public housing in Rotterdam, Oud was, moreover, in a position to apply concepts of standardization and normalization, which he had already begun to articulate in an article published in De Stijl in May 1918. This article, written in response to a call for standardization that had been made by J. van der Waerden to the congress of the Nationale Woningraad (national housing council) in February of that year,[3] stressed the fundamental relationship of architecture to social and technological factors that "impose certain requisites which limit the number of possibilities and its [architecture's] degree of expressive purity." Proceeding from his belief that the machine provided the appropriate means for mass production of utilitarian objects, Oud advocated commercial manufacture of standardized architectural elements, such as doors and windows, which would be used

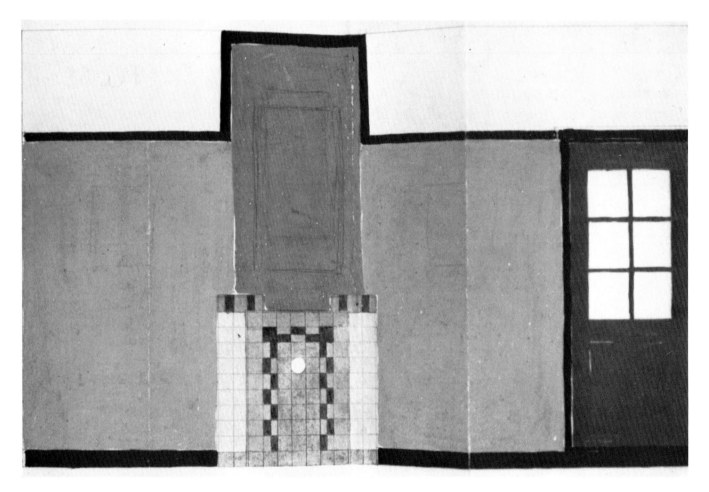

34 Theo van Doesburg, *Color Design for Ground-Floor Interiors, Spangen Housing Blocks IV and V (detail)*, 1920, pencil and gouache on paper, 26.5 × 100 cm. Collection of Mrs. Annie Oud-Dinaux, Wassenaar.

in a limited number of normative housing types, themselves to be "achieved in an aesthetically finished manner." These flats, in turn, could be grouped together in residential blocks whose rhythmic juxtaposition would form the modern, monumental cityscape. Thus, he argued, the aesthetic expression of mass-produced objects would fulfill an urgent need for low-cost housing at the same time that it would lead to a universal style appropriate to modern architecture. "The architect," Oud concluded, "appears here as a producer, as a person who stages the mass products in an architectural setting, i.e., through the art of relationships. Those who still feel the need to express themselves with aesthetic accessories may amuse themselves with private houses."[4] In this last remark, Oud betrayed his contempt for architects who did not view economic and utilitarian considerations as their primary concern and who therefore chose to work in the private sector in order to express their aesthetic individualism. Although in 1918 the statement had been directed against others, by 1920 it could have been construed as a criticism of van Doesburg's increasingly abstract ideas; indeed, in retrospect, it established the context in which Oud's position in relation to De Stijl, and particularly to van Doesburg, would be defined in the next few years.

Between 1918 and 1920 van Doesburg also came to recognize the importance of machine technology in the development of an aesthetic theory appropriate to the modern age, but he dealt with the issue—for example, in his 1922 lecture "Der Wille zum Stil" (the will to style)—in what can only be described as abstract terms. He favored mechanical production over handicraft for primarily formal reasons, and, instead of advocating normalization or standardization to

solve the economic problems of architecture in the postwar period, he focused on aesthetic considerations, stating his belief that "in modern architecture the problem of color and space is the most important, indeed it is the most difficult problem of our age." "In my opinion," van Doesburg declared, "the solution will be found only in a monumental synthesis." The distance that finally separated van Doesburg from Oud's concern for the rationalization of architecture can be measured quite precisely in the words that followed: "A reconciliation between the impulses of space and time can be effected only in chromo-plasticism, that is, in treating three-dimensional space as a painter's composition."[5]

In 1920, however, the break had not yet come. At this point Oud still had reason to be pleased with van Doesburg's relatively conservative designs for his first Spangen blocks, including the stained glass windows van Doesburg designed for the space over each entrance door. In fact, he asked van Doesburg to contribute a comparable design for his next Spangen housing, blocks VIII and IX. On October 1, 1920, van Doesburg wrote Oud that he was about to begin work on the second set of designs, which were to include color schemes for both the exteriors and the interiors of Oud's buildings. He wanted the architect to send him ground plans and a sample of the brick to be used. He asked, "Or will it be *white*?"[6] Evidently he believed that a white background would give him even greater freedom in determining his exterior color design.

In the meantime, in February 1920 van Doesburg had been to Paris, where he had visited Mondrian, who had introduced him to Léonce Rosenberg. Rosenberg was the director of the recently opened Galerie "L'Effort Moderne," and even before he started a journal with the same name he sought to establish himself as a champion of international modern art movements in France by publishing booklets such as Mondrian's *Le Néo-Plasticisme* and acting as distributor of the French version of van Doesburg's *Klassiek–Barok–Modern*. Thus, from the beginning Rosenberg proved to be an enthusiastic supporter of De Stijl. When van Doesburg returned to The Netherlands from Paris, Rosenberg wrote to him requesting photographs of work by De Stijl artists. He published a series of his own articles in *De Stijl* as well. On October 19, 1920, van Doesburg wrote Oud a jubilant letter full of the news that sometime in the next few years Rosenberg wanted to build a model house in the country on which all the De Stijl artists would be expected to collaborate:

He wants to realize completely all our ideals in it! He also wants to have a completely modern garden next to it, etc. A splendid idea, eh? It is not for right away but we can all discuss it at our ease all the better. . . .
In any case the design can be started because his plan seems to stand fast!! This can be a manifestation in which we knock 'em dead!![7]

Several months later, at the end of 1920, van Doesburg made a short trip to Germany on the invitation of Hans Richter and Viking Eggeling, whom he visited in Klein-Kölzig. While in Germany he also met Bruno Taut and the critic Adolf Behne; Behne introduced him to Adolf Meyer and Walter Gropius.[8] Gropius invited him to visit the Bauhaus in Weimar. After spending several days there, van Doesburg returned briefly to The Netherlands, writing to Meyer that he planned to return soon to work in Weimar.[9] In March 1921,

van Doesburg left Holland with Weimar as his eventual destination. After delivering lectures in Antwerp and Brussels he went to Paris, where he visited Mondrian for several weeks. While in Paris, van Doesburg must have had extensive discussions with Rosenberg. By then, Rosenberg had made it clear that for the time being he lacked the funds to build the house he had commissioned from the De Stijl artists. He nonetheless asked van Doesburg to proceed with designs for the house, and told him that they would form the nucleus of an architecture exhibition Rosenberg wanted to present the following year. In April, van Doesburg wrote the following to Oud from Paris:

Now that I have had a really definitive discussion with Rosenberg, and I am very content with it, I can no longer postpone it [a reply]. Tenez donc cher ami: Rosenberg gave me a full explanation of his intentions and all the points have been handled. He himself has made a few "pen scratches" mapping out the house in question. You find them herewith [figures 35–37]. The entire layout is indicated, from the garden to the upper floors. In my opinion it lacks a music-dance room, which R[osenberg] certainly has not considered. Let me quickly go through the various sketches. He imagines the whole surrounded by a garden cut off from the outside world by walls, not actually continuous, but pierced by "grilles." The house itself is situated around a courtyard with a basin in which there is a fountain (my monument, e.g., is very well suited for this).[10] On the upper stories terraces are indicated. . . . I find the terraces a very nice idea, but am afraid that they will harm the exterior aspect. Study these scribbles at your leisure and remember that they are not binding. Rosenberg allows us freedom in everything and these sketches are only intended to indicate what kinds of rooms, etc., there must be. He wants to begin with the exhibition in January or February 1922, and is very, extraordinarily enthusiastic about the affair. He promises that our work will have positive results; it must be a bomb that will explode everything done here. The exhibition will consist of: a. all the designs and photographs of the architecture and painting for this building; b. examples of details in model form, and executed stained glass windows. Furthermore and importantly, a model, made up of various elements that can be taken apart to show the construction and the interior parts. Everything must seem irreproachable. If everyone works with care a splendid whole can come of it. I have already had a discussion with Mondriaan. He is of the opinion that you must get in touch with V[an] 't Hoff because, for such a historic and aesthetic event, all our various, petty differences must be set aside. I am in agreement with this and advise you to do the same as far as Huszar is concerned. Rietveld must help to make the model (which Mondriaan envisions in wood, tinned iron and various colored and uncolored materials). I thought of Vantongerloo but Piet is more or less against that. In any case we three must keep the business amongst ourselves, and discuss and control everything. There are so many rooms that there is a lot of work for the painters to do and I think Huszar can be brought in on the condition that he still works in our spirit and not as earlier, decoratively. Mondriaan will also contribute to make the plan succeed. . . .

Now something else: the exhibition of model and projects must proceed from a group: the Stijl group. The three of us alone would naturally be the best but then Rosenberg would not be enthusiastic. The problem now is to have the right guys in the right place. Piet wants to be responsible for dividing the tasks and he wants to include Huszar among those who execute it. Van der Leck can't be included because his work differs too much from ours.

Furthermore: we are completely free in everything. Layout, material, construction, everything rests in our hands and Rosenberg troubles himself with nothing other than saying how many and what kinds of rooms, and with the launching of

our work in Europe and America. . . . ''Now or never'' should be our motto.[11]

Van Doesburg's letter is important for several reasons. First of all, along with the drawings by Rosenberg, it documents the genesis of the architectural program for Rosenberg's gallery-house, the Private Villa exhibited in ground plan and model form for the first time in 1923.[12] More significant, the letter demonstrates the extent to which van Doesburg and Mondrian were willing to participate in the realization of De Stijl's principles in architecture. Most important in the context of this discussion is what the letter reveals about van Doesburg's concept of the De Stijl group and the collaborative effort he supposedly believed to be a fundamental aspect of De Stijl's architectural aesthetic.

Van Doesburg's primary concern with regard to the eventual exhibition was that De Stijl should appear to be a united group of artists equally responsible for the objects they produced. Nevertheless, at least to Mondrian and Oud, van Doesburg was willing to acknowledge that everyone associated with *De Stijl* was not equally gifted and that, since he and Mondrian and Oud would ''naturally be the best,'' they would need to ''keep the business amongst [them]selves, and discuss and control everything.'' In the exhibition, however, their preeminence would have to be concealed, thus permitting the De Stijl group as a whole to demonstrate the supposed realization of its collaborative ideal. Van Doesburg emphasized the necessity of their not exhibiting as individuals, stating that if they were to do so Rosenberg would be displeased. Evidently, van Doesburg had gone to some lengths to suggest to Rosenberg that there was indeed a united group of artists associated with *De Stijl*. Mondrian

35 Léonce Rosenberg, *Sketch for Private Villa, Ground Floor*, 1921, ink on paper, 22 × 17.3 cm. Fondation Custodia, Institut Néerlandais, Paris.

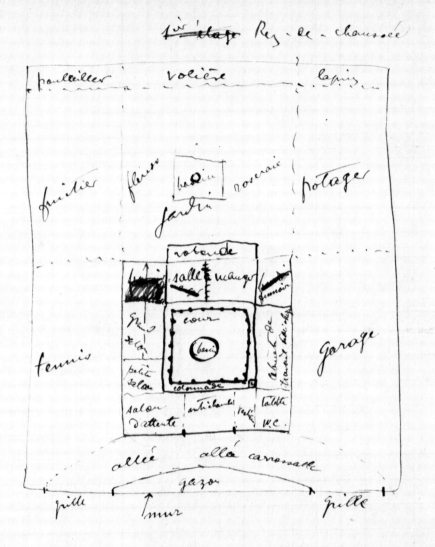

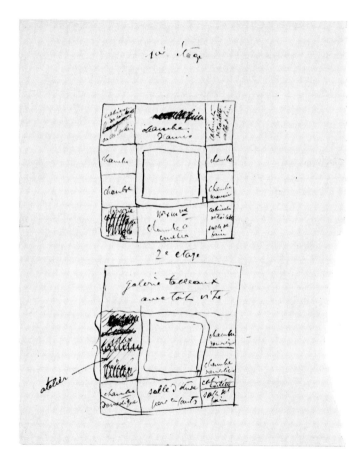

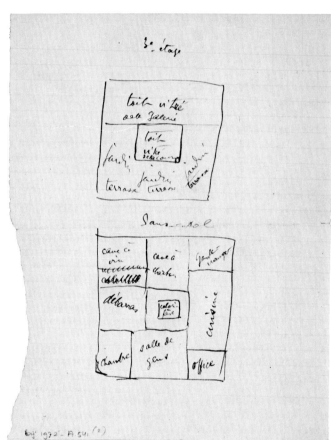

36 Léonce Rosenberg, *Sketch for Private Villa, First and Second Floors (recto)*, 1921, ink on paper, 22 × 17.3 cm. Fondation Custodia, Institut Néerlandais, Paris.

37 Léonce Rosenberg, *Sketch for Private Villa, Third Floor and Basement (verso)*, 1921, ink on paper, 22 × 17.3 cm. Fondation Custodia, Institut Néerlandais, Paris.

hinted at this when he wrote to Oud on April 9, 1921: "You've heard about the big Rosenberg plan. It seems rather impossible to me because there is not yet a Stijl group as a unity, in fact there is no Stijl group. Rosenberg spoke of several architects to me, of V[an] 't Hoff also. He seems to think that all these fellows are still with De Stijl."[13] Indeed, by the spring of 1921 both van 't Hoff and Wils had already left the De Stijl circle, following van der Leck, who had severed his connections several years earlier and whom in any case van Doesburg would not allow to participate in the model project, on the not-unreasonable grounds that his post-1918 figurative work "differs too much from ours." Whatever their reasons for leaving the De Stijl group, whether primarily political, philosophical, or personal or (as seems most likely) a mixture of the three, the departure of van 't Hoff and Wils left De Stijl particularly weak on the architectural side. Of the professionally trained architects, only Oud remained attached to the group—somewhat tenuously, as witnessed by his refusal to sign any of the De Stijl manifestos or petitions even before he also severed connections with *De Stijl* later in the year. Describing the evolution of the Rosenberg project in the tenth-anniversary issue of *De Stijl*, van Doesburg referred directly to the "lack of the desired, collectively developed activity" of the De Stijl artists in order to explain the roles of those who did eventually cooperate.[14]

This situation accounts in part for the willingness of Mondrian and the eagerness of van Doesburg to participate in the architectural decisions related to the model project. From the beginning, these two painters—because they were in Paris—were able to discuss the program with Rosenberg.

Moreover, van Doesburg also felt qualified to express opinions about important architectural considerations, such as problems of heating and the terraces Rosenberg wanted to include. Significantly, it was Mondrian who suggested that the model of the gallery-house be made of diverse materials—consistent with the open, extensive character of his planar understanding of architecture—rather than the traditional plaster, which he associated with an outmoded architecture of masses. In his letter of April 9, 1921, Mondrian described to Oud how he imagined the collaborative work under the existing circumstances:

I said to Does[burg] that it only seems possible to me if you and Does make a plan together, with me as advisor. . . . That way it will be a totality. Perhaps you could even work together with V[an] 't Hoff, but I don't know if that's possible from his point of view. I told Does that the model really must be made of wood and tinned lead or cardboard and not of plaster but later I told him that this would be much too expensive and time-consuming. . . . I would be very pleased to be of as much service as possible but don't get me involved with designing or executing.[15]

This letter reveals that, although at first Mondrian was eager to participate to a limited degree as an advisor in the collaborative effort, he had serious doubts about the Rosenberg project. These doubts were soon to be echoed by Oud, who, van Doesburg wrote to a friend in June 1921, did "not want to take the risk upon himself because it will naturally demand an enormous amount of drafting work."[16] Oud seems, however, to have hesitated at least long enough to correspond directly with Rosenberg, whom he asked for details about the commission, including site specifications for the house and information concerning who was to pay for the model Rosenberg intended to exhibit. On September 1, 1921, Rosenberg wrote to Oud that he could offer the De Stijl artists an exhibition of models and projects but that the cost of making the designs would have to be assumed by them:

. . . I indicated to Monsieur Theo van Doesburg the disposition for a dwelling which would be pleasing to the Parisian public as well as myself. Because, if you aspire to commissions in Paris, it is logical and inevitable that these could only be prompted by works capable of conforming to the taste and habits of the public called to examine them. Since the house—for which I gave indications to Monsieur Theo van Doesburg—corresponds neither to a commission nor to a specific location, it is impossible for me to answer your questions. I therefore leave you free to establish a model which could be adapted to a plot of ground X, Y, or Z. I understand very well that this presents certain difficulties, but as the Parisian public is accustomed to building on flat land, it seems to me that it is possible to establish a project conciliatory to the majority of cases. In sum, I ask you to make your model for a house which you yourself would like to inhabit if you lived in the environs of Paris.[17]

Although Rosenberg wanted to make a name for himself as a promoter of avant-garde art, his letter shows that he also had a subtle understanding of the necessity for progressive artists to compromise with the prevailing taste. His suggestion that in order to be successful the De Stijl artists would have to exhibit works that appealed to French tastes and customs is reminiscent of ideas that had inspired the Maison Cubiste almost ten years earlier. These notions seem to have constituted a particularly French attitude, very much in contrast with the Dutch artists' refusal to make concessions to established norms. It is remarkable that, in spite of Rosen-

berg's desire to please the Parisian public, the vague terms of his proposal eventually enabled the De Stijl artists to produce a series of models and projects so radical and abstract that they seemed to have little in common with the more traditional architecture Rosenberg had invoked.

It was not with Rosenberg's demand for concessions to public taste, however, that Oud eventually found fault. As municipal architect, Oud was increasingly concerned with practical aspects of architecture, and thus he may have appreciated the validity of Rosenberg's requirements in that regard. But Oud's emphasis on practicality led him to decline the Rosenberg proposal because "there was no 'terrain' to build the house on and Oud was opposed to 'Utopian building' which did not start from given facts. . . ."[18] Oud later wrote in *Mein Weg in "De Stijl"* that he "refused because [he] could scarcely imagine a building disengaged from its surroundings."[19] Furthermore, since both Wils and van 't Hoff had left the De Stijl circle, all of the architectural aspects of the project too complex for a painter (even one so avid as van Doesburg) to solve would have devolved upon Oud, and he had made his reservations on that score clear to van Doesburg from the start.

In the meantime, Oud and van Doesburg encountered other difficulties that contributed directly to the breakdown of their collaborative efforts. During the summer of 1921, after his arrival in Weimar (where Adolf Meyer had found him an apartment), van Doesburg began to work on his color schemes for Oud's second set of Spangen housing blocks. In Weimar he had a large studio where he was visited by many Bauhaus students sympathetic to his ideas. While he was designing the Spangen color schemes and clarifying his aesthetic principles with respect to those of the Bauhaus, van Doesburg developed a new working method for his architecture-related projects, starting with interior colors and moving outward "so that interior and exterior can be painted in one color [scheme]."[20] He began to envision color in architecture as a means of connecting interior and exterior surfaces and spaces through a dynamic relationship of loose planes. He no longer felt constrained to limit color to structurally defined elements, and he now understood the various surfaces in a room (particularly the doors) as relief planes; that is, as abstract compositional forms. Through color, van Doesburg now realized, the door could be emphasized as a functional element, like the ones in De Vonk, or it could be treated in the same manner as the wall surface it pierced, thus blending with that surface and denying its own architectural function in the space. He wrote: "I believe (and this in connection with Mondriaan's answer with which I am not in agreement) that in solving an interior, the door does not play so great a role. If by means of color the walls relate well to one another, the door can work either as one color plane or as a wall plane (thus neutrally)."[21] The approach van Doesburg was developing is comparable to Huszar's later design for Til Brugman's music room in The Hague, in which Huszar used color to deemphasize the function of the door by integrating the door surface with the plane of the wall it pierced. Similarly, van Doesburg's desire to compose a single color scheme for both the interior and the exterior of the Spangen buildings can be seen to parallel an issue raised by the problem of the corner: the use of color to relate or connect various surfaces that otherwise constitute discrete architectural planes.

Van Doesburg wrote to Oud that in his Spangen designs he began by working out contrasts, using oblique color relationships to break up the predominantly orthogonal character of Oud's buildings. "My ideal," he declared, "is to follow up the architectonic division with color contrasts and thus to control the whole space."[22] In view of this ambition, which again signals van Doesburg's reappraisal of the nature of collaborative work, it is not surprising that he was soon confronted by the rejection of his coloristic designs.

By the end of October 1921, van Doesburg had sent Oud all the exterior color schemes for Spangen blocks VIII (figure 38) and IX, in which blue, yellow, green, gray, black, and white were intended to create a dynamic movement contrasting with and counterbalancing the static quality of Oud's symmetrical red-brick architecture. Since red was the ground color of the buildings, van Doesburg did not include it among the colors he applied to Oud's designs. He used the other primaries (yellow and blue), together with their intermediary, green (the color-opposite of red). Alongside these colors, which van Doesburg referred to as the "dissonant triad," following Ostwald he also employed the "noncolors," black, white, and gray. He identified the "real" colors blue, green, and yellow with their respective "abstract" counterparts, black, gray, and white, perhaps for the simple reason that a mixture of blue and yellow produces green just as a mixture of white and black produces gray.[23] Continuing to work out his color schemes in musical terms (as he had done in the de Lange Town House window), van Doesburg evidently understood blue, red, and yellow as a consonant triad and introduced green to express dissonance, or contrast. The colors were intended to contrast with one another in order to produce a dynamic effect that would in turn contrast with the static architecture in such a balanced way that equilibrium or "rest"—another quasi-musical term—would ultimately prevail. At the two windowless ends of the facade, van Doesburg proposed to paint large rectangular planes of black (figure 39). These were the only areas where color would be applied on the actual building as flat planes. Although in all his drawings van Doesburg indicated the windows as colored planes, in fact only the window latticework would be colored; the window frames would be white and the panes of glass clear. By using unbroken rectangles to indicate the colors of the woodwork in the windows, van Doesburg wanted not only to strengthen their impact in the color scheme, but also to reinforce his exposition of color moving across architecture in terms of flat planes relating to one another through space.

Van Doesburg also wanted to use color to mitigate the three-dimensional massiveness of Oud's Potgieterstraat facade, the central portion of which was set back slightly behind two wings. His diagram of the color scheme, labeled Schematische voorstelling der abstracte beweging (en tegenbeweging) van elke kleur [schematic representation of the abstract movement (and countermovement) of each color] (figure 40), shows how various groups of colored planes were meant to coalesce into wedgelike shapes that converged in the recessed central area of the facade. This composition, van Doesburg explained, was intended to produce a sense of relief that would make the middle of the building seem to project slightly forward onto the same plane as the lateral wings. The use of color in this manner,

as a means of camouflage intended to alter the viewer's perception of architecture, was extremely bold. The design also demonstrates that, although he was still dealing with rectangular planes of color, van Doesburg was already aware of the enhanced spatial possibilities inherent in color arrangements involving oblique-angled planes.

Shortly after van Doesburg sent his designs to Oud, he received a negative response from the architect. Oud found the color schemes disunified and too much in contrast with his own designs. In a letter written November 3, 1921, under the motto Entweder—oder (either—or), van Doesburg replied with bitter vehemence to Oud's criticism. He cited a letter in which Oud had praised the color schemes and had said that they would all be used. Van Doesburg went on to defend the contrasting quality of his designs, stating that he intended their dynamism to act as a foil for the static nature of Oud's symmetrical facades. He had seen the coloristic and formal design of the block as a whole in which oblique and orthogonal relationships of color and architecture complemented one another. Finally, van Doesburg wrote that he was disappointed not only for himself but also because, in criticizing the designs, Oud had attacked the aim van Doesburg believed they had in common: the development of a coloristic architecture. He reminded Oud that the architect had promised to leave him completely free in his color designs for these Spangen blocks:

Now—according to your latest letter—you want to change the whole thing and murder one of my most successful solutions. Everything fits together beautifully, not only on the exterior but also the interior, which connect with one another.

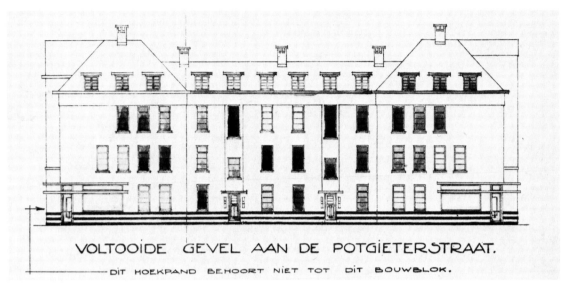

VOLTOOIDE GEVEL AAN DE POTGIETERSTRAAT.

— DIT HOEKPAND BEHOORT NIET TOT DIT BOUWBLOK.

38 Theo van Doesburg, *Color Design, Facade on Potgieterstraat, Spangen Housing Block VIII, Rotterdam*, 1921, ink and watercolor on paper, 15.7 × 25.5 cm. Fondation Custodia, Institut Néerlandais, Paris. Shown in color on page 89.

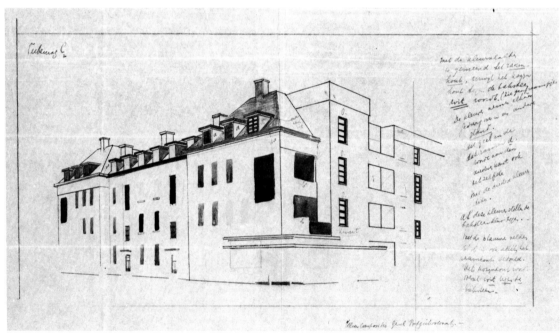

39 Theo van Doesburg, *Color Design, Spangen Housing Block VIII, Rotterdam*, 1921, ink and watercolor on paper, 35.5 × 53.2 cm. Fondation Custodia, Institut Néerlandais, Paris. Shown in color on page 89.

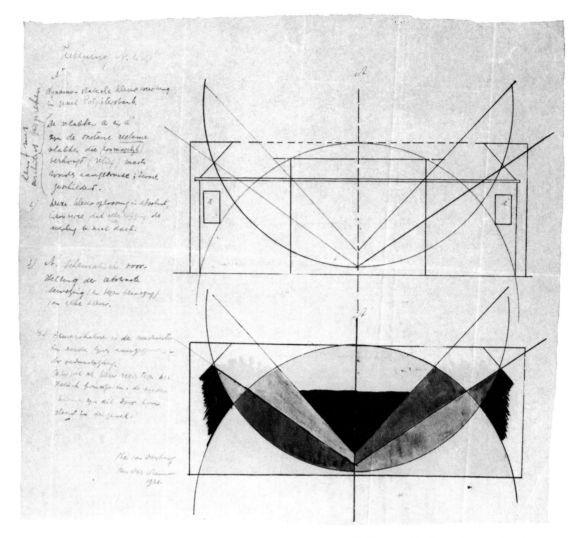

40 Theo van Doesburg, *Diagram of Color Scheme, Spangen Housing Block VIII, Rotterdam,* 1921, ink and watercolor on paper, 29 × 32.3 cm. Foundation Custodia, Institut Néerlandais, Paris. Shown in color on page 90.

Van Doesburg argued that any changes would damage the total effect of his design and stated emphatically that he would not allow any alterations:

. . . given the fact that the execution of the whole was assured; given the fact that I am no house-painter but take these things seriously; given the fact that I am van Doesburg, I have, I seize the right to cry:

NO——NO——NO

Entweder so————oder Nichts.[24]

This explosive letter marks the abrupt end of van Doesburg's collaboration with Oud. Oud did not incorporate the color designs in his Spangen housing blocks, nor did he contribute thereafter to *De Stijl*.[25] Although Oud continued to strive on his own for a coloristic architecture during the next few years (as witnessed by his temporary Superintendent's Shed at Oud Mathenesse of 1923 and his Café de Unie of 1925), he had already criticized the application of brightly colored paint to brick architecture. In "Over de toekomstige bouwkunst en hare architectonische mogelijkheden" (on the future of the art of building and its architectonic possibilities), an essay written in February 1921, before his break with van Doesburg, Oud noted that brick, "like most materials produced according to handicraft techniques," tends to weather by becoming brownish-gray, so that, even if the color value of paint could be made to stay constant, "the color harmony between brick and paint would be subject to change, and therefore what was originally a harmony could become a discord in a matter of weeks." A truly successful application of color to architecture would have to await the development of machine-made materials that could preclude discoloration of the exterior wall surface or peeling of paint due to weathering. For the present, Oud said, the constructive material of the wall would have to be taken into account as the dominant factor in determining the nature of any color scheme applied to brick architecture.[26] Oud thus showed himself to be more and more oriented toward practical attitudes associated with functionalism; for him, material rather than formal considerations were evidently paramount. As Reyner Banham has pointed out, however, Oud's functionalism was not simply a matter of rational pragmatism; as with so many other architects of the period, his functionalist posture was closely bound to his aesthetic intentions.[27] Yet, so far as the issue of color in architecture was concerned, Oud consistently placed greater emphasis on the use of durable, modern materials than on the formal development of abstract coloristic compositions, which was van Doesburg's primary goal in collaborating with Oud. Van Doesburg also emphasized the importance of materials, but he focused on color itself—rather than paint—as a material. In "Van de esthetiek naar het materiaal" (from the aesthetic toward the material), an article written in Weimar in 1922, he explained color "first as 'matter' and second as 'matter in motion.'" Roundly criticizing contemporary architects for neglecting the potential for plastic expression inherent in the materials at their disposal, van Doesburg condemned functionalism as "merely signif[ying] construction without ornamentation." "Plastic architecture," he wrote, "means more than that. . . . The (seemingly) economic organization of space found in standardized town planning actually is in the way of progress of plastic architecture."[28]

Published in September, just before Oud rejected the

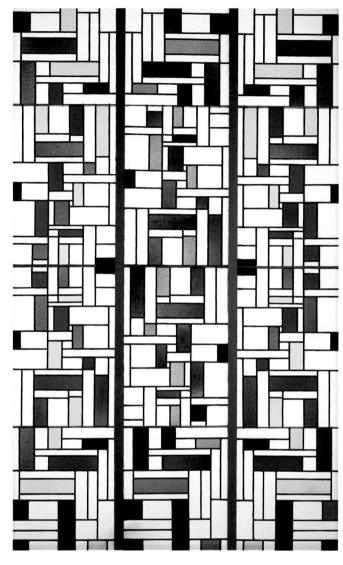

8 Theo van Doesburg, *Composition IV* (in three parts), 1917, stained glass, each panel 286.5 × 56.6 cm. Inv. nos. R5533–R5535, Dienst Verspreide Rijkskollekties, The Hague.

11 Bart van der Leck, *Design for Interior, De Leeuwerik, Laren*, 1918, pencil and watercolor on paper, 70.5 × 76 cm. Graphische Kunstsammlung, Staatsgalerie, Stuttgart.

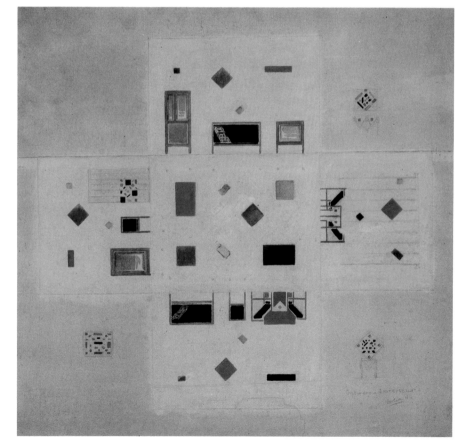

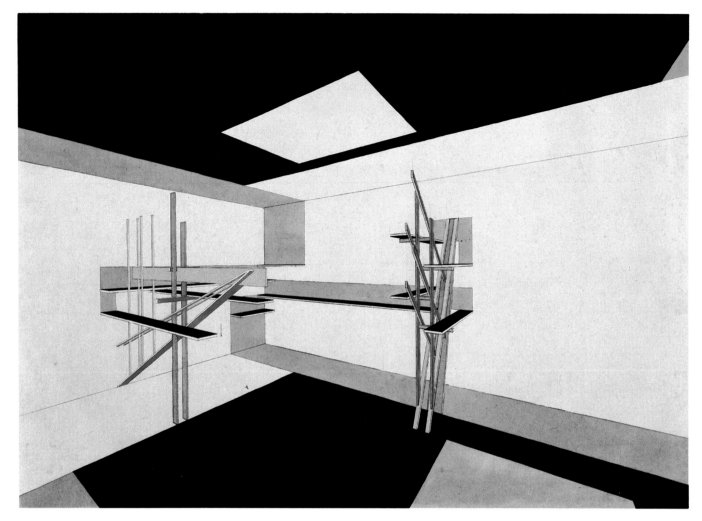

30 Piet Zwart, *Definitive Design for Celluloid
Manufacturer's Stand, Annual Industrial Fair,
Utrecht.* 1921, pencil and watercolor on paper,
45.7 × 64.7 cm. Gemeentemuseum, The
Hague.

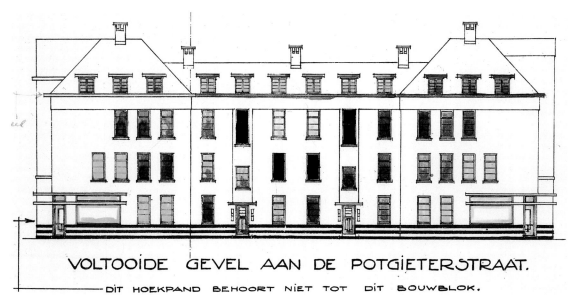

VOLTOOIDE GEVEL AAN DE POTGIETERSTRAAT.

DIT HOEKPAND BEHOORT NIET TOT DIT BOUWBLOK.

38 Theo van Doesburg, *Color Design, Facade on Potgieterstraat, Spangen Housing Block VIII, Rotterdam,* 1921, ink and watercolor on paper, 15.7 × 25.5 cm. Fondation Custodia, Institut Néerlandais, Paris.

■ *89*

39 Theo van Doesburg, *Color Design, Spangen Housing Block VIII, Rotterdam,* 1921, ink and watercolor on paper, 35.5 × 53.2 cm. Fondation Custodia, Institut Néerlandais, Paris.

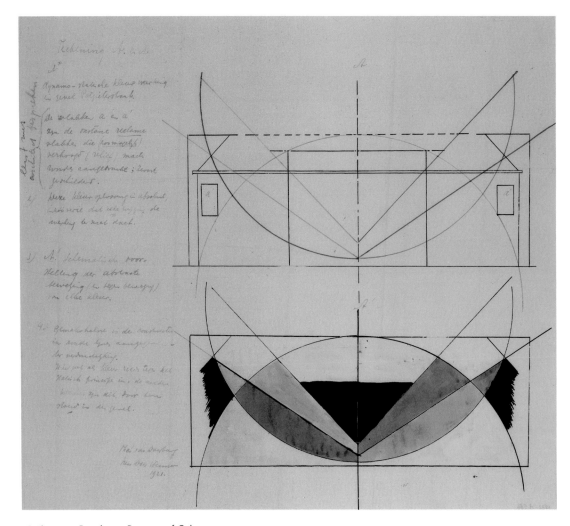

40 Theo van Doesburg, *Diagram of Color
Scheme, Spangen Housing Block VIII, Rotterdam,*
1921, ink and watercolor on paper, 29 ×
32.3 cm. Foundation Custodia, Institut Néerlandais, Paris.

Spangen designs, "Van de esthetiek naar het materiaal" may represent van Doesburg's rejection of Oud's move toward functional considerations. In opposition to the rationalist position Oud took as municipal architect and city planner, van Doesburg posited a theoretical treatment of color as matter that allowed him to ignore practical problems inherent in the discoloration of brick or the mutability of paint, which Oud identified—at least in print—as primary reasons for condemning the application of paint to architecture. In contrast to that of Oud, van Doesburg's attitude toward color was essentially abstract. Van Doesburg noted that "the idea of color as a means of pure plastic expression represented a point of view which made essential demands on the development of architecture"[29]—demands to which Oud was unwilling to accede. Thus the disagreement with Oud over the Spangen colors involved more than a collision between two different attitudes about who should make the ultimate decisions in a project where architecture and color were intended to work together, enhancing one another; it also involved a conflict over the very nature of color and its role in architecture. A viable solution implied—indeed mandated—a harmonious relationship between painter and architect, a collaborative effort necessitating compromises neither Oud nor van Doesburg was prepared to make. Years later Oud wrote a letter to Bruno Zevi that bears indirectly on the issues raised by his disagreement with van Doesburg over the painter's increasingly abstract attitude to color in space:

The spirit of *De Stijl* was, at first, my spirit as well. It was born of an idea of van Doesburg's and my own, and van Doesburg was the driving force in the executive phase. The earliest numbers of the review published some of my works . . . which I regarded as the first examples of a real Cubist architecture. Neo-plastic architecture and also [Dutch architect Willem] Dudok's Cubism derived from these works. . . . But my conclusions were different: through the process of decomposition I gained a sense of space, atmosphere, line and mass, color and construction, but I realized that the building that later derived from it was developing the most superficial aspect of my early works. Such a development seemed to me superficial for architecture: it had really more to do with painting. . . . I abandoned it and began to move in another direction: a healthy, broad, universal, social architecture could never come from this, i.e., from so abstract an aesthetic.[30]

The split with Oud was perhaps the most compelling of several factors, including his Bauhaus experience and his encounter with El Lissitzky in 1921–22, that together catalyzed van Doesburg's development of his own architectural concepts. Clearly it marked a turning point in his career as an architectural colorist. An additional factor was van Doesburg's collaboration at about the same time with another architect, C. R. de Boer. While in Weimar, van Doesburg designed color schemes, similar to those for Spangen, for an agricultural school and a block of middle-class housing units that de Boer built in the small Friesian town of Drachten in 1920–21.[31]

Van Doesburg's designs for de Boer's buildings were even more ambitious than those he proposed almost simultaneously for Oud's Spangen blocks. To both the interior and the exterior of de Boer's block of sixteen residences van

Doesburg applied the primary colors, red, yellow, and blue, each in what he said was a "logical proportion relative to the character of the architectural construction" (figure 41).[32] Although van Doesburg never explained why he chose a proportional relationship of eight parts blue, five parts red, and three parts yellow, the ratio can almost certainly be traced to his frequent invocation of musical structures as a model for organizing abstract color compositions. The ratio shares the same internal relations as the tones of a musical chord in the fundamental position, and van Doesburg must have felt that the interaction of the colors in these proportions with each other and with the architecture would produce an effect of harmony, of simultaneous movement and rest, similar to that experienced in chordal music.

As at Spangen, it was van Doesburg's intention to use color as a foil for the long, low form of de Boer's structure. He indicated how the colors were supposed to be perceived in motion across the facade and around the corners of the building, linking its various sides in a single coloristic whole. He suggested color schemes for the ceilings, floors, walls, doors, hallways, and staircases of the sixteen interiors, and once again he paid particular attention to the colors of the window woodwork. By painting the wood of each window the same color on the exterior as in the interior, van Doesburg intended color to suggest the continuity of interior space and exterior facade. Striving for even greater control over the whole design than the application of color to constructed form alone might allow, he also planned the gardens in front of each dwelling, indicating which areas were to be planted with grass, flowers, and

trees, laying out the footpaths, and providing a scheme of primary colors (again in the proportions 8:5:3) for the garden fence.

For the facades and the interior of the Drachten agricultural school across the street from the residential block, van Doesburg suggested the application of secondary colors, the color opposites of blue, red, and yellow—that is, orange, green, and violet—in the same proportional relations (figure 42). Again he drew a schematic rendition of the design for the exterior (figure 43) in order to illustrate how the movement and countermovement of color would develop across space, resulting here as well in a sense of equilibrium. "Violet and green work against each other," he explained, "while orange works eccentrically [excentrisch] in agreement with the architecture. Black, white, and gray work as noncolor, or rests."[33] The planar manner in which the three facades were rendered in sequence in the drawings (figure 42) again emphasized the continuity of the design, which was also reinforced by van Doesburg's use of lines to show how the planes of each color were linked not simply by juxtaposition but in a complex series of arching and diagonal relationships extending across all the surfaces. The long horizontal format of the schematic drawing makes an interesting comparison with the abstract scroll drawings and film experiments done at the same time by Hans Richter and Viking Eggeling. Van Doesburg was well aware of their work; it had provided the impetus for his first trip to Germany at the end of 1920. He was fascinated by the musical elements involved in the scrolls (which, following their creators' practice, he referred to as visual "scores"), and the same analogy with temporal, musical progression is evident in his Drachten designs.

Like van Doesburg and many other artists of the period, Mondrian too invoked a musical analogy in his painted work.[34] His interest in music can be traced at least as far back as 1912, when he met Jacob van Domselaer in Paris. Four years later van Domselaer published "Proeven van Stijlkunst" (essays on style), seven works for piano that were based on the music of Bach and further inspired by Mondrian's so-called "Plus-Minus" compositions of 1914–1916.[35] Mondrian himself mentioned van Domselaer's attempts to arrive at a less naturalistic, more abstract kind of musical expression in *Le Néo-Plasticisme*, the 1920 essay that contains his first really substantive discussion of the new music. In it Mondrian praised "the *jazzband* which dares brusquely to demolish melody and to oppose the roundness of sound with its own dry, strange noises." "Although it has not yet abandoned traditional instruments," he wrote, "it nevertheless contrasts other, more modern ones to them."[36]

Mondrian adumbrated the basic ideas about music expressed in *Le Néo-Plasticisme* in four subsequent essays published during the 1920s.[37] He repeatedly stated his reasons for favoring jazz in spite of the fact that, in his opinion, it had not completely superseded the naturalistic element of tonal harmony and therefore did not fulfill his requirements for the new music, which would be based on the pure plastic means of sound. Still, Mondrian appreciated jazz music for the qualities he believed it had in common with Neo-Plastic painting: asymmetry, lack of repetition, and an intuitive, improvisational manner of composition. The indigenous, Black American character of jazz also appealed to him because,

he said, the traditional structure of the arts begins to break down when art or music is made by a nonprofessional. Finally, he wrote that the best qualities of jazz were brought out by the kinds of dance steps being done to it—the tango, the shimmy, and the fox trot—in which "straightness is dominant." He explained that "the straight element plasticizes in space what the greatest speed plasticizes in time."[38] Just as the rapid succession of different sounds in jazz music represented to Mondrian the destruction of, or opposition to, the first sound by the second, so in modern social dances such as the fox trot the steps followed each other so quickly that one was immediately neutralized by the next. Mondrian associated these aspects of jazz and modern dance directly with Neo-Plastic painting; already in 1920 he had used *Fox Trot* as the title of a painting that the newspaper correspondent visiting his studio on the rue du Coulmiers saw on the easel there:

It is divided into little rectangular blocks filled with the primary colors: bright red, blue, black. It does not represent anything. No regularity can be discovered in the image. Nevertheless, there is a not unpleasant equilibrium. . . . the painter revealed the name of his creation: Fox Trot. There is the same modern-rhythmic vitality in the regular forward- and back-stepping. . . . the painter explained to me, briefly and clearly, how he had proceeded from the fox trot to arrive at his [or its] rendition or formation, and how naturalistic representation has, in a mysterious way, completely disappeared. It is the history of the last half century of painting.[39]

Although that history is well beyond the scope of this study, it is clear that Mondrian conceived of his own work within a

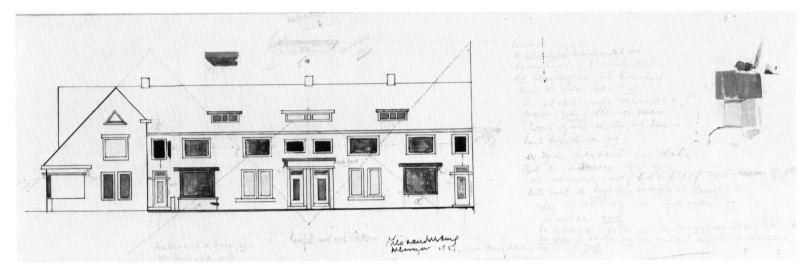

41 Theo van Doesburg, *Color Design for Exterior of Middle-Class Housing, Drachten*, 1921, ink, pencil and gouache on paper, 30.2 × 70.5 cm. Collection of D. Rinsema, Meppel. Shown in color on page 155.

42 Theo van Doesburg, *Color Design for Exterior of Agricultural School, Drachten*, 1921, ink and watercolor on paper, 27.9 × 112.5 cm. Museum It Bleekerhûs, Drachten. Shown in color on page 156.

43 Theo van Doesburg, *Diagram of Color Scheme, Agricultural School, Drachten*, 1921, ink and watercolor on paper, 27.8 × 93 cm. Museum It Bleekerhûs, Drachten. Shown in color on page 156.

long-established tradition of the association of the arts. He continued to give musical titles to his paintings throughout his life, not because he was simply visualizing specific kinds of musical composition in painterly terms, but rather because the evocation of music induced the viewer to consider the formal rhythms of Neo-Plastic painting in the familiar terms of jazz. The musical title was, in a sense, juxtaposed with the painting, just as the painting in Mondrian's studio was juxtaposed with that space as a whole. The literal and figurative proximity of music, painting, and environmental design pervaded Mondrian's work; one must have felt this all the more when Mondrian played his jazz records and allowed music to fill out the Neo-Plastic design of his atelier.

In 1922 Mondrian wrote in *De Stijl* that he envisioned an art "between painting and music" that could be attained by projecting planes of colored light one after another, thus expressing the unity of space and time: "It will be painting because it plasticizes through color and noncolor, but because it appears in time and not in space, it approaches music. Since space and time are scarcely different expressions of the same unity, plastic music (spatial plasticity) and plasticity in time are both possible in the conception of Neo-Plasticism."[40] Although in this characteristically recondite passage Mondrian did not allude specifically to abstract film, his conception of an art between painting and music could have been assimilated to the kind of work being done by Richter and Eggeling, and it clearly developed out of concerns shared by van Doesburg, who was at the time trying to realize a fusion of his coloristic and musical concepts in the context of de Boer's architecture in Drachten.[41]

The Drachten projects are particularly remarkable because they provided an opportunity for van Doesburg to experiment with color designs that were not limited to a single building. For the first time he was really able to confront the issues involved in creating coloristic architecture on an environmental scale. He relied on his chosen system of rhythmic, musical proportions to organize the use of color opposites and thus to relate the buildings standing opposite one another through space.

Although van Doesburg presented his plans in a series of intricate annotated drawings, the essence of his proposal for the two buildings—the contrast of primary and secondary colors in a single proportional system—was actually rather simple. Indeed, it is reminiscent of the window triptych he designed in 1917 for the de Lange Town House, and it reflects the same interest in colors arranged in consonant and dissonant triads that can be found not only in his paintings but also in some of his earliest design work.[42] Still basically in keeping with the original premises of collaboration, van Doesburg limited his exterior color schemes to the windows and doors of de Boer's relatively conservative buildings. Nevertheless, and in spite of van Doesburg's effort to explain his intentions in a lecture delivered in Drachten on December 22, 1921, the designs provoked bitter controversy as well as a prolonged debate in the local press.[43] The public condemned the idea of brightly coloring de Boer's buildings, derisively referring to the housing as the Papegaaienbuurt (parrot neighborhood). The art correspondent of the *Dragster Courant* pointed out that the radical character of van Doesburg's coloristic principles was not in accord with de Boer's architecture. He also criticized the attempt to create a stylistically harmonious unity in the interiors because, he claimed, it would force the inhabitants to abandon their own tastes and to replace their furniture with objects consistent with the style imposed by van Doesburg.[44] Although van Doesburg would undoubtedly have welcomed such a chain of events, the citizens of Drachten remained steadfast in their opposition to his proposals. The colors applied to the housing block were removed almost immediately and no photographs remain to document their appearance; thus van Doesburg's designs for Drachten met much the same fate as the color schemes he made for Spangen, which remained on paper and for more than fifty years were largely unknown. Now, however, we are in a position to appreciate their importance for the evolution of van Doesburg's abstract, environmental design concerns.

As a result of the repeated failure of his attempts to collaborate with established architects, van Doesburg began to develop his own architectural credo. In his essay "Van de esthetiek naar het materiaal," which was based on a series of lectures he delivered in Germany in 1922, van Doesburg elaborated on his concept of architecture as "the organization of plastic means as an unmistakable unity":

Only in our own times has painting, the most advanced form of art, shown the path by which architecture might reach, like painting and sculpture, the mechanical and disciplined realization in *material* form of what the other arts have already achieved in an imaginary (aesthetic) manner.

It is not surprising that painting, the art which at the beginning of the twentieth century took over the leading role among the arts, first created an ideal aesthetics. The new vision of life demands that the world of duality be abandoned . . . and it exhibits both a desire for unity, *an indivisi-*

ble unity of the world, and the will to materialize in architecture the ideal aesthetics established by the "liberal" arts.[45]

Van Doesburg felt that it was the task of everyone, not only architects or engineers, to work toward the realization of ideal aesthetics in modern material form. In response to this self-imposed challenge, he began to direct his own efforts toward the combined expression of painting and architecture in designs over which he himself might exercise ultimate control. He managed to do this by collaborating with a young architect named Cornelis van Eesteren, who was fourteen years his junior and, although already somewhat experienced professionally, was still a student when van Doesburg met him in Weimar in May 1922.

Born in 1897, van Eesteren was the son of a building contractor and municipal councilor responsible for housing in the area of Alblasserdam, a small town southeast of Rotterdam. Around 1915, van Eesteren decided that he wanted to become an architect. After obtaining an honors diploma from the Academy of Fine Arts and Technical Sciences in Rotterdam, in 1919 he went to Amsterdam to enroll in a course in advanced and higher architectural studies. In 1921 he was awarded the gold medal in the Dutch equivalent of the Prix de Rome architecture competition for his design for the Royal Netherlands Academy of Sciences, a structure whose basically conservative character led van Eesteren's biographer to describe it as "an architectural work which even today would be quoted approvingly as a model example of the Amsterdam School, if it had ever been built."[46] Van Eesteren did not begin to move away from his academic approach to architectural design until after 1922, when, traveling in Germany, he met van Doesburg as well as other avant-garde artists and architects.

Over the next several years van Eesteren worked closely with van Doesburg, who, at least in the beginning, was easily able to dominate van Eesteren because of his more advanced age and his position as a relatively established, mature artist. For many years, the exact nature and degree of van Eesteren's contribution to their collaborative efforts were often obscured and van Doesburg usually received the lion's share of credit for their work together. In several instances van Doesburg apparently implied that he was in some way responsible for architectural designs actually produced by van Eesteren.

When he met van Doesburg, van Eesteren was working on his final student project, a series of buildings for Amsterdam University that were to be grouped around a large connecting hall (figure 44). Reinder Blijstra writes: "This design was sketched out in The Netherlands, and received its definitive form in Weimar and Berlin between May and August 1922. Via a radial treatment of the building program, a simple three-dimensional composition arose with a spatial effect which was new for that time."[47] While working on the university designs in Weimar in the spring of 1922, van Eesteren heard van Doesburg give several lectures on De Stijl to a class attended mostly by Bauhaus students, and in October he was present at the Weimar Constructivist Congress hosted by van Doesburg. It was not, however, until after van Doesburg left Germany at the end of 1922, eventually settling in Paris late in the spring of the following year, that he began to work on color schemes for van Eesteren's university buildings. He concentrated on the interior of the large central hall.

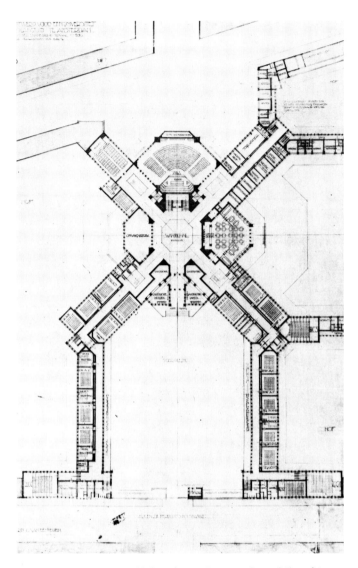

44 Cornelis van Eesteren, *Ground Plan of Amsterdam University Hall and Connecting Buildings*, 1922, pencil, ink and chalk on paper, 149 × 99 cm. Van Eesteren-Fluck & van Lohuizen Foundation, Amsterdam.

Van Doesburg must have been aware that the University Hall, van Eesteren's final project for a degree in architecture, had never been a real commission. In the summer of 1923, when he decided to compose colors for the building,[48] he would also have known that the designs had recently been rejected and that as a result van Eesteren did not receive his architecture diploma. Unlike Oud, who refused to become involved in a project that might never be realized, van Doesburg apparently felt that the absence of a real commission could become an advantage by allowing him, with van Eesteren's help, to develop abstract architectural and coloristic concepts without having to take their functional or technical feasibility into account. As Oud later wrote of van Doesburg in *Mein Weg in "De Stijl"*, "his views proceeded from an unhampered painterly impulse, while I already recognized the restraints that society imposes on a practical construction of form as one of the foundations of the new architecture."[49]

As a painter who in 1922–23 was only beginning to learn about architecture, van Doesburg naturally saw the experimental nature of the University Hall, and especially of the more ambitious Rosenberg project with which he was engaged at the same time, as an opportunity to learn about the architectural design process while working out an abstract architectural credo consistent with the principles he had already established in painting and applied design. It is also possible that he wanted to collaborate in the University Hall design in order to include it as a product of teamwork in the De Stijl architecture exhibition he was preparing for Léonce Rosenberg in 1923.

Van Doesburg's contribution to the University Hall design included color schemes for a large stained glass skylight (figure 45) as well as planes of primary colors loosely arranged across broad sections of the interior such as the floor, walls, and undersides of the balconies (figure 46). The design for the floor (figure 47) illustrates his working method: Separate compositions were brought together, interpenetrating to form the central octagonal plan with four outstretched wings and the somewhat smaller entrance area. That van Doesburg treated individual areas of the floor as independent compositions is demonstrated by his willingness to reproduce the central portion alone on the cover of *De Stijl* in 1925.[50] Designs for the ceiling were achieved in a similar manner; the colored planes under the balconies in the central hall formed an octagonal composition which van Doesburg hung in his Paris atelier.[51] He also mounted one of the watercolor designs for the stained glass skylight on board and inscribed the title *Étude pour une composition* (study for a composition) (figure 45).

The composition of the University Hall skylight is particularly interesting because it involves a Neo-Plastic design of clear, black, and primary-color glass rectangles within a reinforced concrete grid set at a 45° angle with respect to the primary architectural axis established by the main entrance to the hall. The composition relates orthogonally to the secondary axes formed by the radial wings that meet in the hall. Thus the structure of the stained glass skylight created a dynamic series of diagonals relating the central hall to all the areas it joined. Van Doesburg had begun to explore the use of interpenetrating rectangles and diagonals in earlier stained glass windows. For example, each of the

45 Theo van Doesburg, *Study for a Composition*, 1923, gouache on paper mounted on board, 17 × 17 cm. McCrory Corporation, New York.

etude pour un composition.   Theo van Doesburg. Paris 1922

46 Theo van Doesburg, *Color Design for Amsterdam University Hall*, 1923, ink, tempera, and
collage on paper, 63 × 145.5 cm. Van Eesteren-Fluck & van Lohuizen Foundation, Amsterdam. Shown in color on page 157.

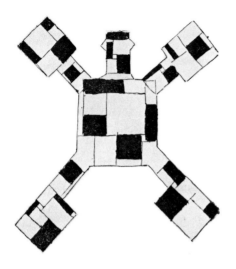

47 Theo van Doesburg, *Color Design for Floor, Amsterdam University Hall*, 1923. Illustrated in *L'Architecture Vivante* (autumn 1925), plate 12.

48 Theo van Doesburg, *Window for House at Maasdam*, 1917. Photograph: Van Doesburg Archive, Dienst Verspreide Rijkskollekties, The Hague.

square windows (figure 48) he executed in 1917 for a house in Maasdam designed by Jan Wils had a second, relatively broad square frame set at a 45° angle within it. The stained glass composition retained its orthogonal relationship to the outer frame while the inner one created thick diagonal bands dividing the design into a series of radiating triangles. It is as though the possibility of interpenetration suggested only tentatively in the windows of 1917 was brought to fruition in the University Hall stained glass design, where the multiple axes of the building's central area provided a rationale for their reflection in the structure of the skylight.

In his color designs for the wall surfaces of the University Hall, van Doesburg began to experiment with his recently formulated concept of color planes as material forms independent of and contrasting with the given architectural surfaces. His large, asymmetrically arranged, rectangular planes of red, blue, yellow, black, and gray seem in their freedom from structural delimitations to hover in the space of the design. This lends to the interior architecture a light, floating quality that is particularly apt for the balconies located in the hall. To emphasize further the independence of the colored planes from the supporting architectural structure, rather than applying paint directly van Doesburg envisioned attaching enameled slabs or plaques to the wall. This novel approach may have been due to the influence of Mondrian, who consistently avoided using paint to apply color (other than gray) directly to the walls of his studio and employed rectangles of pasteboard instead. Van Doesburg's plaques, presumably to be made of metal, would have enabled him to eschew the provisional qualities of

Mondrian's studio and produce instead the kind of durable colored surface that Oud had been demanding. Van Doesburg realized that the University Hall would never be built, and thus he must have felt free to propose new or unusual materials such as glass brick for the ceiling skylight and rubber for the floor as well as the enameled plaques for the walls.[52]

At the time he was working on the University Hall design, van Doesburg still adhered for the most part to common techniques of indicating color in architecture by means of either a symmetrical perspective view (figure 46) or an exploded-box plan emphasizing flat planes (figure 49).[53] However, one design has survived (figure 50) in which van Doesburg made a distinct break with past practices of indicating color in space and experimented with a new method that conveyed a sense of the perspective view of the colored planes as they might have appeared to a spectator in the actual University Hall interior. In this tiny ink and gouache sketch, he attempted to analyze the relationship of the flat planes of color on the floor and on portions of the walls by including them together in a single design where no architecture at all was indicated. The sketch retains some qualities of both the perspective view and the exploded-box plan, and it may represent van Doesburg's attempt to fuse the two drafting techniques. It suggests that van Doesburg was searching for alternative means of rendering color in architecture at just about the time he began working directly with van Eesteren on designs for several houses that were eventually exhibited in Léonce Rosenberg's gallery. Not until then did van Doesburg learn about the technique of axonometric projection, which was to influence him profoundly.

By 1923, the project proposed by Rosenberg had grown from the design of a model house with a gallery attached to the design of three buildings: the original Private Villa for Rosenberg, a second Private House whose conception was closely associated with the first house, and a House of an Artist. The precise chronology of the evolution from a single house to three separate structures is not certain, but apparently the motivation for it came from van Eesteren and van Doesburg. Van Eesteren was at the time already preoccupied with designs for a private house, and van Doesburg, who had recently moved to Paris, was hoping to build a home for himself and his wife. The division into three separate parts was also a logical result of Rosenberg's original tripartite suggestion that the De Stijl artists (1) design a house with gallery that would (2) be a model house and (3) still satisfy their own needs as artists. It seems likely that Rosenberg's house with gallery involved too many specifications to be acceptable as an ideal, model house, but the work in which van Eesteren was already engaged could exemplify a De Stijl private house. Presumably this second design also accorded with Rosenberg's requirement that the house be reconcilable to the tastes and habits of the Parisian public. The third design, including a large atelier and a music room, responded to Rosenberg's proposal that the house be one that the De Stijl artists themselves might like to inhabit if they lived in the environs of Paris. Indeed, the House of an Artist was designed to fit the needs of van Doesburg and his wife, Nelly, who was a musician. At the time van Doesburg was using an overcrowded, previously furnished atelier that he hoped to exchange for one complying with his own aesthetic principles, which he later described poetically in his diary:

49 Theo van Doesburg, *Color Design for Amsterdam University Hall*, 1923, pencil, ink, and gouache on paper, 16.5 × 25 cm. Inv. no. AB5110, Dienst Verspreide Rijkskollekties, The Hague, Schenking van Moorsel.

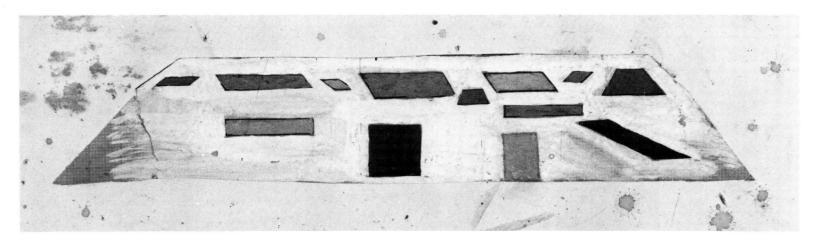

50 Theo van Doesburg, *Color Design for Amsterdam University Hall*, 1923, ink and gouache on paper mounted on cardboard, 7 × 32.5 cm. Inv. no. AB5112, Dienst Verspreide Rijkskollekties, The Hague, Schenking van Moorsel. Shown in color on page 157.

Your atelier must be like a glass cover or like an empty crystal. It must have an absolute purity, a constant light, a clear atmosphere. It must also be white. The palette must be of glass. Your pencil sharp, rectangular and hard, always free of dust and as clean as an operating scalpel. One can certainly take a better lesson from doctors' laboratories than from painters' ateliers. The latter are cages that stink like sick apes.

Your atelier must have the cold atmosphere of mountains 3000 meters high; eternal snow must lie there. Cold kills the microbes.[54]

This extraordinary passage, clearly evocative of Bruno Taut's 1919 *Alpine Architektur*, follows the House of an Artist by seven years, yet it is an accurate reflection of van Doesburg's long-standing attitude toward the artist's creative process. Although he strongly opposed the romantic tradition of the artist as priest or creative genius, van Doesburg clung to the expressionist vision of a crystalline, mountaintop architecture, positing a notion of the modern artist as a scientist working in a hygienically controlled environment of modern materials made by modern methods. Although the House of an Artist was never built, its design came very close to satisfying the conditions van Doesburg had in mind.

It is difficult to reconstruct exactly the sequence of events that led to the design of Rosenberg's house with gallery, the Private Villa. In 1921, Oud had already refused to participate in the development of the design, and apparently van Doesburg received a similar response from Wils and Rietveld when he invited them to submit plans.[55] Only van Eesteren agreed to cooperate when van Doesburg approached him about the Rosenberg project on March 31, 1923.[56] According to van Eesteren, at that time he was preparing to build a house for a widow in Alblasserdam and was therefore already studying the problem of the private house.[57] He saw the project for Rosenberg as an opportunity to work out his ideas more fully and present them formally in the context of an exhibition. Accepting the lack of site specifications, he imagined that the Private Villa would be situated on a corner lot somewhere near the Bois de Boulogne in Paris.[58] Working in Holland, van Eesteren proceeded to develop ground plans and elevations of the villa, described by Jean Leering as "marked by a striving for a '*plan libre*,' i.e., a free groundplan, in which the various spaces were no longer pressed into the total form as determined by the exterior, but had a freer position in relation to each other."[59] Leering and Joost Baljeu agree that van Doesburg had no direct involvement in the development of the villa designs, which did not include the application of color; he played an intermediary role between Rosenberg, with whom he discussed the program, and van Eesteren, who, both scholars state, was alone responsible for the architectural form.[60] There is evidence, however, that van Doesburg participated more actively in the final phase of the design process. When van Eesteren had nearly finished his drawings, he must have gone to Paris to discuss them with van Doesburg and only later sent the designs back to Holland, where Rietveld constructed the model (figure 51). This speculation is supported by a letter van Doesburg wrote to Rietveld on August 10, 1923, in which he implied that he and van Eesteren had worked together to complete the designs: "Last night we worked through the entire night; the drawings of the Rosenberg project are ready and have been blueprinted. They have been sent; you should receive them one of these

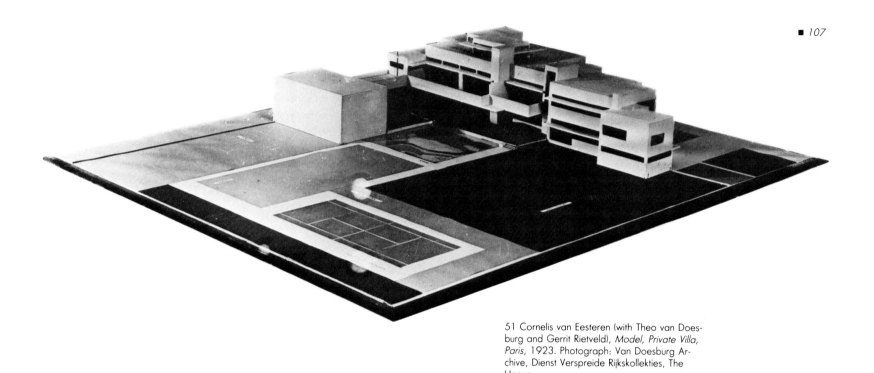

51 Cornelis van Eesteren (with Theo van Doesburg and Gerrit Rietveld), *Model, Private Villa,
Paris*, 1923. Photograph: Van Doesburg Archive, Dienst Verspreide Rijkskollekties, The
Hague.

days. . . . I assume that you are too busy to make any models. If you cannot find time for the Rosenberg model, write us <u>in time</u>, and we will try to tinker with it ourselves."[61]

In view of van Doesburg's previous plan to enlist the collaboration of all the De Stijl painters, as well as the architects, it is interesting that no one aside from van Doesburg, van Eesteren, and Rietveld participated once the model projects were under way. Even Mondrian, who lived in Paris, chose not to be involved as an advisor after 1921, although many of his initial suggestions were eventually realized in the projects and models exhibited by Rosenberg in 1923.

Although one cannot be sure exactly when or on which project they began working together, it is certain that after van Eesteren joined him in Paris van Doesburg had an impact on the second and third model projects. However, the authorship of these projects too remains in dispute. Baljeu states that the ground plan of the Private House "clearly derives from van Doesburg's hand,"[62] while van Eesteren claims that the Private House represents a more advanced development of his own ideas related to the house he was building in Alblasserdam. According to van Eesteren, he made the plans alone and provided van Doesburg with axonometric drawings and analyses, which van Doesburg then traced in order to come to terms with the architecture. Through a process of abstraction, van Doesburg stripped the architecture of all references to function and instead emphasized the surfaces as independent planar forms suspended in space (figure 52). These remarkable, highly original drawings constituted the basis for his "counter-constructions" (figure 53), colored axonometric projections in

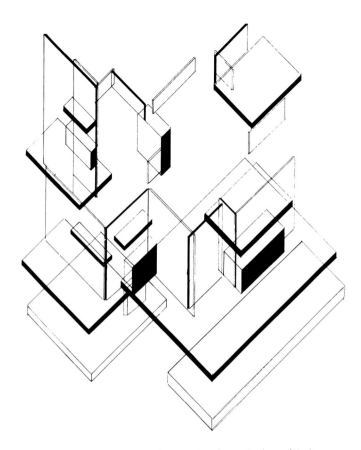

52 Theo van Doesburg, *Analysis of Architecture, Private House*, 1923, ink on paper, 55.7 × 59 cm. Van Eesteren-Fluck & van Lohuizen Foundation, Amsterdam.

53 Theo van Doesburg, *Color Construction: Project for a Private House*, 1923, gouache and ink on paper, 57 × 57 cm. Museum of Modern Art, New York; Edgar Kaufmann, Jr., Fund.

which van Doesburg demonstrated how red, blue, yellow, black, and gray might be applied to the white model (figure 54) van Eesteren says he constructed on his own.[63] Van Eesteren's description of the collaborative design process corresponds to van Doesburg's previously established practice (exemplified by his early working relationship with Oud), in which the architect, who was responsible for the structural form of the building, supplied black and white ink drawings to which the painter would then add his color scheme. However, one must bear in mind that, as a result of his frustrations with Oud, van Doesburg was anxious to play a more active role in the determination of the architectural designs to which his colors would be applied. It therefore seems most likely that the development of the Private House involved a continuous dialogue between van Eesteren and van Doesburg, who worked together on the project in van Doesburg's Paris atelier. Thus their respective contributions cannot be entirely isolated in terms of color and form.

Leering has written that in the Private House ''the all-sided orientation of the Private Villa was realized even further'':

Whereas in the first project there was still an indication of front, back, and side in relation to the site, in this project the ground plans seem to show the development of space from the center, the stairwell, outward to the periphery of the building.

Therefore the corners of the building block disappear. From this building block different groups of rooms form loose, independent units interlocking with one another. They are brought into contact with each other at different levels via flights of stairs, landings, etc.[64]

Leering goes on to state that in van Doesburg's colored counter-constructions ''the ideas concerning loosening, inde-

pendence, and interpenetration of the various constructive elements were developed even further.'' Although these drawings provide a sense of three-dimensional space, they are basically ideal images of colored planes suspended in space, and they bear little resemblance to the architectural structure to which they ultimately referred. They do not indicate any functional apparatus, nor do they show the windows or doors that would puncture the surface planes of the house. Moreover, in spite of their analytical purpose, the counter-constructions did not proceed from any concrete or utilitarian organization of the architectural spaces. And whereas the axonometrics made by van Eesteren were technically correct architectural studies, van Doesburg's counter-constructions, although based on those axonometrics, were neither projected correctly in every instance nor meant to be used directly in the process of formulating architectural aspects of the building project. Indeed, when he applied color to the model of the Private House, van Doesburg determined the placement of hues according to formal, fundamentally painterly considerations, without respect to the functions of the spaces inside. That the counter-constructions had only a tenuous connection with their origins in van Eesteren's architectural designs is further demonstrated by the fact that van Doesburg made a number of them in 1924, and probably produced some even later, well after the model projects were completed. By that time, the highly abstract nature of the counter-constructions prompted van Doesburg to apply some of their characteristics in a series of paintings he called ''counter-compositions.'' He thus brought the process of the counter-constructions full circle by adapting architecturally derived formal principles to easel paintings.

It is fair to say that van Doesburg's counter-constructions constituted abstract proposals for a coloristic architecture whose conception, as far as he was concerned, was based on its independence from the realities of situation, construction, material, and other technical considerations. Indeed, van Doesburg's counter-constructions might be said to express Mondrian's vision of Neo-Plastic architecture as a multiplicity of flat planes not bounded by space or time. They also share a great deal with the images and ideas behind Lissitzky's notion of Proun, lying somewhere between painting and architecture and drawing elements from both in an attempt to fuse the two domains of art into a new and revolutionary unity. Van Doesburg had met Lissitzky in Germany during the winter of 1921–22, and the two had become close friends as well as artistic allies. Knowledge of Lissitzky's work clearly played an important part in the development of van Doesburg's approach to coloristic architecture, just as his art as a whole would have been inconceivable without the example of Mondrian. But it is also necessary to see van Doesburg's design projects in the context of his own earlier work.

In applying color to the Private House, van Doesburg drew on his experience with the University Hall. In both cases the coloristic treatment involved an attempt to apply flat planes of primary color plus black and gray in a manner independent of structural framing devices, suggesting a construction of colored planes suspended in space. Like van Doesburg's ink and gouache sketch for the University Hall (figure 50), but going even further, the counter-constructions took this to an extreme, doing away with everything extrinsic to the relational study of color itself as architectural matter.

54 Cornelis van Eesteren and Theo van Doesburg, *Model, Private House*, 1923. Photograph: Van Doesburg Archive, Dienst Verspreide Rijkskollekties, The Hague.

Whereas on the model of the Private House van Doesburg's treatment of color once again involved the application of paint to architectural surfaces and therefore had to take the presence of elements such as doors and windows into account, in the counter-constructions, composed exclusively of unbroken planes, color itself was treated as a constructive element (indeed, the only constructive element). Here it was possible for van Doesburg to suggest that color was no longer a superficial addition applied only to certain parts of the building, but rather that color actually *was* the material of which the structure was composed.

In the counter-constructions van Doesburg took advantage of the axonometric projection technique, which allowed him to show multiple planar dimensions in the same view, and he treated each plane as an uninterrupted field of color. By these means he was able to fuse his color scheme with the abstracted architectural forms and make a design in which all the coloristic relations could be apprehended simultaneously in a single view. He thus took his ideas about movement and contrast of color in architecture one step beyond the designs for Drachten, in which the movement of color was still understood in terms of music, as a progression in time applied to space. The counter-constructions fulfilled the same function as the schematic rendition of the color designs he made for the earlier Drachten project (figure 43), but they demonstrate that now he was not thinking of color in the same temporal connection with music. A comparison of these drawings reveals that in 1923 van Doesburg no longer conceived of color relationships in terms of sequential, linear progressions across architectural surfaces, but rather in terms of the identification of color with those sur-

faces, perceived simultaneously in space and time. For van Doesburg this constituted an architectural rather than a musical understanding of color, and it represented an important break with his previous design work. His notion of coloristic movement had changed in a fundamental way because it no longer involved a viewer moving around a building. It was understood not simply as movement in space or movement through time, but as the fusion of these concepts in a far more abstract realm where color functions to reveal time as the fourth dimension of space.[65] Having arrived at a new conception of coloristic movement that subsumed the temporal in the architectural, van Doesburg no longer needed to resort to musical analogies or proportional relations in order to determine his abstract color scheme.

The lessons van Doesburg and van Eesteren had learned from the counter-construction studies were applied in the design of the third model project exhibited in 1923, the House of an Artist. "Here," Leering notes, "the color fields and the construction of the exterior planes merged completely together: the color fields were seen as planes in the outer surface, bounded by edges which clearly separated one color field from another or from the adjoining window or door surface. The model [figure 55] was put together in a similar manner: a plumber made zinc frameworks which were soldered together and in which panels, some of glass, were installed."[66] The structure was conceived as an integration of vertically oriented spaces connected in a zigzag formation involving cantilevered sections, which in the model seemed to hover in space. Given the construction methods available at the time, the design would have been impossible to realize without the addition of more structural sup-

55 Cornelis van Eesteren and Theo van Doesburg, *Model, House of an Artist*, 1923. Photograph: Van Doesburg Archive, Dienst Verspreide Rijkskollekties, The Hague.

ports. Van Eesteren and van Doesburg accepted this, but, far from seeing it as a disadvantage, they emphasized the experimental, utopian character of this particular project. In its purity and its freedom from technical considerations, the House of an Artist provided an opportunity for them to present a coloristic architecture—indeed, a very abstract environment—that may have been impossible to realize but nonetheless suggested how De Stijl architecture would eventually look once it had overcome the material limitations of conventional building practices.

In a sense the House of an Artist is comparable to Mondrian's atelier, and for more reasons than the simple fact that it housed a studio. It was, after all, in the model for this project that Mondrian's suggestion about using diverse materials rather than plaster was most fully realized. In "De Realiseering van het Neo-Plasticisme in verre toekomst en in de huidige architectuur," an article he wrote during the early planning stages of the model projects and thus while he was probably thinking about them, Mondrian mentioned the importance of the right kind of model to the process of developing Neo-Plastic architecture as art, free from the limitations of conventional building:

. . . even as a "work of art," Neo-Plastic architecture can only be realized under certain *conditions*. Beside *freedom*, it demands preparation of a kind unfeasible in customary building practice. . . .
Execution in which every detail must be *invented and worked out* is too costly or impossible under present circumstances. *Absolute freedom for continuous experimentation* is necessary if art is to be achieved. How can this come about within the complex limitations of conventional building in our society? . . . Today the architect is compelled to create a

"work of art" more or less hastily and constrictedly, that is, he can only evolve it on paper.
How can he meet every new problem *a priori*? A plaster model is no real study for an interior design; and there is neither time nor money for a large scale model in metal or wood.[67]

In addition to the fact that the model of the House of an Artist corresponds to Mondrian's proposals, the abstract character of the design as "an image of the new architecture," an architectural work of art, recalls Mondrian's studio and the challenge implied in his entire conception of the harmonious, abstract environment: ". . . after all it is for the new man that it exists. He alone will be able to give concrete existence to the spirit of the new age both in society and in art."[68]

The Rosenberg house, the Private House, and the House of an Artist formed the nucleus of the De Stijl architecture exhibition held at the Galerie "L'Effort Moderne" in Paris between October 15 and November 15, 1923.[69] In the checklist van Doesburg and van Eesteren were credited with equal responsibility for all aspects of the architectural designs and color schemes for the houses. This full sharing of responsibility was an indication of the fundamental premise underlying the exhibition: the necessity for collaboration in the creation of modern architecture. In the exhibition as a whole (which in addition to work by Oud and Wils included designs by Ludwig Mies van der Rohe and Willem van Leusden, who were at most only tangentially related to De Stijl), every effort was made to present all the objects shown as the work of individual artists united behind a common set of aesthetic principles. When the show was reconstituted at the

École Spéciale d'Architecture several months later, a manifesto entitled "Vers une construction collective" (toward collective construction) and signed by van Doesburg, van Eesteren, and Rietveld was distributed. Introducing the manifesto in the pages of De Stijl, where it was signed only by van Doesburg and van Eesteren, the authors wrote the following:

Since the formation of the "De Stijl" movement in Holland (1916) painters, architects, sculptors, etc., have arrived during the course of their practical work at the definition and application of laws which lead to a new unity of life. It is through the new conception born of mutual cooperation that these distinctions between the practitioners of the various arts will cease to exist.

Today, we may speak only of the builders of the new life.

The exhibition of the "De Stijl" group in the salles de l'Effort moderne (Léonce Rosenberg) in Paris had as its aim the demonstration of the possibility of collective creation on this universal basis.[70]

Baljeu has stated that Rietveld's name was added to the manifesto circulated at the École Spéciale d'Architecture and also appeared alongside those of van Doesburg and van Eesteren when the drawings and models were reproduced in L'Architecture Vivante,[71] "as a result of the De Stijl desire to be seen as a collective creative force." However, Rietveld played no part in composing the manifesto, and his only contribution to the three projects consisted in making the model of the first house. According to Baljeu, "this attitude also explains why Oud and Wils participated in the exhibition, although by this time neither was any longer actively involved with De Stijl."[72] Van Doesburg doubtless urged Oud and Wils as well as the other participants to allow examples of their work to be included in the exhibition in order to demonstrate the half-truth that De Stijl could still claim the allegiance of a like-minded group of established architects, colorists, and designers.

Van Doesburg spoke repeatedly of the need for collaboration in order to achieve his ideal of an abstract, coloristic architecture. But for him the call for collaboration remained a conceptual goal that he was unable to achieve to any profound degree. Even in 1921, when he wrote to Oud about the participation of all the De Stijl artists in the realization of a model house for Rosenberg, he was already undermining the collaborative ideal by suggesting that he and Oud and Mondrian ought to retain ultimate control over the eventual design, distributing only aspects of lesser importance, such as responsibility for individual rooms, to the rest of the group. Furthermore, van Doesburg repeatedly allowed personal antagonisms to intervene and subvert his professed aims. For instance, when he learned that Rietveld had joined Oud and Wils in agreeing to contribute to a large Bauhaus exhibition held during the summer of 1923, van Doesburg took it as a personal offense as well as an attack against the principles of De Stijl. Apparently he presumed that Rietveld, who continued to associate with De Stijl, would share his own animosity toward the Bauhaus, and that like a good collaborator he would support van Doesburg's notion of the "Stijl-idea" in opposition to the Bauhaus. In what seems to have been a moment of intense paranoia, van Doesburg wrote the following to Rietveld on August 10, 1923:

I was stunned . . . that you had joined in the exposition of the Bauhaus in Weimar, thus working against "De Stijl." That Wils and Oud joined does not surprise me very much;

they are constantly advertising themselves. But what advantage can you see in exhibiting <u>there</u>. I feel very miserable and now realize that I must give up the Stijl-idea because I am gradually, due to encircling intrigues, standing alone. This entire Bauhaus display results from the struggle which I had there; the exhibition is intended as an immediate revenge against my influence and my person.

In a postscript van Doesburg added this remark: "I have given up completely the desire to work toward a collective goal. I am very sad because of this kick from <u>you</u>, from whom I <u>least</u> expected it."[73]

The nature of van Doesburg's relationship to the Bauhaus, particularly the question of whether or not Gropius ever invited him to join the faculty, has long been an issue of contention.[74] In the context of the present discussion, the frustration of van Doesburg's ambitions with respect to the Bauhaus is important because it contributed to his disappointment in De Stijl's collaborative ideal. As disclosed by his letter to Rietveld, even while van Doesburg was in the final stages of preparing the model projects and the Rosenberg exhibition, which together were intended to demonstrate the strength of De Stijl as a group, the fact that Oud, Wils, and Rietveld had contributed to the Bauhaus exhibition made him feel abandoned and in danger of defeat.

The conclusion one inevitably draws from the apparent discrepancy between van Doesburg's repeated advocacy of a collaborative ideal and the way he actually handled whatever teamwork was called for in the model projects and the Rosenberg exhibition is that a subtle change occurred in his use of the term "collaboration." Previously this had been used to describe the working relationship between architect and colorist, on the basis of the premise that each restricted his activities to his own area of expertise. By the end of 1922, the impossibility of van Doesburg's own participation in such a relationship had become amply apparent. Nevertheless, he was not immediately prepared to deny the original premise completely. For instance, in "De Beteekenis van de kleur in binnen- en buitenarchitectuur" (the significance of color in interior and exterior architecture), published in *Bouwkundig Weekblad* in May 1923, van Doesburg called for an "even distribution of tasks between engineer, architect and painter": "Many a misunderstanding or mistake has resulted when painter and architect did not sufficiently respect one another's field. On the one hand architects restricted painters; on the other hand they presented them with *too much* freedom. A compromise resulted from the former type of relationship, while painting, which retained a separate function, dominated in the latter. . . . In both cases, color led to the destruction of architecture." In the same essay, however, he also insisted on the intrinsic interrelationship of color and architecture, intimating that architecture could not be successful in an aesthetic sense unless coloristic and constructive solutions were arrived at simultaneously: "The problem of color's role in architecture is too important to be determined summarily, as is usually done only when the building is finished." Furthermore, van Doesburg stated that color in architecture "represents an intrinsic part of the material expression,"[75] thus emphasizing the closest possible identification of color and architecture, which in turn implied a more thoroughly integrated relationship of those working in the two media. Finally, in his architectural program "Tot een beeldende architectuur" (toward plastic architecture), written in Paris in 1924, van Doesburg stated explicitly that "the plastic architect . . . might also be a painter."[76] Thus he tacitly admitted his own aspirations in that regard, and simultaneously acknowledged both his agreement with Mondrian's similar statement of 1922 and his departure from his original conception of collaborative work—a conception that had at one time been fundamental to De Stijl theory and practice.

De Stijl painters were not alone in questioning the wisdom of dividing responsibility for the abstract environment between colorists and architects. Oud also clearly grew to doubt this aspect of the collaborative ideal, and Rietveld embarked on his first large-scale architectural project without seeking the advice or contribution of any colorists. Mrs. Truus Schröder, for whom Rietveld designed the Schröder House in 1924, has remarked that when he was in his early twenties Rietveld wanted to become a painter, although since the age of eleven he had been making furniture, which eventually led him into the architectural profession.[77] Carel Blotkamp writes that "apparently Rietveld did not feel it necessary to associate with painters because he himself was quite capable of integrating color in his work."[78]

Ever since he had applied primary colors to the chair whose basic form he had established around 1918, thus transforming it into the Red-Blue Chair, Rietveld had consistently treated color as a means of emphasizing or differentiating structural forms. Although he certainly had a well-developed sense of coloristic composition, he understood and used color in an architecturally determined manner, primarily as a means of accentuating plastic forms already defined by material construction. In this sense—and this sense only—his color schemes are analogous to those first de-

vised by van der Leck and van Doesburg in 1916 and 1917. This is particularly evident in the exterior of the Schröder House (figure 56), Rietveld's major contribution to the coloristic architecture of De Stijl. The exterior wall planes of the house were painted in solid fields of white, broken white, and four tones of gray. Other elements, including pipes, window frames, balcony supports, and railings, were painted either white, black, gray, blue, yellow, or red. The color of each element seems to have been decided in terms of its material character, shape, and spatial relationship to the whole. However, because the exterior of the house already involved a loose composition of independent planes in space, Rietveld was not obliged to use color in contrast to the architecture, to give it a sense of extension and movement, as the De Stijl colorists generally did. He was not in the position of the monumental painter described earlier by van Doesburg. Unlike Oud's Spangen blocks, for instance, Rietveld's architecture was not a symmetrical, constructionally closed mass to which highly dynamic coloristic compositions would have to be applied in order to convey an aesthetic effect of openness and movement. Theodore Brown has described the "visually weightless elements" of the Schröder House, which seem to be "independent of gravitational pull . . . suspended in a state of equilibrium with no greater pull in any one direction":

The sense of weightlessness, heralded by the painters, marks an important shift in the vocabulary of our architectural vision, because traditionally we "read" an unbroken surface as the boundary of a mass. But by means of overlapping planes, of separation of parts and of color Rietveld helped to dispel not only the massiveness of this building but also our mass-oriented vision. Volume in the Schröder

56 Gerrit Rietveld, *Schröder House, Utrecht,* 1924. Photograph: collection of Mrs. Truus Schröder, Utrecht.

House, staked off from the continuum of outside space, is not sharply defined and discretely limited by massive materials but merely suggested by the weightless elements of line and surface.[79]

Because Rietveld's architecture was stylistically advanced, he could afford to be comparatively conservative when dealing with color. This should not be taken to mean that Rietveld's approach to color was similar to the 1916–17 style of van Doesburg or van der Leck in every respect. He did not, for example, produce designs involving internal patterns or the division of structural planes into framed compositions resembling easel paintings, as they had; rather, his use of color in the Schröder House was indebted to van Doesburg's 1923 planar color schemes for the House of an Artist and to the counter-constructions in general. But whereas van Doesburg was by 1923 already well advanced in the development of a notion of color working against architecture, Rietveld consistently employed color to enhance architecture by delineating structure. To that extent, his work was comparable to the earliest colored architectural designs of De Stijl.

Although the quality of his own architectural work enabled Rietveld to maintain his independence from the De Stijl colorists and still achieve the ideal of a coloristic architecture, his attitude toward collaboration was generally parallel to that of Oud, who for many years felt a need for collaboration yet insisted on retaining control over every aspect of his building designs, including the application of color. According to Mrs. Schröder, "at first Rietveld felt that architect and painter could work one after the other," the architect setting aside discrete surfaces for the colorist to work with. In applying color to the Schröder House, however, Rietveld

"wanted to use color less as a *painter* [that is, one who applies paint to a given flat surface] and more in direct connection with the *simultaneous* creation of color and architecture."[80] Like Oud, who provided color schemes for his own designs on several occasions after his break with van Doesburg, Rietveld came to the conclusion that if color was to be used at all, a single individual—the architect—ought to be responsible for both the coloristic and the architectural aspects of a given design.

Van Doesburg had reached a remarkably similar conclusion by 1924. He too began to deemphasize the distinction between the roles of colorist and architect that had previously informed his conception of the design process as a whole. Much like Rietveld and Oud, van Doesburg wanted to exercise complete control. In order to do so—in order to justify his desire to claim the prerogatives of both colorist and architect—he had to abandon the underlying premises of De Stijl's collaborative ideal.

The collaborative ideal had been a basic tenet of van Doesburg's aesthetic credo before 1923. It had been, and to a certain extent it remained, central to the thinking of all De Stijl artists who believed in the eventual unity of painting and architecture in the modern environment. In practice, however, collaboration between painter-colorist and architect-builder was rarely achieved in a project in which each played an equal role. The House of an Artist might be cited as one example of the successful integration of constructive and coloristic contributions, but the abstract character of the design already involved a degree of compromise in terms of architectural viability, and this, one might argue, attests to the predominance of van Doesburg's conceptual role in the project. Moreover, in 1924 van Eesteren was beginning to argue with van Doesburg over his refusal to acknowledge the architect's contribution to certain ideas they had developed together. On August 25, 1924, van Eesteren wrote a letter to van Doesburg in which he protested van Doesburg's recent publication of "Tot een beeldende architectuur" in *De Stijl*. He claimed that the essay should not have been credited to van Doesburg alone because it was the result of all their discussions since they had first met in Weimar: "The important point is really that it is said, not by whom it is said. What it contains is really the conceptualization, the clarification of what we have achieved in our collaborations." Here van Eesteren seems to be saying that his individual contribution was not the main issue, but he nevertheless wanted very definitely to be acknowledged and he went on to tell van Doesburg exactly how this should have been done: "It would therefore have been more just to have a caption as follows: Tot Een Beeldende Architectuur (in large print). In small print: Result of a collaboration between C. v. Eesteren, Théo van Doesburg, by Théo v. Doesburg." Finally, he said that he expected his suggestion to be followed if the essay was to be reprinted or translated in another publication.[81]

Evidently, when it suited him to do so, van Doesburg took advantage of van Eesteren's avid desire for collaboration, asking the younger architect to cosign certain articles (such as "− □ + = R$_4$," a text for which Baljeu says van Doesburg alone was responsible[82]) but not acknowledging the role van Eesteren played in formulating others (such as "Tot een beeldende architectuur"). Furthermore, when they were exhibited in 1923, the plans for the first Rosenberg house were assigned to van Doesburg as well as van Eesteren,

suggesting the clearly erroneous notion that van Doesburg was equally responsible for them. Later publications of these and other designs compounded the questions of authorship, which van Doesburg made little or no effort to resolve.

By that time, however, van Doesburg's interest in architecture had led him in large measure to reject the original premises of the collaborative ideal that had confined him to the role of colorist. He now embraced the less easily pinned down notion of collectivity, which did not connote a specific assignment of roles in a common task. With its much broader implications, collectivity could involve all those united behind a given set of ideals, rather than just those individuals literally working together, each engaged in a specific, well-defined activity subsumed in a larger whole. Whereas the accepted meaning of collaboration had forced van Doesburg to tolerate limitations on the nature of his artistic pursuits, by making the rather subtle yet apparently crucial transition to collectivity he could justify his desire—intimated in "Tot een beeldende architectuur" and made manifest in his work—to fuse the once strictly separated functions of painter and architect. In "− □ + = R$_4$," published in *De Stijl* in 1924, van Doesburg argued for collective rather than collaborative work, stating in the first section of the article that "during the course of our collective efforts we have studied architecture as a plastic unity of all the arts (excluding technique and industry) and we have found that the result would give a new style."[83]

Although van Doesburg's advocacy of collectivity rather than collaboration can thus be understood as a development paralleling the growth of his desire to claim exclusive control over the shape of his coloristic spatial designs, collectivity was not merely the reincarnation in a new form of the failed collaborative ideal. It was a concept shared by many avant-garde artists with whom van Doesburg associated during his stay in Germany in 1921–22. Van Doesburg's evolution toward total abstraction in interior design must also be examined within that international context. It was, after all, also in response to his interaction with an international range of avant-garde artists, El Lissitzky in particular, that van Doesburg began to recognize collectivity instead of collaboration as his ultimate goal. Lissitzky too was involved in promoting such an ideal. Indeed, his original purpose in coming to Germany on behalf of the new Soviet government in 1921 was to strengthen the ties between progressive Russian artists and their colleagues working in Western Europe.[84]

Lissitzky was introduced to van Doesburg in Berlin during the winter of 1921–22, and the two artists remained in close contact for the next several years. Lissitzky was associated with De Stijl until the mid-1920s; his work was published in the magazine and he participated with van Doesburg in artists' congresses held in Dusseldorf and Weimar in 1922. The purpose of these two meetings was to establish an association uniting avant-garde artists throughout Europe; they provided an important forum for Lissitzky and van Doesburg to promote their common belief in the need for collective international cooperation. At the first congress van Doesburg read a statement to the International Union of Progressive Artists in which he claimed that progressive Dutch artists had "taken an international view from the very beginning," even during the war. Furthermore, he said, "This international outlook was imposed by the very way our work

developed, which was out of the practice of our art."[85] A proclamation to the congress published in *De Stijl*, where it was signed by Lissitzky and Richter as well as van Doesburg, stated emphatically the common goal of creating an international organization aimed at realizing the principle of collectivity uniting them all: "We must fight to make this assertion good, and we must be organized for the fight. This is the only way to liberate our collective energy. In this way our principles and our economic needs become as one."[86]

International implications notwithstanding, the fact remains that in emphasizing the relatively vague ideal of collectivity van Doesburg found a means of avoiding both the theoretical and the practical dilemmas that accompanied actual artistic collaboration with architects. The fundamentally abstract character of his architectural conception of color was in any event becoming unacceptable to most architects, who were increasingly concerned with pragmatic social issues rather than problems of pure form. As the model projects demonstrated, the development of a totally abstract environment such as van Doesburg and other De Stijl colorists envisioned could only proceed if pragmatic issues were not of primary importance. For the most part, such a situation was available only in the context of exhibitions or in the artists' own ateliers. In order to grasp fully the importance of this fact and to understand how it affected the further development of totally abstract coloristic designs, it is helpful to examine De Stijl exhibition and atelier environments of the 1920s against their historical background in the latter part of the nineteenth century.

4   Total Abstraction: Color in Space

During the 1870s, when the Aesthetic Movement was at its height in England, James McNeill Whistler became famous for the settings he designed as backgrounds for his paintings. The correlation between Whistler's paintings and his interior designs, both indebted to *japonisme*, was made especially explicit in the exhibition spaces he installed. These were conceived as environments with which his paintings would harmonize, and the artist treated them almost as works of art in their own right. The later Art Nouveau phenomenon of exhibiting interior ensembles grew in part out of Whistler's practice. It too was intended to promote the individual objects displayed, as was the case with Siegfried Bing's L'Art Nouveau gallery in Paris and the showrooms of Dutch design workshops such as Arts and Crafts and 't Binnenhuis. In all of these instances, emphasis was placed on the harmony of the whole in order to suggest that good design principles not only were applicable in the realm of fine art but could also be adapted to every aspect of daily life in the home. Interiors such as the dining room and bedroom that van de Velde exhibited at the opening of Arts and Crafts in The Hague were expressly designed and meant to be shown as ensembles for everyday use.

This treatment of the exhibition space as an approximation of the intimate environment of the home was due in part to a new appreciation for the aesthetic value of applied art. It also involved a reaction against the often chaotic manner in which paintings were hung in official salon exhibitions. The repercussions of this reaction lasted well into the early twentieth century, as demonstrated in 1912 by the display of easel paintings by Marcel Duchamp, Roger de la Fresnaye, Albert Gleizes, Fernand Léger, Jean Metzinger, and Paul

Vera in the controlled environment of the Maison Cubiste.[1] In Holland, too, many artists and critics favored the presentation of exhibition interiors as if they were living spaces. For example, in 1907 the Haagse Kunstkring organized an exhibition in cooperation with the Nederlandsche Vereeniging voor Ambachts- en Nijverheidskunst (the Dutch association for technical and applied art, commonly referred to as VANK) in which seven interior ensembles were shown. In a review comparing the exhibition with one he had recently seen in Cologne, Willem Kromhout described the positive impression made by the German interiors, which had been displayed as units unto themselves: "No single space had an overhead light, all had ceilings, and therefore one really imagined himself in a room. Each contributor was free to use as much light as he felt necessary. As a result the idea 'exhibition' was reduced to a minimum. In the future we would be pleased to see a similar exhibition arranged by VANK in order to reassert the intimacy of rooms. The manner in which it is now done . . . [makes] people feel too much as though they are at an exhibition. . . ."[2]

Kromhout praised the Cologne exhibition because the interiors displayed there had succeeded in simulating the environment of a home. Like many of his contemporaries, he criticized the prevailing practice of exhibiting objects in overcrowded and confusing circumstances that precluded their aesthetic appreciation. Kromhout was primarily concerned with applied art, but similar attitudes were also expressed by critics of fine art, including Theo van Doesburg. In a review of the 1916 Amsterdam painting exhibition of De Onafhankelijken (the independents), van Doesburg began by saying that when he had visited the show he had imagined

himself in the position of an average spectator rather than an exhibiting artist or a critical reviewer. In doing so, he explained, he confronted two problems: "1st, the psychology of the exhibition visitor; 2nd, the painting in its environment."

My visit to the "De Onafhankelijken" exhibition convinced me that this manner of seeing and exhibiting paintings next to and in contrast with one another is one of the greatest absurdities of modern society.

Art and Intimacy are very close to one another; however in painting exhibitions, particularly this time at the "De Onafhankelijken" show, they are so far apart that we can barely recognize either.

One expects something different from a painting exhibition than from a fair, a market, an auction, or a corner store. It should give you the impression of permanence; you want to be surrounded by deep spiritual values. If a painting is merely hanging crooked on a wall, you are already shocked and the illusion of spirituality and the intimacy are replaced by a kind of disconsolate acquiescence in the "transitory." You don't permit even the simplest things in your house—tables, chairs, benches, etc.—to stand crookedly, because they would put you in an unpleasant frame of mind. Why then should you permit this with objects which are intended to express certain spiritual attitudes? Well, I have had to endure this nevertheless. That is why I am writing in this vein; perhaps it will contribute to an amelioration of the situation: the exhibition and care of works of Plastic Art.[3]

Van Doesburg's remarks reveal his strong desire to control the environment in which works of art were exhibited. He recognized that the way objects were treated, especially the setting in which they were displayed, had a profound effect upon the ability and the willingness of the spectator to perceive their aesthetic value.

That many other artists shared van Doesburg's concern for the exhibition environment is demonstrated by the fair-stand interiors that Huszar, Klaarhamer, and van der Leck designed in 1918 and 1919. But it was Piet Zwart's review of the 1919 industrial fair and his subsequent design of a stand for the 1921 fair that evidenced a new development in the attitude of progressive artists toward exhibition design. In his article, and later in the exhibition interior constructed according to the principles outlined in it, Zwart broke away from the analogy between the exhibition space and the domestic interior that even van Doesburg was still invoking in 1916. By emphasizing only those qualities peculiar to exhibition design (especially its temporary, transitory status, as opposed to the sense of permanence van Doesburg had called for), Zwart helped to initiate the phenomenon of the exhibition interior as a completely independent demonstration space. In 1923, first Lissitzky and then Huszar and Rietveld designed interiors that took Zwart's achievement one step further. Unlike Zwart's stand for the celluloid firm, the interiors they produced were not intended as backgrounds for the display of objects. They were totally abstract interiors designed expressly as demonstration spaces for temporary exhibitions. These interiors were displays in and of themselves.

Alan Birnholz has shown that Lissitzky's activity in the field of interior design can be traced as far back as 1916, and that even earlier, as a student at the Technical High School in Darmstadt, Lissitzky must have been aware of "all the varied interests pursued by Olbrich and his colleagues at the Darmstadt Künstlerkolonie, perhaps the most significant [of which] was their concern with exhibition and interior design."[4] After leaving Darmstadt in 1914, Lissitzky helped install the Egyptian collection of the Pushkin Museum in Moscow. At the same time he was also examining the art and structure of synagogues, which, Birnholz suggests, may have contributed to the development of his later interior-design concepts.[5] Lissitzky also designed the dining and reading rooms for the Congress of the Third Communist International held in Moscow in the summer of 1921.[6] The following year he helped organize the Erste Russische Kunstausstellung (first Russian art exhibition), which opened at the Van Diemen gallery in Berlin in October 1922.

Lissitzky was closely associated with van Doesburg throughout the latter's stay in Germany. The two artists may have had occasion to meet again before van Doesburg moved to Paris when Lissitzky accompanied the Erste Russische Kunstausstellung to Amsterdam, where it was shown in the Stedelijk Museum between April 28 and May 28, 1923. In view of his own long-standing interest in interior design, Lissitzky must have been aware of van Doesburg's efforts in this domain, as well as those of other De Stijl artists which van Doesburg doubtless made known to him and which he would have learned about from De Stijl. Indeed, Birnholz suggests that "the impetus toward Lissitzky's creation of an actual environment according to the Proun concept probably came from van Doesburg, who was close to Lissitzky at this time."[7]

Lissitzky's Prounen Raum (Proun Space) (figure 57) was a small interior, approximately 3 × 3 × 2.5 meters, which he designed as a demonstration of his abstract spatial concepts for an exhibition held in Germany during the summer of 1923. Although Lissitzky had been involved in designing in-

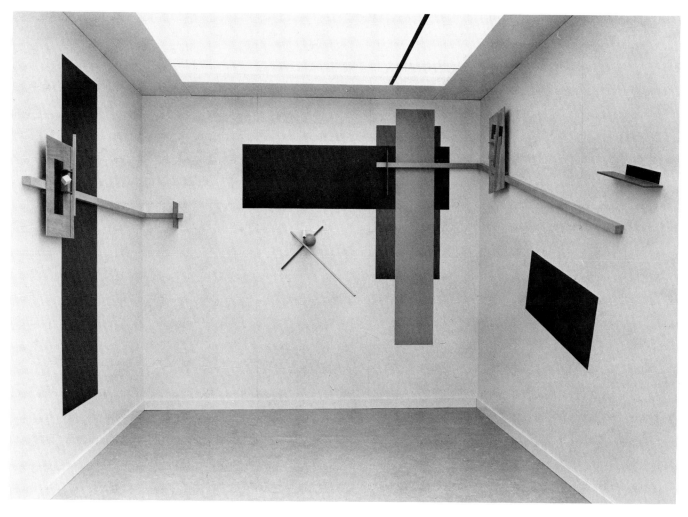

57 El Lissitzky, *Proun Space*, 1923 (1965 reconstruction), painted wood, 300 × 300 × 260 cm. Stedelijk Van Abbemuseum, Eindhoven.

teriors for some time, the exhibition provided him with his first opportunity to create a harmonious expression of the unification of the arts—a ''halting point on the way to constructing the new form''[8]—in three dimensions. The *Proun Space* was expressly designed not as a functional ''living'' room, but as a temporary exhibition space in which the viewer's process of perception was an important factor. In an article about the *Proun Space* written while he was in Holland in May 1923, Lissitzky explained its design as follows:

One keeps on moving round in an exhibition. Therefore the room should be so organized that of itself it provides an inducement to walk around in it.

The first form, which ''leads in'' someone coming from the large hall, is placed diagonally and ''leads'' him to the broad horizontals of the front wall and from there to the third wall with its verticals. At the exit—HALT! There down below is the square—the primary element of the whole design. The relief on the ceiling, lying in the same field of vision, repeats the movement. For material reasons the plan for the floor could not be realized.

The room (as an exhibition room) is designed with elementary forms and materials; lines, flat surfaces and bar, cube, sphere, and black, white, gray, and wood; and surfaces which are spread flat on to the wall (color) and surfaces which are placed perpendicular to the wall (wood). The two reliefs on the walls provide a problem-situation and the crystallization of the entire wall-area (the cube on the left wall in relation to the sphere of the front wall, and both in relation to the bar of the right wall). The room is not a living-room.

I have shown here the axes of my design for the room. I want to express in it the principles which I consider essential to the fundamental organization of room space in itself.[9]

In the *Proun Space* Lissitzky attempted to make painting, architecture, and sculpture work harmoniously. In contrast to the De Stijl practice of applying fields of bright, primary colors to given architectural surfaces, Lissitzky used only black, white, and gray paint on the walls. In some cases, however, he took advantage of the natural color and texture of the wood reliefs projecting from the walls. He wrote that the reliefs provided the theme and focus for all the wall surfaces, thus emphasizing that physical matter projecting into real space was central to his concept of how the viewer apprehended his environment. Kenneth Frampton has written that Lissitzky ''attempted optically to destroy . . . the constraining walls of the given space,'' organizing the forms in the interior so as to suggest what Frampton has referred to as ''dematerialized'' space. But Lissitzky did not deny the physicality of the materials he employed. Rather, he managed to suggest an ''amaterial-materiality'' that Frampton says was at the heart of Lissitzky's work as an architect and designer.[10] In this respect Lissitzky's concept of the *Proun Space* bears some similarity to van Doesburg's coloristic analyses of architecture in his counter-constructions stemming from the Private House and the House of an Artist. Van Doesburg also stressed the material, but unlike Lissitzky he did so by wedding color so completely to architectural form that he was able to suggest that color itself could be used as a physical, structural material. Van Doesburg's conception of color can thus be understood as a means of emphasizing its materiality in space. In practice, however, van Doesburg used color in much the same way Lissitzky used form in his interior: to dematerialize and optically destroy the limitations imposed by architecture. By manipulating the materials they chose in completely novel ways, both artists sought to make their audiences more aware of the environment and of their reactions to it.

In 1923, van Doesburg was only beginning to perceive the wealth of possibilities inherent in oblique relationships of colored forms, although his manipulation of dissonant color relationships in his earlier work might also be discussed in terms of the discordant potential of the oblique in a general sense. Although he had experimented with diagonal movement in his color schemes for Spangen and Drachten, he had not yet taken advantage of the literal oblique forms he discovered especially in his counter-constructions of the last two model-house projects (figure 53). Lissitzky's characteristic forms, on the other hand, included diagonal and spherical shapes, signs of his Suprematist heritage and his belief that the universe "knows no straight elements, only curves."[11] With its white background and tenuously hovering forms, Lissitzky's temporary little interior was endowed with the sense of vast, nonterrestrial space one finds in Suprematist easel paintings. The *Proun Space* was also comparable to the floating skeletal structure composed of active diagonal elements that Piet Zwart had used in his fair stand of 1921. Lissitzky met Zwart in Holland in 1923,[12] and it possible (though unlikely) that his own demonstration space reflected the influence of Zwart's earlier design, which was also intended to be a temporary interior for an exhibition rather than an inhabitable room. Furthermore, like Zwart, Lissitzky used color and form to unite the interior walls of the *Proun Space* in order to create a single, continuous optical experience. That this was indeed his intention can be seen in a touched-up photograph of the *Proun Space* (figure 58)

that Lissitzky published in 1923. Here four distinct views—one of each wall—were merged in a single image to emphasize the continuity of painted rectangles and strips of wood extending across the corners of the room. Any sense of discrete wall surfaces was suppressed; instead, the walls seem to blend together, creating an encompassing spatial shell.

Lissitzky's emphasis on materials and his treatment of the corners in the *Proun Space* bring to mind the early Constructivist work of Vladimir Tatlin. Developed in response to Picasso's Cubist reliefs in 1914–15, Tatlin's reliefs incorporated fragments of actual objects and were suspended in corners of rooms, where they seemed to float freely in space. Here again one is reminded of the importance corners assumed in the development by many painters of a fully three-dimensional conception of abstract spatial composition. Tatlin too became involved with interior design. In 1917 he was one of several contributors to Georgii Yakulov's interior arrangement of the Café Pittoresque, an artists' rendezvous in Moscow that Lissitzky must have known. John Bowlt has called attention to the striking features of this café:

Although the Café did not open until January, 1918, by which time it had been renamed the Red Cockerell, and even though it existed as such only for a few months, the Café Pittoresque served as an important platform for proto-Constructivist ideas—as one observer later recalled: "The interior of the Café Pittoresque struck young artists by its dynamism. There were all sorts of fantastic figurations made out of cardboard, plywood and fabric: lyres, wedges, circles, funnels, spiral constructions. Sometimes light bulbs were inside these bodies. All this was interfused with light, everything revolved, vibrated—it seemed that the

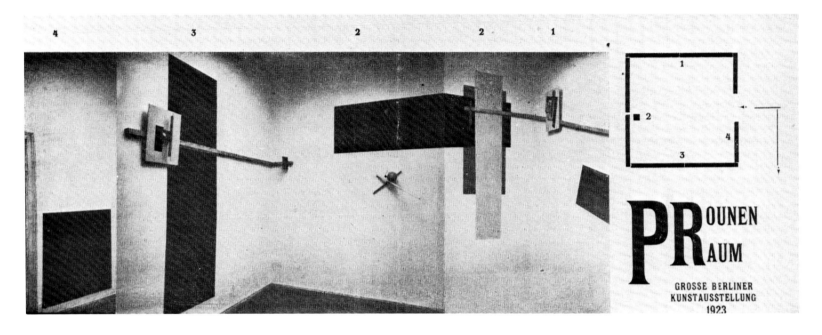

58 El Lissitzky, *Proun Space*, 1923. Illustrated in
G 1 (1923).

whole decoration was moving. Red and yellow-orange tones predominated and by way of contrast cold tones. The colors appeared to be on fire. All these things were hanging from the ceilings, from the corners and from the walls and they struck you with their extraordinary audacity."[13]

Camilla Gray describes the Café Pittoresque in terms that emphasize the properties it shared with Lissitzky's later *Proun Space*: " . . . dynamic constructions in wood, metal and cardboard clung to the walls, squatted in the corners, hung from the ceiling of this tiny interior, destroying the idea of a room as an enclosed space with solid walls. Pillared construction-fittings were attached to the lights, forming rods and shafts of light with their cupping intersecting planes, thus further breaking up and 'dynamizing' the interior."[14]

Although the Café Pittoresque was undoubtedly an important precedent for Lissitzky's environmental designs, there was little formal resemblance between his *Proun Space* and the café's interior. The many eclectic elements that combined to give the café its Dada atmosphere had more in common with the found objects Kurt Schwitters used when he began to assemble the *Merzbau* in his home in Hanover around 1923.

Lissitzky's *Proun Space* was shown in the Grosse Berliner Kunstausstellung (great Berlin art exhibition), an international exhibition held in the Landesausstellungsgebäude am Lehrter Bahnhof in Berlin from May 19 to September 17, 1923. In addition to Lissitzky's interior (and likewise included in the Novembergruppe section of the exhibition) were paintings by van Doesburg, designs for coloristic interiors by Huszar, and architectural designs or photographs of executed work by Dutch architects and designers, including Willem van

Leusden, van 't Hoff, Wils, Oud, Rietveld, and C. R. de Boer.[15] There is no evidence in the exhibition catalog to support Birnholz's contention that Willi Baumeister, Erich Buchholz, and Vilmos Huszar, as well as El Lissitzky, "were each given a room to design for the exhibition."[16] Rather, it seems likely that some or all of these artists were asked to design interiors for the Juryfreie Kunstschau (nonjuried art exhibition) that was held in the same building after the close of the Grosse Berliner Kunstausstellung in the fall of 1923. It is known that in May 1923 Hermann Sandkuhl, one of the organizers of the Kunstschau, invited Buchholz to construct an exhibition space. However, because of lack of coordination between the closing of the Grosse Berliner Kunstausstellung and the opening of the Juryfreie Kunstschau, the interior was never realized.[17]

Although it is not certain that Sandkuhl also invited Huszar to participate in the Kunstschau, this was probably the exhibition for which Huszar and Rietveld collaborated to produce a *Ruimte-Kleur-Compositie voor een Tentoonstelling* (spatial color composition for an exhibition) (figure 59), in which Huszar applied color to a structural form for which Rietveld was supposedly responsible. There is still considerable room for debate about the nature of this project, particularly the relative degrees to which Huszar and Rietveld were involved in it. All the surviving photographs appear to have been made of a small model rather than a full-size interior. An inscription visible in some of these photographs indicates that it was "realized" in an exhibition, but the circumstances that prevented Buchholz from producing his interior probably affected the plans of Huszar and Rietveld as well. This may explain why, in contrast to the critical re-

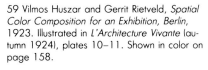

59 Vilmos Huszar and Gerrit Rietveld, *Spatial Color Composition for an Exhibition, Berlin*, 1923. Illustrated in *L'Architecture Vivante* (autumn 1924), plates 10–11. Shown in color on page 158.

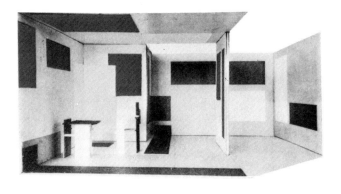

sponse to Lissitzky's *Proun Space* in the earlier exhibition, reviews of the Juryfreie Kunstschau made no mention of abstract interior designs.[18]

In any event, two versions of the ground plan of the interior have survived: one published in *L'Architecture Vivante* in 1924 (figure 60) and the other known only in the form of a slide once belonging to Huszar that is labeled Huszar-Rietveld Plattegrond voor RKC Berlin (Huszar-Rietveld ground plan for S[patial] C[olor] C[omposition] Berlin).[19] Neither version indicates dimensions or the kinds of materials that were to be employed—information one might expect to find if Rietveld, who was particularly concerned with materials and their practical manipulation, had indeed been responsible for the architectural design.[20] The manner in which the ground plan is rendered looks complex at first glance, as if it were a projection of a three-dimensional parallelopiped on a flat surface. In fact, however, it was a simple, straightforward plan of the irregular, six-sided room. Within that area, as indicated in the published version, coloristic and structural elements (including furniture) were deployed so as to organize the spectator's movement through and experience of the space. It was especially the coloristic treatment that gave the interior its complex character and special appeal as one of the most interesting and beautiful abstract environments produced by artists associated with De Stijl.

By examining several photographs of the model (figure 59) together with the published ground plan (figure 60), in which a broken line and arrows indicate the spectator's intended path, one can reconstruct the coloristic and spatial sequences, which complemented one another. The visitor would enter on one side of the room into a small corridor

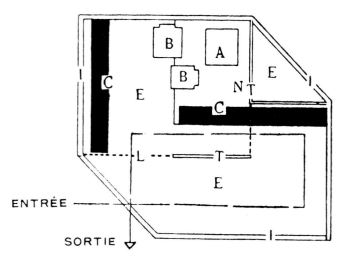

60 Vilmos Huszar, *Ground Plan, Spatial Color Composition for an Exhibition, Berlin*, 1923. Illustrated in *L'Architecture Vivante* (autumn 1924): 14.

The key translates as follows: "(I) existing walls, (T) new partitions, (L) ceiling, (E) gray floor, (A) square painted red on white ground, (N) white floor, (C) bands painted black, (B) furniture. Lighting from above."

formed by a partition on which a painted arrow indicated the direction he was supposed to follow. In this area the walls of the room were painted with rectangular planes of black and white and one plane of yellow. These neither overlapped one another nor crossed the boundaries of the surfaces to which they were applied. Upon rounding the corner, the spectator was confronted by a wall on which a red rectangle partially overlapped a running band of black that crossed over to the wall now to the spectator's right, thus suggesting that he had entered into a different, more complex kind of space. Another black band, passing from one wall onto and across the floor behind the partition, propelled the visitor into a larger area, where Rietveld's furniture, including his "Berlin Chair," was arranged on the right. Here painted rectangles including all of the primary colors were disposed not only on the walls, overlapping each other and the boundaries between the surfaces, but on the ceiling and the floor as well. In this part of the interior the spectator experienced the culmination of the design in the joining of the arts to form a total, abstract environment: the application of pure primary colors plus gray, black, and white to elementary architecture and to a kind of functional sculpture in the form of Rietveld's furniture. From here another black band along the floor conducted the visitor past a vertical red rectangle and back to the entrance of the room. The interior thus provided a sense of sequential development in its increasingly complicated and intricate interrelationship of color and form. In an almost didactic manner, it introduced the viewer to the multifarious possibilities and means of joining the arts to form a harmonious whole.

The Berlin interior was similar to Lissitzky's *Proun Space* in that it involved not only the joining of the arts but also the process of the viewer's perception of space as he moved through it. In this respect Christopher Green has noted that the Berlin interior, whose spatial form he attributes to Rietveld, can also be related to the almost exactly contemporaneous model projects by van Eesteren and van Doesburg:

The spaces of the 1923 De Stijl villa projects were designed to be moved through, their corners opened up to encourage movement, so that the experience of "concrete" and "abstract" space created by the overlappings of colored wallplanes constantly changed; the factor of time was engaged as a crucial element. Rietveld's Berlin room was designed to be moved in as well, and so Huszar's color-planes turned corners to impel the eye from one wall-plane to another as well as to destroy all sense of enclosure.[21]

Huszar was among the first De Stijl artists to express interest in the mutual interaction of color and viewer in the interior. In an article dealing with various attitudes toward Cubism, published in *De Stijl* in March 1919, Huszar had stated that the "realistic" Cubist seeks "perfection in the function of things": "He first wants to determine the essence of one object with respect to another. He does not see each thing apart, but in influential connection with the others. If a man moves in his interior, so the interior moves with the man."[22] This essentially abstract attitude toward the modern interior was one of many concepts that the De Stijl artists distilled from their experience of French Cubism; it was focused upon in particular by van Doesburg, who developed it from a notion of simple sequential movement to a complex idea of time as a fourth dimension in architecture. As such it formed a fundamental point in the architectural program, "Tot een beeldende architectuur," that van Doesburg published in 1924. Rietveld also seems to have been interested in this concept, although he approached it in a significantly different way. In the Schröder House he managed to give functional purpose to the same abstract notion of coloristic movement integrated with structural form: By using sliding partitions, Rietveld made it possible to create seven different arrangements of the single interior space of the living quarters on the upper floor. Whereas Huszar and van Doesburg developed their concepts of movement without regard to functional requirements, the flexibility of Rietveld's Schröder House responded to specific demands made by the patron. Indeed, it was apparently at Mrs. Schröder's insistence that Rietveld agreed to use sliding wall panels here.[23]

It has already been mentioned that the Schröder House was Rietveld's first major architectural commission. In the several years before 1924, Rietveld had designed two shop interiors that, as permanent exhibition spaces rather than temporary displays of abstract spatial possibilities, came closer than the Berlin interior to achieving the goal with which he was generally concerned, first as a furniture maker and then as an architect: to employ modern aesthetics in the fulfillment of practical requirements. The Berlin exhibition space had no such utilitarian implications. Rather, it served as a temporary demonstration of the kind of ideal, unified, abstract interior Huszar and other De Stijl colorists, as well as Lissitzky, had been developing in previous projects. As a demonstration space whose impact was due to its coloristic treatment, the Berlin interior does not seem to reflect Rietveld's approach, which proceeded from the requirements of furniture design and was therefore always grounded to some degree in practical, structural considerations. The Berlin exhibition space seems closer to the idea of abstract, coloristic architecture envisioned by Huszar.

Rietveld's emphasis on structural efficacy should not, however, be equated with a purely functional approach to design. In the early 1920s he did not believe that the design of a building should depend upon an evaluation of its functional purpose alone. As Rietveld later wrote: "I did not think that function as a point of departure was a sound approach. Function was an accidental, casual need that would change with the time and indeed always changes in the course of time." On the other hand, he continued, "I have never opposed it, as, after all, I thought much of it and did not see that function merely in the light of today, but also in the perspective of the future." Eventually, he acknowledged, his own work became "keyed to the function."[24] The point to be emphasized is that even when function was not Rietveld's primary consideration, structure always was. Any realized structure, whether a chair or a house, has to be sound; its parts must function in order for it to exist. To that extent, Rietveld's desire to create a sense of movement in real architectural space was tied to the functional integrity of his constructions.

Of course Rietveld too was concerned with the integration of color and architecture. He was able to achieve this to a significant degree in the Schröder House of 1924. But because the Schröder House (like Rietveld's shop interiors) was designed in a completely different context than the Berlin exhibition space, certain characteristics—including its particular coloristic treatment—distinguished it from the kinds of designs for which Huszár was responsible. Rietveld's stylistically advanced architecture and highly developed sensibility for the way color might be used to enhance a building enabled him to integrate color and structure without resorting to the collaborative effort that proved so troublesome for other De Stijl artists. His professed aversion to division of tasks between colorists and architects may further help to explain why Rietveld did not play a more active role in determining the form of the Berlin interior he and Huszár supposedly realized together in 1923.[25]

When a ground plan of the Berlin exhibition space was published in an article entitled ''Intérieur, par V. Huszár'' in 1924, it was signed ''V. Huszár, inv.,'' indicating only Huszár as inventor of the design (figure 60). The article was written by Jean Badovici, who stated (rather vaguely for present purposes) that Huszár had realized the interior ''with the collaboration of the architect G. Rietveld.'' However, Badovici discussed the conception of the space as a whole in relation to Huszár's ideas, not those of Rietveld: ''Huszár wants to renew the architecture of the interior by putting painting and the other plastic arts in its service. . . . His goal is to create 'an abstract space with compositions and combinations of different colors in a given concrete space.' The excessive liberty expressed in easel painting is excluded by the very fact of collaboration between painting and architecture.''[26] Huszár must have provided Badovici with notes from which to write this brief text. It bears a marked similarity to the summary Huszár distributed before his lecture, ''Het Wandvlakprobleem in de beeldende kunst'' (the prob-

lem of the wall plane in plastic art), delivered to the Haagse Kunstkring on December 15, 1922. In the last point of the summary he stated: ''With abstract forms and primary, real colors, modern architectural art [that is, architecturally related painting] creates an abstract, plastic space in the concrete space, independent yet at the same time of similar disposition to the artistically conceived building structure, which also plasticizes the spirit of the age.''[27]

Not only the ground plan but also three photographs of the Berlin interior (figure 59) were attributed to Huszár alone when Badovici published them in *L'Architecture Vivante* together with his article. The available documentary evidence thus suggests that Huszár was primarily responsible for shaping the ''given concrete space,'' as well as for determining the colors applied, leaving Rietveld's role to the design and execution of the furniture included in the interior.

In the final analysis, attribution is a minor issue in comparison with what Huszár and Rietveld achieved in the Berlin interior. They not only created a totally unified abstract space integrating all the visual arts, they also brought the development of exhibition design to its culmination as far as De Stijl was concerned. Like Lissitzky's *Proun Space*, the Berlin interior was not a background for the exhibition of objects; rather, it was an object, an aesthetic experience in and of itself. The abstract character of the room reflects the fact that it was designed without deference to any structural or functional requirements in an artistically controlled situation made possible by the exhibition context.

Insofar as the demonstration space was a kind of interior that was developed in response to the consideration of exhibition-design problems and depended in part on the fact that exhibitions provided an arena in which artists could avoid issues extrinsic to their particular aesthetic concerns, the demonstration space can be compared to the artist's atelier. Of course, in his own home or atelier the artist could exercise even greater control over the setting in which his work was seen. In a sense the conscious aesthetic determination of the studio environment, first as a background for the making and private exhibition of paintings and eventually as a work of art in its own right, paralleled the development of the abstract demonstration space. Like the demonstration space, this kind of atelier also reversed the trend, established in Art Nouveau exhibitions, of making the exhibition space seem like a habitable room. Instead, artists made parts of their own homes into works of art that functioned simultaneously as exhibition areas. Thus, although Mondrian submitted his work to temporary exhibitions whose installation he could not hope to control to any significant degree, he also made his own atelier into an exhibition space reflecting the same principles upon which his easel paintings were based. The studio itself, as well as the work displayed there, became an expression of the artist's environmental concerns.

That Mondrian conceived of his atelier as an appropriate locale for exhibiting his paintings is demonstrated by a succession of photographs he allowed to be taken in his Paris studio beginning as early as 1924. In many of these photographs the central position is occupied by an easel upon which one or more paintings are displayed. One photograph dating from about 1929 (figure 61) shows four canvases arranged as if in an impromptu exhibition in front of the long wall of the studio, with which they maintain a har-

monious relationship. Another photograph shows Mondrian standing beside two paintings displayed on the easel, as if exhibiting them to the viewer. In several pictures the easel stands empty to emphasize that no individual work but the environment itself, like a demonstration space, was on display (figure 62). Here the easel, placed directly in front of one wall, is reminiscent of a Constructivist sculptural object, implying its own extension outward to incorporate the entire atelier.

Mondrian did not take these photographs, but he permitted them to be made and willingly provided them for publication. Undoubtedly he also played a large part in determining their composition and content. Several of them substantiate the proposition that Mondrian's paintings and the design of his studio were generated by a common set of ideas. For example, the book published on the occasion of the Société Anonyme's International Exhibition of Modern Art in 1926 contained two photographs supplied by Mondrian. In addition to a portrait of the artist, there was a photograph of his atelier, which appeared alongside a reproduction of one of his diamond-shaped paintings, calling attention to the relationship between the two.[28]

Max Bill has written about what he refers to as Mondrian's "acute" paintings, pointing out that, of about twenty works in this diamond format ("a square standing on a corner") included in his oeuvre, Mondrian painted most in 1925 and 1926: ". . . his principle of the dynamic rhythm extending beyond the boundary of the image becomes exceptionally effective in the 'acute' pictures. A horizontal-vertical structure accords itself with a horizontal-vertical environment. However, a square placed on a point cannot be assimilated

61 Four paintings by Piet Mondrian displayed in
the artist's studio, Paris, ca. 1929. Paul Citroen,
Palet (1931), p. 77.

62 Piet Mondrian, *Studio of the Artist, Paris,*
1926. Photograph: Documentation Archive, Gemeentemuseum, The Hague.

to this order, but develops as another form of activity, which extends itself on the wall surrounding it in four horizontal and vertical directions."[29] According to Bill, a desire to express extension played a crucial role in the development of Mondrian's Neo-Plastic style, particularly in his use of intersecting lines not only to determine rectangular areas on the canvas but at times also to imply their continuation beyond the picture plane. Of all Mondrian's paintings, Bill notes, those in the diamond format most effectively establish a relationship with their environment. Bill's interpretation of the diamond paintings has been subject to some dispute, but in light of his argument it is significant that Mondrian painted a series of these pictures around 1926, during the period of his most intense activity in the evolution of an abstract, Neo-Plastic, colored environment.[30]

Whereas the apparently fortuitous juxtaposition of a diamond painting and a photograph of Mondrian's atelier in the Société Anonyme publication merely implied a relationship between the two images, Mondrian was able to make the connection explicit in an interview published in the Dutch newspaper *De Telegraaf* on September 12, 1926. In the interview Mondrian specifically referred to a diamond painting as an "abstract surrogate" of the studio space, which, in turn, he understood as a microcosm of the world view to which Neo-Plasticism aspired. The interviewer wrote:

On the easel stands the artist's latest painting: in a white square on its point, three, four horizontal and vertical lines cross each other, cutting off small slices of yellow and blue. . . . But as the canvas is against the wall, which is itself resolved in a coloristic way, it is redoubled and overdone; I asked Mondriaan about his ideas on the relationship of the two.

"With me there is no absolute opposition as with Léger, who discriminates between easel painting as condensed innerness and the superficially pleasing decorative wall. As my painting is an abstract surrogate of the whole, so the abstract-plastic wall takes part in the profound content that is implicit in the whole room. Instead of being superficially decorative, the entire wall gives the impression of the objective, universal, spiritual condition that comes to the fore in the most severe style forms."[31]

As he had done already in 1920, here again Mondrian made it clear that in his paintings and studio environment he endeavored to manifest the same aesthetic relations and proportions, which were to be organized constructively rather than decoratively. For him, as for other De Stijl painters, "decoration" was a pejorative term implying an arbitrary arrangement of forms that could not result in the exact expression of balanced relations necessary for the achievement of harmony. The denigration of the "merely decorative" on the part of Huszar, van Doesburg, and van der Leck grew primarily out of their attempts in applied design to arrive at a monumental style in direct relation to architecture. Mondrian's antidecorative attitude was instead indebted to the French Cubists. Like them, he never doubted the efficacy of individual easel painting, although he did foresee its disappearance in the future.

Mondrian's reference to Léger also reflects his belief in the continuity between easel painting and painting in an architectural context. He criticized Léger for making a distinction between the two, and particularly for approaching the application of color to architecture with a primarily decorative intention. In 1925 Léger himself had written the following: "I have collaborated in doing some architectural designs, and have then contented myself with being decorative, *since the volumes were provided by the architecture and the people moving around.* I sacrificed volume to surface, the painter to the architect, by being merely the illuminator of dead surfaces. In works of this kind, it is not a question of hypnotizing through color but of refining the surfaces, of giving the building, the town *a joyful countenance.*"[32] In light of such a statement it is not surprising that Mondrian expressed opposition to Léger's approach. But Léger's attitude to painting in architecture is a complex issue meriting further examination in comparison with Mondrian's ideas.

At the time he wrote the passage quoted above, Léger was experimenting with a series of nonfigurative paintings he called *Peintures murales.*[33] It is difficult to categorize these images exclusively in terms of either mural or easel painting; they share attributes of both genres. As Christopher Green has noted, "Léger's murals may have been abstract and may have declared a new alliance with architecture, but they did not announce the death of easel painting." Virtually the same could be said of Mondrian's Neo-Plastic paintings, and Green points out their similarities with Léger's work. He also goes on to describe the fundamental difference between them: "In one further crucial way Léger's approach to painting for architecture differed from that of De Stijl: he did not see the experience created by the marriage of color and construction as self-sufficient. His murals and the walls on which they might hang were no more than a setting for the main drama—the drama of real life, of people and things."[34] Instead of intending color in architecture to conform to the compositional principles of easel painting, Léger

wanted his murals to function more or less as neutral backdrops—as decoration. This helps to account for the "superficially pleasing" quality Mondrian condemned in Léger's architecture-related work.

Mondrian's initial interest in architecture resulted from his search for neutral subject matter, such as that provided by building facades. A. B. Loosjes-Terpstra has suggested, with respect to Mondrian's paintings of 1913, that "the facade motif *as such* could hardly call up any emotional reaction—and apparently it was attractive for just that reason."[35] It was not until several years later, when Mondrian had an opportunity to organize his own studio environment, that he began to consider the problem of decoration and the relation of painting to architecture in terms of actual, three-dimensional space. As he wrote in connection with a discussion of his atelier in "Natuurlijke en abstracte realiteit": "It is as difficult to paint a room as to make a painting. It is not enough to set a red, a blue, a yellow, a gray, etc., next to each other. That would be merely decoration. . . . It is all in the *how*: how the elements are placed, how the dimensions are worked out, how the colors of the various elements are interrelated. . . . The abstract-realist picture will disappear as soon as we can transfer its plastic beauty to the space around us through the organization of the room into color areas."[36] In the same essay Mondrian established the principles upon which he based his concept of the Neo-Plastic environment and, more specifically, the arrangement of his studio: ". . . a room should not be an empty space, limited by six empty planes which are merely opposite each other: a room should be a divided space, hence a space already partially filled, limited by six surfaces which are also divided,

63 Piet Mondrian, *Studio of the Artist, Paris,* 1926. Photograph: Documentation Archive, Gemeentemuseum, The Hague.

and which balance each other in their relations of position, dimension and color. . . . The distribution of the space should not be effected primarily by objects brought into the room from outside: everything should contribute to the harmony."[37]

Mondrian seems to have gone to considerable lengths to suggest for the purposes of individual photographs that his rue du Départ studio was a regular, rectangular shape. A comparison of the floorboards visible in two pictures (figures 62 and 63) belies that assumption. By the same token, some photographs show oblique angles formed by objects and furniture that might appear to have been deliberately placed repoussoir elements; however, these angles, though exploited to that end, were in fact a result of the actual shape and arrangement of the room (figure 64). One entered through the only door. To the left of the doorway was a wicker chair, and beyond that a stove that heated the room. Immediately in front of the door was a small table next to a couch (barely visible in the background of figure 65) that faced a cupboard and an easel, the latter covered on one side with pasteboards. A diamond-shaped canvas hung on the back of the easel. On the far side of these dividing elements were hidden a bed and a cratelike chest that stood beside the studio's large tinted windows on the courtyard side (figure 66). The wall in this area was a continuation of the wall Mondrian faced as he painted, at a table jutting out below the window overlooking the rue du Départ.

In the course of time Mondrian moved a few of these elements around to achieve new and occasionally very specific compositional ends. One such instance was an arrangement

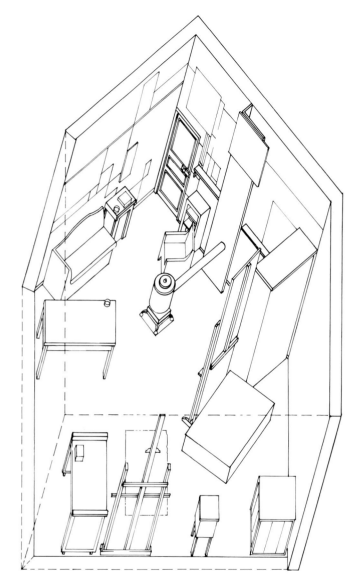

64 Approximate layout of Mondrian's studio, Paris, 1926.

made in 1926 for a photograph in which he paid homage to Michel Seuphor, whose book *Diaphragme intérieur et un drapeau* (interior diaphragm and a flag) lies on a table in the foreground. Mondrian's model stage design for Seuphor's play *L'Éphémère est éternel* (the ephemeral is eternal) stands on a table by the opposite wall (figure 67).[38] Seuphor wrote *L'Éphémère* in Rome in February 1926. When he returned to Paris he presented Mondrian with the recently completed manuscript of *Diaphragme intérieur* and the text of *L'Éphémère*. He visited Mondrian several days later and was surprised to find in the studio "a charming construction of gay colors: an eventual model for my little theatrical piece, with the three removable decors."[39] Several months later Mondrian remarked: "I made the model for a play by him [Seuphor] that will be performed in Lyon (not really a play but more a critique of the theater, very good) but again there is no money for decor work. I am still happy that I made it because now I see that in it there is a whole field to cultivate."[40] At the last moment the performance of *L'Éphémère* originally planned for November 1926 at the Théâtre du Donjon in Lyon, and thereafter possibly in Brussels and Rome, was canceled because of financial difficulties;[41] the unrealized model remained in Mondrian's studio and he had no other opportunities to realize his ideas for a Neo-Plastic space in stage design.[42]

The failure to produce *L'Éphémère* was not the only disappointment Mondrian experienced in his attempts to construct a Neo-Plastic environment outside his own atelier. At about the same time, he designed but was unable to carry out an interior for the Dresden collector Ida Bienert. The frustration of this plan too undoubtedly influenced his subse-

65 André Kertész, *Piet Mondrian and Friends in Mondrian's Studio, Paris*, 1926. Photograph: Collection of Michel Seuphor, Paris.

66 André Kertesz, *Piet Mondrian's Studio, Paris,*
1926. Photograph courtesy of André Kertesz.

67 Piet Mondrian, *Studio of the Artist, Paris,*
1926. Photograph: Documentation Archive, Gemeentemuseum, The Hague.

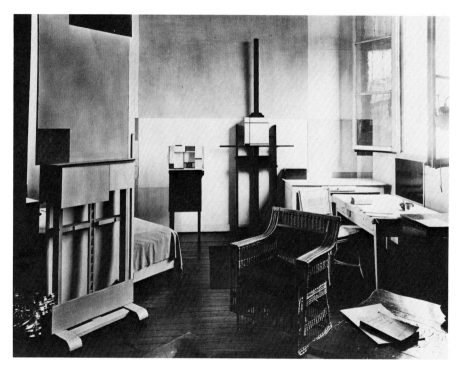

quent decision to concentrate his interior-design efforts on his studio, where he could exercise complete control. Ida Bienert was the daughter of a wealthy businessman and the wife of a successful industrialist. She promoted social causes, such as the establishment of Dresden's first public library in 1905. Around that time she began to assemble a small art collection, which included engravings by Dürer and etchings by Rembrandt. In 1911 she began collecting modern art, eventually amassing an important collection that included the work of Chagall, Kandinsky, Klee, Malevich, and Moholy-Nagy.[43] In the early 1920s Bienert became friendly with Lissitzky, and it was apparently upon the advice of his future wife, Sophie Küppers, that she acquired work by Mondrian after seeing an exhibition of his paintings at the Kühl und Kühn gallery in Dresden in 1925.[44] Shortly thereafter, again through the mediation of Lissitzky and Küppers, she asked Mondrian to design a room in her home in Plauen, a suburb of Dresden.[45] According to Bienert's friend, the art historian Fritz Löffler:

The house on the Würzburger Strasse in the suburb Plauen, where the Bienerts had lived since 1890, was not built by them. It was one of the typical Renaissance-style villas of the "Dresden School" influenced by Gottfried Semper, a brick structure with sandstone facing, with a ground floor for the social rooms, and a mezzanine. In the center was a large hall with a skylight. The ground plan of the whole was very grand and reserved. In this hall Ida Bienert received her guests. A big painting by Kandinsky and two Chagalls were hung here. However Ma-Ida [as she was called by family and friends] was not really content with this traditional space. So in 1925 she asked Lissitzky to put her in touch with Mondrian, who at that very moment in his Bauhaus book, *Neue Gestaltung*,[46] had expressed himself forcefully

on the subject of architecture and the environment. Mondrian sent very interesting designs for the renovation of the hall, but did not himself come to Dresden. For various reasons the plans remained unrealized. The designs have disappeared.[47]

Although it seems logical that Ida Bienert would have commissioned Mondrian to redesign an interior as important as the hall in which she customarily received visitors, among whom were many modern artists whose work she collected, this was not the case. It is possible that she thought of asking Mondrian to design a stained glass window for the hall skylight Löffler described, as suggested by a letter of October 18, 1925 from Lissitzky to Sophie Küppers: "You write about a glass window by Mondrian for Bienert. Is that supposed to mean that he is to make a design for it?"[48] However, there is no convincing evidence that Mondrian ever made a design for either the window or the reception hall.[49] Rather than a large space with furnishings appropriate for such a room, the interior Mondrian redesigned was relatively small. It had no skylight, and except for a table and a lamp, the only furniture it contained was a single bed and two built-in cabinets (figures 68–72). Early in 1926 Mondrian wrote to Oud that the Bienert room, on which he had already been working for some time, was intended to be a study (kamerbibliotheek).[50] The narrow oblong cabinet that Mondrian would have placed against one wall of the room must have been intended as a bookcase. That Mondrian's designs for Bienert were destined for a private study is confirmed by several related drawings for the same room by another artist, which include shelves and a desk as well as a bed.[51] Furthermore, as Mondrian wrote to Alfred Roth in

1937, he was obliged to adapt his design to the existing "old architecture," and "the table was also prescribed by the person who asked me to do the project."[52]

Never having seen the room itself, Mondrian must have worked from architectural plans and descriptions provided by Bienert. This undoubtedly contributed to the way he conceived the project at first in terms of the spatial distribution of rectangular forms. He thus began, in a manner characteristic of his sketches for easel paintings, by making a black and white line drawing with written indications of color (figure 68). Here, in addition to ink and pencil, he used white gouache as a corrective device to block out lines and thereby alter the boundaries of several rectangular areas. This exploded-box plan was retained by the artist throughout his life; it is the only drawing for the Bienert interior whose location has always been known to scholars of Mondrian and De Stijl. It provided the basis for a full-scale Formica model of the otherwise unrealized interior that was produced by the Pace Gallery in New York and in 1970 (figure 69).

Recently, three other large and impressive color drawings for the Bienert interior—those Fritz Löffler believed to have disappeared—were rediscovered in the Kupferstich-Kabinett of the Staatliche Kunstsammlungen in Dresden. Like the ink and pencil version described above, one of these ink and gouache drawings is an exploded-box plan in which all six surfaces of the room are depicted as flat rectangular planes (figure 70). The two other Dresden drawings are axonometric views, unique in Mondrian's oeuvre because they do not maintain strict planarity on the page. Instead the artist employed an architectural drafting technique involving a 30°

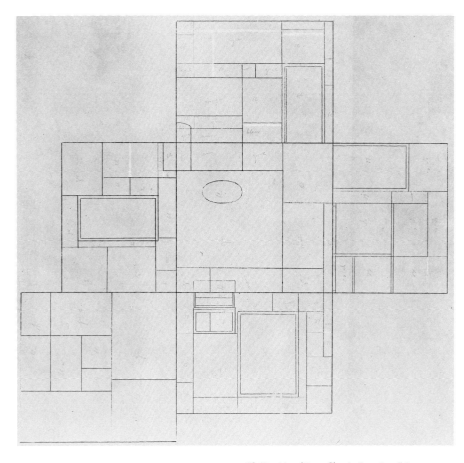

68 Piet Mondrian, *Classic Drawing #5*, ca. 1926, ink and pencil, with gouache corrections on paper, 76.3 × 75.5 cm. Private collection, West Germany.

■ 146

69 *Interior Executed by the Pace Gallery, New York, After* Classic Drawing #5 *by Piet Mondrian*, 1970, Formica on wood, 305 × 366 × 427 cm. Collection of Sidney Singer, New York.

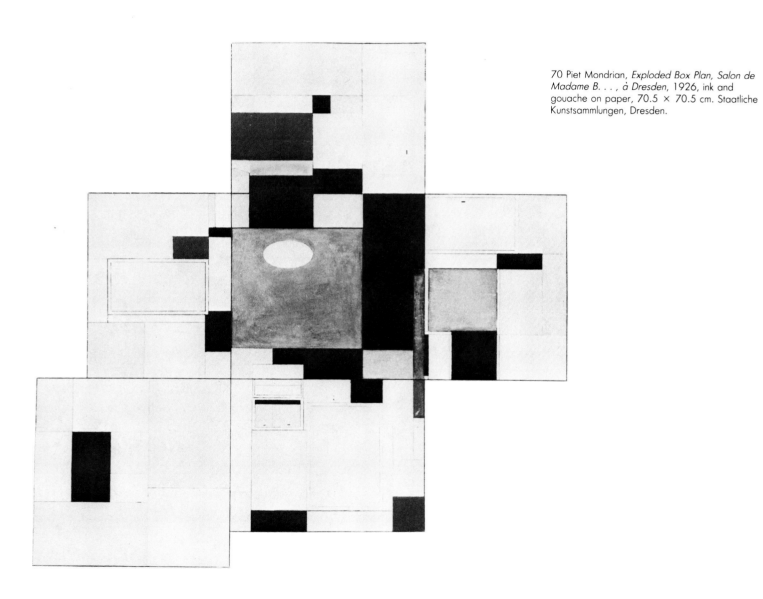

70 Piet Mondrian, *Exploded Box Plan, Salon de Madame B. . . , à Dresden*, 1926, ink and gouache on paper, 70.5 × 70.5 cm. Staatliche Kunstsammlungen, Dresden.

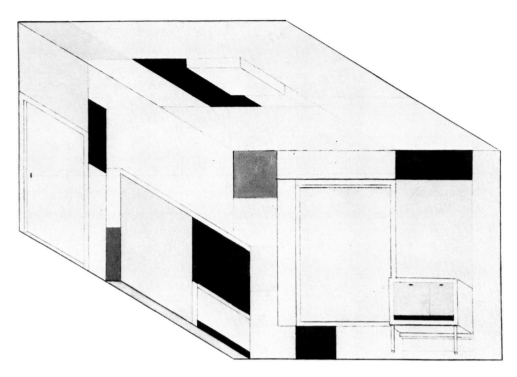

71 Piet Mondrian, *Geometric Perspective, Salon de Madame B. . . , à Dresden*, 1926, ink and gouache on paper, 37.5 × 57.8 cm. Staatliche Kunstsammlungen, Dresden.

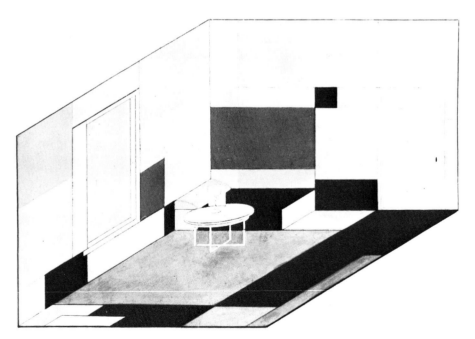

72 Piet Mondrian, *Geometric Perspective, Salon de Madame B. . . , à Dresden*, 1926, ink and gouache on paper, 37.5 × 57 cm. Staatliche Kunstsammlungen, Dresden.

angle of projection that enabled him to show the room to scale in three dimensions. One view shows two walls and the ceiling of the interior from below (figure 71), while the other shows the remaining two walls and the floor from above (figure 72).

Mondrian may have decided to employ axonometry because, although it involved the use of perspective—which he otherwise avoided consistently—this drafting technique allowed him to give an illusion of three-dimensional space while still providing accurate information about the scale of most elements in the proposed interior. It must have seemed appropriate to submit some kind of perspective views so that his patron could imagine how the room would look when it was completed. Whereas traditional perspective is based on a single, stationary point of view and reproduces the optical image of converging parallel lines and of objects whose size diminishes in proportion to their distance from the frontal plane, in axonometry, "Parallel lines are *really* parallel . . . there are no vanishing points and consequently no diminishments; a thing does not change its size or dimensions by reason of position or distance. . . . What it amounts to is the correlation in a single drawing of plan and elevation, but in a somewhat distorted form."[53]

In choosing axonometric views, Mondrian was probably also influenced by van Doesburg's counter-constructions of several years earlier. By 1926 a kind of rivalry had developed between the two artists, who were in the process of redefining their relationship to one another. Although van Doesburg's painting style had for many years been largely indebted to Mondrian, in the sphere of interior design van Doesburg was both more sophisticated and far more experienced than Mondrian (who was, of course, aware of van

Doesburg's architecture-related work).

Initially, Mondrian seems to have approached the Bienert designs in a manner more or less consistent with his paintings of the same period. He used thin black lines to organize each surface of the nearly square interior, including the bed, the enclosed bookcase, and the cabinet, into rectangular planes. He then applied primary colors, black, white, and several shades of gray to every element of the room, filling each rectangular area completely so that, unlike in his paintings, in the room itself the dividing lines would hardly be visible. One cannot fail to be impressed by the rigor of the interior's horizontal and vertical planar composition, which is interrupted only by the small lamp and the oval table Bienert had asked Mondrian to include in his plans. The rest of the sparse furnishings seem to have been pressed up against the walls in an effort to integrate them with the overall Neo-Plastic design. Mondrian thus created tension between the treatment of the ceiling, the floor, and the walls as individual, planar compositions, resembling his easel paintings, and the suggestion of a real, three-dimensional space in which all those surfaces would interact.

The colors, red, yellow, and blue, were used quite sparingly. There are four areas of each hue, judiciously distributed in an asymmetrical arrangement that enlivens the remaining grisaille treatment of forms. The largest area of color is a rectangle of red placed on the wall above the length of the narrow daybed as if to deny any possibility of rest by the sheer force of visual stimulation and coloristic impact. The subtle orchestration of tonal values—which Mondrian only hinted at in his annotated line drawing, by making a distinction between *gris* (gray) and *gris clair* (light gray)— becomes very powerful in the Dresden gouaches. Close examination reveals three shades of gray, each probably corresponding in Mondrian's color theory to one of the primary colors. By juxtaposing these grays with rectangles of color, black, and white, Mondrian was able to achieve a complex relationship of tones and an active interplay of forms to which no black and white reproduction can do justice. Mondrian asked that a note to this effect be placed alongside the drawings when they were published in 1927.[54]

Max Burchartz's design for his atelier of about 1922 (figure 73) is comparable to Mondrian's plans for the Bienert interior. Around the time he made his design Burchartz was closely associated with van Doesburg;[55] thus he would have been familiar with Mondrian's interior-design ideas, about which he probably read in *De Stijl* as well. Like Mondrian's later interior, Burchartz's studio design involved the application of rectangular planes of primary color plus black, white, and gray to the ceiling, the floor, the walls, and the furnishings. However, Burchartz's drawing technique was significantly different: He included the ceiling, the floor, and most of three walls in a single perspective view. The ceiling was rendered as if folded back, in a manner resembling Lissitzky's 1923 *Proun Space* lithograph (figure 74). Burchartz's design nevertheless seems remarkably similar to Mondrian's designs of years later. Although there is no evidence that Mondrian had seen Burchartz's drawing, he could have been made aware of it by van Doesburg or by Burchartz himself, who knew French and was responsible for translating Mondrian's essay "Die neue Gestaltung in der Musik und die futuristischen italienischen Bruitisten" (Neo-Plasticism in music and the Italian Futurist noisemakers), published in *De Stijl* in 1923.

It seems likely that Mondrian's three gouache drawings were a source of Georges Vantongerloo's *Design for a Dining Room* of 1926. Vantongerloo also made an exploded-box plan of his interior, and his two perspective views (figure 75) are almost identical to those by Mondrian: One indicates two walls and the ceiling of the interior viewed from below, while the other shows two walls and the floor from above. Although many details are common to both designs, Vantongerloo's interior was more conservative than Mondrian's Bienert room; the massive furniture Vantongerloo provided was arranged more symmetrically with respect to the coloristic solution of the walls in large planes of white and gray. (These planes bring to mind the coloristic treatment of Mondrian's long studio wall in the early 1920s, for which Vantongerloo was partially responsible.) According to Seuphor, Vantongerloo was Mondrian's "closest painter friend" during this period.[56] He had been in Paris visiting Mondrian until early September 1925, just around the time that Mondrian must have begun working on the Bienert designs.[57] It may even have been Mondrian who urged Vantongerloo to exhibit several of his dining room designs in the Société Anonyme International Exhibition of Modern Art of 1926; ink versions of Vantongerloo's perspective views were published in the accompanying book, in which a photograph of Mondrian's studio also appeared.[58] In 1927, a painted wood model of Vantongerloo's interior was illustrated in the same issue of the French magazine that first published Mondrian's gouache drawings for the Bienert room.[59]

Despite the fact that Mondrian's plans for Bienert's study were completed and approved sometime before March 1926,[60] it was not possible to carry them out. The apparent reason was neither that Mondrian spoke no German[61] nor that he harbored an intense dislike of the German people and was therefore unwilling to travel to Dresden.[62] The designs were not realized because, in Mondrian's own words, "the financial compensation was too little for me to go there myself for the execution. I do not think that someone else can direct it."[63]

Mondrian evidently felt that his personal supervision was vital to the successful realization of his plans. This is especially interesting in light of the fact that, when a full-scale Formica model of the Bienert interior was produced in 1970 (figure 69), its rigidity alone might have made one conclude that it failed to do justice to the many nuances of Mondrian's drawings. However, there is a tightness about Mondrian's designs—a harsh, impersonal quality that is heightened by the angularity of the bed and the fact that all the books in the study were to be hidden behind the Neo-Plastic facade of the bookcase. Mondrian made no provision for an adequate table, a desk, or chairs, so it is difficult to imagine how the room could have fulfilled its function as a study unless furniture were to be added by Bienert. When Lissitzky first saw photographs of Mondrian's designs, he too was puzzled by their apparent lifelessness: "I had expected something clearer. It is more reminiscent of his earlier works than of his most recent. And once again it is really a still-life of a room, for viewing through the key-hole. Should Ida Bienert have the design put into effect it will certainly be a document of his work. Perhaps the finished room will make a more convincing impression than the design."[64]

Although the Formica model is not particularly faithful to Mondrian's intentions (the oval table, for instance, was mis-takenly interpreted as a small rug next to the bed), it does evoke the harsh, still-life quality Lissitzky and others have perceived, particularly in reproductions of Mondrian's designs. The decision to make the model in Formica was prompted by a text by Mondrian himself. He wrote in "Le Home—la rue—la cité," an essay accompanying publication of the Bienert designs in 1927: "If our material environment is to be pure in its beauty and therefore healthy and practical, it can no longer be the reflection of the egotistic sentiments of our petty personality. In fact it need no longer be lyrical in expression, but purely plastic." Mondrian believed that, in order to establish a material environment reflecting universally valid moral and aesthetic principles, it would be necessary to abandon the use of natural materials because they evoke subjective individuality:

In architecture, matter can be denaturalized in various ways, and here technology has not said its last word. *Roughness, rustic appearance* (typical of materials in their natural state) *must be removed.* Therefore:

1. Surfaces will be smooth and bright, which will also relieve the heaviness of the materials. This is one of the many cases where Neo-Plastic art agrees with hygiene, which demands smooth, easily cleaned surfaces.

2. The natural color of materials must also disappear as far as possible under a layer of pure color or of non-color (black, white or gray).

3. Not only will materials be denaturalized in their use as plastic means (constructive elements), but so will architectural composition. Neutralizing and annihilating opposition will destroy natural structure.[65]

Mondrian's mention of hygiene (typical of many statements concerning architecture in the 1920s) and his emphasis on

73 Max Burchartz, *Design for the Studio of the Artist*, ca. 1922, pencil, tempera, and collage on paper, 44 × 59 cm. Private collection, Cologne.

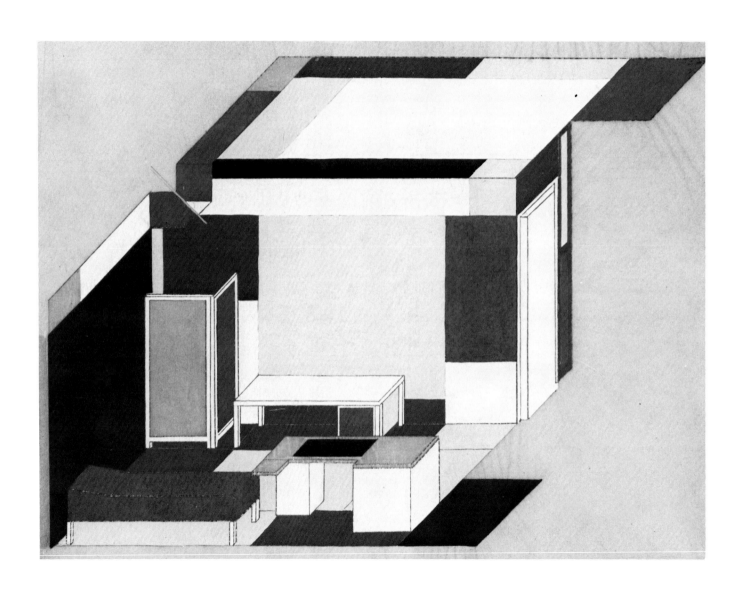

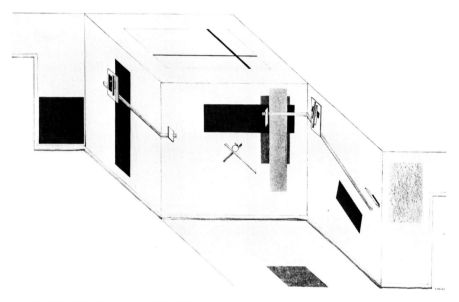

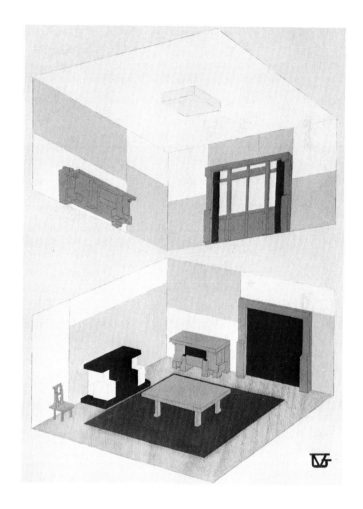

74 El Lissitzky, *Proun Space (No. 5 from 1st Kestner Portfolio)*, 1923, lithograph on paper, 43.8 × 60.3 cm. Stedelijk Museum, Amsterdam.

75 Georges Vantongerloo, *Design for a Dining Room*, oil on panel, 71.5 × 56.5 cm. Estate of the artist. Courtesy of Max Bill, Zumikon.

denaturalization of both color and material bring to mind van Doesburg's remark (quoted on page 106 above) about the form he would have liked his ideal studio to assume.

The Formica model of the Bienert room was intended to realize the image of modern, machine-made architecture possessed by Mondrian, van Doesburg, and many other artists and architects of the 1920s. However, the model fails to capture the sense of experimentation and evolution—indeed, subjective individuality—that made Mondrian's studio such a lively space. Ironically, although Mondrian wanted to see a Neo-Plastic environment like his studio—which was a source of inspiration for the Bienert designs[66]—realized in modern materials according to technological methods, it was only because his studio was neither machine-made nor scientific but evolved intuitively under his own supervision that it was a successful interior composition. In Mondrian's studio, as in his Neo-Plastic paintings, "there was no program, no symbols, no 'geometry' or system of measure; only intuition determined the total relationships, by trial and error."[67] That is why, in contrast to the Formica model of the Bienert study and many other more recent attempts to realize coloristic architecture in machine-made materials on an environmental scale, Mondrian's studio always maintained a personal character, a degree of intimacy, notwithstanding the strictness with which at any given moment Mondrian may have guarded its compositional arrangement.

Mondrian's three ink and gouache drawings for the Bienert interior (referred to as the *Salon de Madame B . . . , à Dresden*) were published in a special number of the French review *Vouloir* devoted to the subject of "Ambiance." The designs illustrated Mondrian's article "Le Home—la rue—la cité," which set the tone of the entire publication and constituted the artist's most cogent discussion of the Neo-Plastic environment and its value for modern society. In that essay Mondrian succinctly expressed ideas that lay at the foundation of his oeuvre and were particularly relevant to the environmental designs in which his aim was to make those ideas manifest in real space:

. . . the home can no longer be sealed, closed, separate; nor can the street. While fulfilling different functions, home and street must form a unity. To achieve this we must cease regarding the home as a box or a void. The idea of the "home"—"Home, Sweet Home"—must be destroyed at the same time as the conventional idea of the "street."

Home and street must be viewed as the city, as a *unity formed by planes composed in neutralizing opposition that destroys all exclusiveness*. The same principle must govern the interior of the home, which can no longer be a conglomeration of rooms—four walls with holes for doors and windows—but *a construction of planes in color and non-color unified with the furniture and household objects, which will be nothing in themselves but which will function as constructive elements of the whole.*[68]

Mondrian was well aware that the achievement of his goal, a "harmonious material environment," would have to wait for the transformation of society from an individual to a universal outlook: "That is the dream of the future. . . . But we cannot expect this of the great masses. Today everything is created in and by the individual."[69] Mondrian's oeuvre, and his studio in particular, must be viewed in this light: as the work of an individual artist produced in what he felt was a period of discord but intended to express a universal harmony to be achieved collectively in the future. Be-

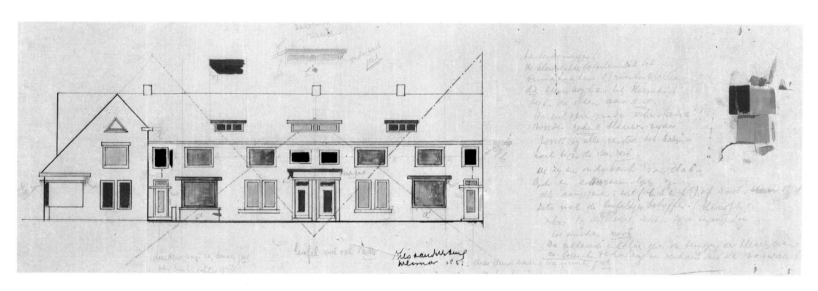

41 Theo van Doesburg, *Color Design for Exterior of Middle-Class Housing, Drachten*, 1921, ink, pencil and gouache on paper, 30.2 × 70.5 cm. Collection of D. Rinsema, Meppel.

42 Theo van Doesburg, *Color Design for Exterior of Agricultural School, Drachten*, 1921, ink and watercolor on paper, 27.9 × 112.5 cm. Museum It Bleekerhûs, Drachten.

43 Theo van Doesburg, *Diagram of Color Scheme, Agricultural School, Drachten*, 1921, ink and watercolor on paper, 27.8 × 93 cm. Museum It Bleekerhûs, Drachten.

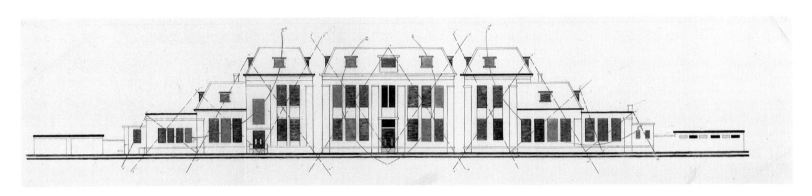

1

46 Theo van Doesburg, *Color Design for Amsterdam University Hall*, 1923, ink, tempera, and collage on paper, 63 × 145.5 cm. Van Eesteren-Fluck & van Lohuizen Foundation, Amsterdam.

50 Theo van Doesburg, *Color Design for Amsterdam University Hall*, 1923, ink and gouache on paper mounted on cardboard, 7 × 32.5 cm. Inv. no. AB5112, Dienst Verspreide Rijkskollekties, The Hague, Schenking van Moorsel.

59 Vilmos Huszar and Gerrit Rietveld, *Spatial Color Composition for an Exhibition, Berlin,* 1923. Illustrated in *L'Architecture Vivante* (autumn 1924), plates 10–11.

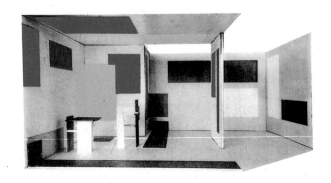

cause he was unable to ignore the fact that society was not prepared to accept the new Neo-Plastic order, Mondrian continued to believe in the validity of individual easel painting throughout his career. Moreover, it was probably because of the failure to realize either the designs for Seuphor's *L'Éphémère est éternel* or those for the Bienert salon that after 1926 Mondrian no longer concentrated with the same intensity on Neo-Plastic interior design.

It should be emphasized, however, that the Bienert commission coincided with a crucial period in Mondrian's career when he was intensively exploring possibilities for relating his easel painting style to architecture and interior design. It has been mentioned that in 1925 and 1926 Mondrian painted a number of pictures in a diamond format. He seems to have liked this shape partly because it enabled him to establish an especially strong relationship between the painted composition and the wall in front of which it would be seen. The diamond format was central to Mondrian's artistic development in the mid-1920s because it engaged him in issues associated with both painting and architecture; these problems were similar to those he encountered in his interior designs.

Possibly an outgrowth of Mondrian's Cubist experiments with an oval format in the teens, the diamond format eventually became a focal point of Mondrian's argument with van Doesburg about the role of the diagonal in their respective work. Years later Mondrian described this problem to James Johnson Sweeney:

Doesburg, in his late work, tried to destroy static expression by a diagonal arrangement of the lines of his compositions. But through such an emphasis the feeling of physical equilib-rium which is necessary for the enjoyment of the work of art is lost. The relationship with architecture and its vertical and horizontal dominants is broken. If a square picture, however, is hung diagonally, as I have frequently planned my pictures to be hung, this effect does not result. Only the borders of the canvas are on 45° angles, not the picture.[70]

The late work of van Doesburg to which Mondrian referred in this statement was the series of counter-compositions developed out of the several architectural projects with which van Doesburg had been involved in 1923, his counter-constructions in particular. In several of his counter-composition paintings of 1924 and later, van Doesburg oriented the compositional structure of rectangular forms at a 45° angle in relation to the framing edge of the canvas (figure 76). He thus departed from the horizontal-vertical orientation that constituted a fundamental compositional principle of Mondrian's Neo-Plasticism.[71] Even in his diamond paintings, as he explained to Sweeney, Mondrian always retained the orthogonal relationship of planar elements, introducing an oblique angle only by implication in the limits of the canvas support.

Although Mondrian first painted diamond compositions in 1918 and continued to explore this format throughout the rest of his career, his relatively frequent use of the diamond shape in 1925 and 1926 deserves particular attention because it seems to have embodied a response to the counter-compositions van Doesburg was painting at about the same time. Just as the counter-compositions were related to van Doesburg's architectural interests, so Mondrian's diamond compositions of this period played a special role in the development of his own interior-design concerns. He was particularly pleased that one such painting was hanging

76 Theo van Doesburg, *Counter-composition V*,
1924, oil on canvas, 100 × 100 cm. Stedelijk
Museum, Amsterdam.

in the Dresden studio of Ida Bienert's daughter-in-law, the modern dancer Gret Palucca. Early in 1926 Mondrian wrote to Oud that he had just sold a painting for 400 marks "to a dancer who apparently has a white dance studio." "Now," Mondrian remarked, "my canvas is hanging there as a focal point when the dancer is at rest, so I am told. That's rather nice, eh."[72] Furthermore, Mondrian's axonometric projections for the Bienert interior may be understood as an attempt to rival van Doesburg's counter-constructions of 1923. The particular nature of the relationship among all of these works deserves more attention than the context of this discussion allows. Here it is sufficient to note that the paintings and architectural projects of Mondrian and van Doesburg involved a complex dialogue that affected both men profoundly.

Mondrian's Bienert designs must therefore be considered not only in the context of his own work, but also in relation to that of van Doesburg. It seems significant, for example, that van Doesburg's most ambitious interior-design project, the Café Aubette in Strasbourg, was begun at the end of 1926. The Aubette was the ultimate expression of van Doesburg's aesthetic ideals and may be seen as his final statement in the dialogue he carried on with Mondrian's work. If their respective careers are viewed in these terms, Mondrian's designs for Ida Bienert assume an importance far greater than one might expect of an isolated, unrealized project.

The Bienert commission gave Mondrian an opportunity to express his ideas about interior design in drawings and plans as well as in words. This process seems to have affected his thinking about the relationship between his easel paintings and their architectural setting while also reinforcing his emphasis on the horizontal-vertical structure, which was fundamental to Neo-Plasticism as he always construed it. Finally, when compared with van Doesburg's counter-constructions, the drawings Mondrian produced for the Bienert commission may be seen as one indication among many of the gulf that separated him from van Doesburg. Their argument over the diagonal in painting was in part a manifestation of their different approaches to architecture and interior design.

Mondrian was evidently disappointed that neither the stage designs nor the Bienert salon could be realized. After 1926, his only work on an environmental scale was for his own atelier. In a letter of August 26, 1927, to Félix Del Marle, the artistic editor of *Vouloir*, he mentioned that he had been busy for more than two months with changes in the studio interior.[73] It may have been at this time that the large cupboard and the second easel received a coat of white paint over the original black.[74] Pictures taken in the studio in subsequent years register its transformation alongside that of his easel-painting style. Throughout this period Mondrian's studio continued to function as an exhibition space. People interested in promoting his paintings—among them Sophie Küppers and the American collector Katherine Dreier—and many fellow artists were received there. The profound impression of such an experience has been described by Ben Nicholson and Alexander Calder, both of whom testified to the influence not only of Mondrian's paintings but also of his studio environment on their work. Calder wrote the following about his 1930 visit:

It was a very exciting room. Light came in from the left and from the right, and on the solid wall between the windows there were experimental stunts, with colored rectangles of cardboard tacked on. Even the victrola, which had been some muddy color, was painted red.

I suggested to Mondrian that perhaps it would be fun to make these rectangles oscillate. And he, with a very serious countenance, said:

"No, it is not necessary, my painting is already very fast."

This visit gave me a shock. A bigger shock, even, than eight years earlier, when off Guatemala I saw the beginning of a fiery red sunrise on one side and the moon looking like a silver coin on the other.

This one visit gave me a shock that started things.[75]

In a letter to John Summerson written on January 7, 1944, Nicholson described his first meeting with Mondrian in the studio ten years earlier:

His studio . . . was an astonishing room: very high and narrow . . . he'd stuck up on the walls different sized rectangular pieces of board painted a primary red, blue and yellow and white and neutral gray. . . . The paintings were entirely new to me and I did not understand them on this first visit (and indeed I only partially understood them on my second visit a year later). They were merely, for me, a part of the very lovely feeling generated by his thought in the room. I remember after this first visit sitting at a café table on the edge of a pavement almost touching all the traffic going in and out of the Gare Montparnasse, and sitting there for a very long time with an astonishing feeling of quiet and repose (!)—the thing I remembered most was the feeling of light in his room and the pauses and silences during and after he'd been talking. The feeling in his studio must have been not unlike the feeling in one of those hermit's caves where lions used to go to have thorns taken out of their paws.[76]

The studio had perhaps an even greater impact on Jozef Peeters, Félix Del Marle, Cesar Domela, and Jean Gorin, all of whom responded, often with Mondrian's encouragement, by creating similar environments in their own homes or ateliers.

The Belgian painter Jozef Peeters was the first of these artists to visit Mondrian, during a two-month stay in Paris in the summer of 1921. Even earlier, as is shown by correspondence dating from May 1919, Peeters had been in contact with van Doesburg, whom he soon invited to Brussels to deliver a lecture ("Classique–Baroque–Moderne") in February 1920. Peeters also corresponded with architects, including Wils, Oud, and Berlage, and from 1922 on he was engaged in applied art and interior design.[77] As he wrote in November 1922: "We, as artists, want to create an environment for the masses that would adapt itself to contemporary demands. . . . We concern ourselves with the formation of the new environment. . . ."[78] Peeters's relationship with Mondrian was never particularly intense; he found Neo-Plasticism too systematic, limited by its strict adherence to the orthogonal relationship of primary color rectangles on a single plane. His early visit to Mondrian's studio nevertheless coincided with the genesis of his interest in furniture and interior design, and may have influenced his decision (not realized until 1927–1932) to paint the walls of his studio and his entire apartment at Statiekaai 7 (now Gerlachekaai 8), Antwerp, in an abstract composition of light blue, pink, yellow, and green rectangular planes (figure 77).[79]

Félix Del Marle may have met Mondrian and van Doesburg as early as 1922;[80] however, the influence of Neo-Plasticism was not evident in his own work until several years

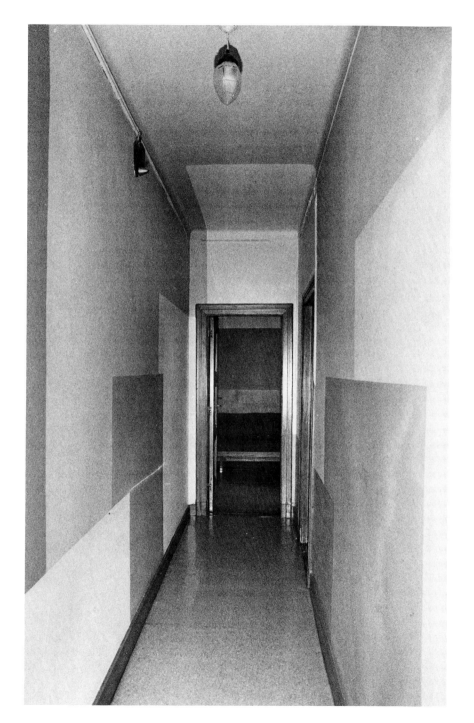

77 Jozef Peeters, *Hall of Peeters Apartment, Antwerp*, ca. 1932.

later. In the tenth-anniversary issue of *De Stijl* van Doesburg wrote that, after seeing the Paris exhibition L'Art d'Aujourd'hui in November 1925, Del Marle began to promote the ideas of De Stijl in *Vouloir*.[81] It was not until 1927 that the subtitle of *Vouloir* was changed from the original *Organe constructif de littérature et l'art moderne* (constructive organ of literature and modern art) to *Revue mensuelle d'esthétique Néo-Plastique* (monthly review of the Neo-Plastic aesthetic), as a sort of homage to Del Marle's friend Mondrian.[82] Del Marle's earliest correspondence with Mondrian dates from 1926, the year in which Mondrian and van Doesburg first published articles in *Vouloir*. It was probably then that Del Marle visited Mondrian's studio in Paris for the first time.[83] Shortly thereafter Del Marle redesigned the living room of his own home as a Neo-Plastic interior. He made chairs and tables, a lamp, and a hanging tapestry, and he applied rectangular planes of color to the walls (figure 78). Mondrian congratulated Del Marle for this achievement, remarking: "What I like best is your furniture; when I have the pleasure of seeing you I will make a few little observations about the interior itself. But all my compliments for your effort, which is already so successful."[84] Del Marle's daughter recalls, however, that the members of her family found the room cold and uninviting. They hardly ever used it, and spent most of their time in the dining room instead.[85]

The Neo-Plastic interior that Cesar Domela designed in 1927 for his apartment in Berlin posed a similar problem. Domela had been introduced to Mondrian and van Doesburg when he was in Paris in the spring of 1924. He was deeply impressed by his initial experience of Mondrian's studio, as he demonstrated two years later when he made his first interior design for the Amsterdam home of Arthur Lehning, editor of *i10*, a journal whose inaugural issue contained a Dutch version of Mondrian's essay "Le Home—la rue—la cité."[86] When Domela moved to Berlin in June 1927 he arranged his own apartment at Kantstrasse 149 (figure 79) in much the same way, with rectangular planes of primary color and noncolor inspired by what he had seen in Mondrian's studio. However, when he and his family moved to the Roscher-Strasse in 1928, his interior design for the new apartment was much less severe; having once had the experience, Domela decided that one "really can't live in a painting."[87] In an interview many years later, Domela described how he had come to feel about Mondrian's studio, expressing particular objection to the rigidity of its arrangement: "If you lit a cigarette in his atelier and you put the box of matches down in a different place, he would get up to put it back in its original position. Otherwise the composition of the atelier wouldn't work anymore."[88] Apparently Domela and his wife decided that, however beautiful it might be, a Neo-Plastic interior was suitable only for the kind of bachelor life that Mondrian led. Like the Del Marle family, the Domelas concluded that it was inappropriate for a household with small children and a more active social life. In the work space of his second Berlin apartment Domela used only gray tones, reminiscent of the earlier form of Mondrian's studio. He felt that, unlike the primary colors, gray would not impose itself prominently in his visual field and thus complicate the process of working with color in individual compositions.[89]

Jean Gorin first encountered Mondrian's work in 1926, when he bought a copy of *Vouloir* that included Mondrian's

article "*Art* pureté + abstraction."[90] The following year, he met Mondrian in his rue du Départ studio. Almost immediately Gorin "created a Neo-Plastic environment in his own home by applying orthogonal lines and planes of primary color to the walls and floor," and he also designed several tables, chairs and lamps.[91] In imitation of Mondrian's practice, Gorin even went so far as to display an easel as a construction against one wall of his atelier (figure 80). Like Del Marle, Gorin was interested in the application of Neo-Plastic principles to the design of functional objects; his subsequent architectural designs reveal debts to van Doesburg, van Eesteren, Huszar, and Lissitzky, as well as to Del Marle and Mondrian.

Although the several ateliers Mondrian created in Paris and later in London and New York were undoubtedly the most influential, he was not the first, even among the artists associated with De Stijl, to treat his studio as an arena for coloristic, plastic manipulation: "Ever since 1912 van der Leck [whom Mondrian had met in 1916, and at whose house he had been a frequent visitor] lived in white-walled surroundings, in which accents of primary color were placed by means of rugs, curtains, upholstery, cushions."[92] Furthermore, the long-established tradition of painters depicting themselves in their studio environments, or the studios alone, testifies that the atelier was often considered to be like a self-portrait, a reflection of the artist and his aesthetic concerns. It is also possible that the prevalence of still-life subject matter in the work of artists such as Cézanne, van Gogh, and the Cubists, like the interiors of Vuillard and Matisse, was similarly related to a widespread trend toward concentration on the intimacy of the artist's everyday life

80 Jean Gorin, *Studio of the Artist, Nort-sur-Erdre*, 1928. Photograph: collection of Suzanne Gorin, Nort-sur-Erdre.

and his personal environment in particular.

Even the photographer Henri Berssenbrugge, who fancied himself a progressive artist, wanted his atelier to be an appropriate setting in which to make the so-called moderne fotographie on which his reputation in Holland was based. When he decided to renovate the atelier (at Zeestraat 65, The Hague) in 1920–21, Berssenbrugge employed Jan Wils and Vilmos Huszar to create an interior according to the principles of De Stijl, with primary colors applied to ceiling, floor, walls, and furniture (figure 81). Many reviews greeted the opening of the atelier, testifying to its success not only as a painted abstract environment but also as a means of advertising Berssenbrugge's "artistic" portrait photography.[93] Until July 1921, Berssenbrugge had been a member of the Haagse Kunstkring, in which Wils was very active and Huszar was also involved. In December 1921, six months after Wils and Huszar had completed the renovation of his atelier, Berssenbrugge offered it to members of the Haagse Kunstkring as a temporary exhibition space.[94]

The dual role of the artist's atelier as both a private and a public space, where art was first created and then shown, made it a particularly appropriate forum for the promotion of advanced aesthetic ideas. Indeed, during the latter half of the nineteenth century, the artist's house, with the studio as its focal point, had been much copied by patrons who wanted their own homes to express the artistic tastes they acquired on visits to actual studios. Collectors were reminded that just "as the value of a picture consists in the expression of an artist's mind and is an index of the owner's artistic sympathies, so is a beautiful house the manifestation of its owner's artistic temperament."[95] Mark Girouard has

81 Vilmos Huszar, *Color Applications, Atelier Berssenbrugge, The Hague*, 1920–21, Photograph: Nederlands Documentatiecentrum voor de Bouwkunst, Amsterdam.

written about the popularity of the "artistic house" in England, noting that "although many of these houses were built for artists, even more were built for those of the rich who enjoyed the company and neighborhood of artists."[96] In a sense, Ida Bienert's desire for Mondrian to redesign a room in her villa was yet another instance of a collector wanting to acquire a work of art representative of the artist's oeuvre. Had it been carried out, the *Salon de Madame B . . . , à Dresden* would have been a harmonious yet individual ensemble, comparable on a certain level to every other object in Bienert's art collection.

In spite of all pretensions to universality, it was the ironic fate of the abstract interior that for the most part it remained an exhibitable, collectable entity, subject to much the same treatment as many abstract easel paintings produced during the 1920s. But unlike easel paintings, which could be taken off the wall and put away, the few interiors that had been realized were dismantled or destroyed when tastes and circumstances changed. With rare exceptions, as a group they are known today only through descriptions, photographs, preliminary drawings, or reconstructions.

The interior of the Café Aubette in Strasbourg, designed and executed between 1926 and 1928 by Theo van Doesburg together with Hans Arp and Sophie Taeuber-Arp, illustrates this point particularly well. In 1926, van Doesburg, still lacking a studio like Mondrian's that he could arrange according to his own interior-design principles, seized the opportunity to make the Aubette into a reflection of his aesthetic ideas. Where all previous attempts had failed, he hoped to succeed in changing what he felt were the petty, individual demands most people made on the environments they used or inhabited: "All 'isms' which originated here in recent decades have failed largely because of the narrow-mindedness of their dogmas, compromise or a chauvinistic tendency. All the gains in aesthetic insight of the last twenty years could not dislodge either the individual or collective mankind from its exclusive interest in material prosperity. Only material and physical well-being has served, and still serves, as a criterion of success."[97]

It may have been Taeuber-Arp who actually secured the Aubette commission,[98] and although she and her husband (a native of Strasbourg) were individually responsible for roughly half the interiors, van Doesburg exercised ultimate control over all the designs. Taking even the smallest details into consideration, he designed new lettering for signs on the exterior and interior and applied the same typographical forms to objects such as the ashtrays used throughout. He even made the arrangement of the master light switches into an aesthetically pleasing composition. All in all, the transformation of the café, which occupied one wing of an eighteenth-century building on the place Kléber in the center of Strasbourg, was an enormous undertaking. The original facade had to be preserved, but, in addition to a passageway linking the place Kléber to the rue de la Haute-Montée behind the Aubette, and a large stairway inside, there were ten public rooms at the artists' disposal, including various bars and cafés, a billiard room, and two dance halls.[99] Like several similar establishments in Glasgow that C. R. Mackintosh decorated for Catherine Cranston at the turn of the century, the idea here was to create an ambiance appropriate to the social or gastronomic activity that went on in each room, while at the same time uniting all the designs in a harmonious whole that conveyed the dynamic quality of modern urban life.

As director of the entire project, van Doesburg had an especially challenging task that involved the incorporation of Arp's ''premorphist,'' Surrealist-related style as well as the geometric configurations that characterized his own and Taeuber-Arp's work.[100] By dividing initial responsibility for the various interiors among the collaborators, it was possible to preserve the integrity of each artist's contribution. However, they all tried to use the most modern, machine-made materials, so that, for example, the nickel-coated tubular chairs in one room would correspond to the nickel-coated tubular light fixtures in another. At first van Doesburg had hoped to avoid what he called ''illusionistic materials'' and to introduce light not as painted color but as an energy inherent in the durable, functional materials he proudly listed as evidence that the latest technical advances had been exploited in the designs.[101] Indeed, standardized furniture and fixtures as well as lighting considerations in general played an important role in every Aubette interior. Centralized light sources were eliminated in an attempt to achieve ''a regular, full lighting which, nevertheless, would not dazzle the eyes and which should avoid shadows.''[102] Shiny nickel, aluminum, and electroplated elements, mirrors, glass, and enamel were manipulated to reflect light and color and thereby intensify the dynamic character of the painted compositions that, van Doesburg said, had been applied to all the wall and ceiling surfaces because of financial limitations restricting the use of expensive new materials he would have preferred.

Each Aubette interior was designed with its intended function clearly in mind. The organic, curving forms of Arp's mural in the ''caveau-dancing'' (figure 82) proved particularly appropriate for its basement location, where the exclusively artificial light could be regulated to produce a vivid yet still somewhat mysterious atmosphere of nocturnal, subterranean life. This was in marked contrast to Taeuber-Arp's arrangement of the tea room (figure 83) on the ground floor, which was intended for daytime patronage. Here the neutral gray ceiling and wall planes were divided asymmetrically by wide bands of silver leaf whose glossy surface was meant to complement the proposed use of shiny mosaics (in practice, paint was used) for the coloristic compositions of black, gray, and red rectangles on a white ground that were located at irregular intervals throughout the large room. As in Arp's caveau-dancing, mirrors were placed so as to correspond with the rest of the arrangement, adding another shiny surface to enhance the various ways color and light were actively manipulated in the room.

In the cinema–dance hall (figure 84) on the first floor above ground level, van Doesburg demonstrated still other possibilities for many of these same materials, combining them in a masterful design that liberated the potent energy of contrasting colors and abstract forms. By virtue of its large size and central location, the cinema–dance hall was the most important of all the Aubette interiors. The dual function of the room made it particularly well suited to van Doesburg's notion of the dynamic role of color employed so as to activate an otherwise ''expressionless, blind''[103] architectural space:

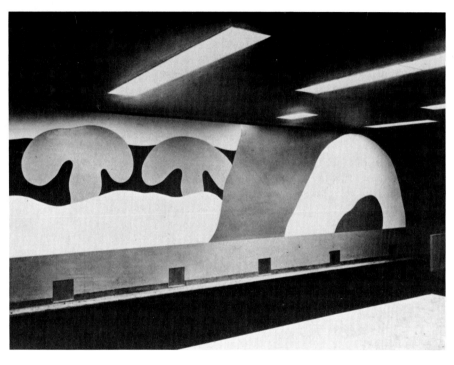

82 Hans Arp, *Caveau-Dancing, Café Aubette, Strasbourg*, 1926–28. Photograph: Documentation Archive, Musées Municipaux, Strasbourg.

It was very difficult to animate this room by the use of colors. I did not have any unbroken surface at my disposal. The front wall was interrupted by the screen and the emergency exit, the rear wall by the entrance door, by the door of the small banqueting hall and by the openings for the cinematic projectors, as well as by the reflector. The left-hand wall was broken up by the windows extending almost to the ceiling, and the right-hand wall by the door to the kitchen offices. Now, since the architectural elements were based upon orthogonal relationships, this room had to accommodate itself to a diagonal arrangement of colors, to a counter-composition which, by its nature, was to resist all the tension of the architecture. Consequently, the gallery, which crosses the composition obliquely from the right-hand side, was an advantage rather than a disadvantage to the whole effect. It accentuates the rhythm of the painting.

The surfaces are raised 1 1/2 in. [4 cm] above the plaster and separated from one another by bands 1 1/2 in. deep and 14 in. [35 cm] wide. If I were asked what I had in mind when I constructed this room, I should be able to reply: to oppose to the material room in three dimensions a supermaterial and pictorial, diagonal space.[104]

The designs for the cinema–dance hall involved broad compositions of colored rectangular planes in relief oriented at 45° angles to the orthogonal architecture. Mirrors were placed between the windows to reflect the ceiling and the three other walls, all treated in a manner that turned the architectural surfaces into a kind of plastic, relief sculpture. Van Doesburg's use here of high relief was a further development of his plan to attach colored enameled plaques to the walls of the University Hall in order to achieve a sense of color floating free from architectural form. An independent composition was applied to the ceiling and the three windowless walls, and, rather than extend colors across the

83 Sophie Taeuber-Arp, *Tea Room, Café Aubette, Strasbourg*, 1926–28. Photograph: Documentation Archive, Musées Municipaux, Strasbourg.

84 Theo van Doesburg, *Cinema-Dance Hall,
Café Aubette, Strasbourg*, 1926–28. Photograph: Documentation Archive, Musées Municipaux, Strasbourg.

boundaries of each surface, van Doesburg allowed the architecture to determine the limits of the individual designs. He seems to have conceived of the walls and ceiling as gigantic fields of radiating compositions clashing with one another at their junctures. The corners functioned as the edges of the compositions, slicing off splayed rectangles to create a variety of irregular forms in a manner similar to that of the diamond paintings Mondrian was producing around the time that the remodeling of the Aubette got under way. But whereas Mondrian's images retained their strict horizontal-vertical character and the oblique was only implied by the limits of the canvas support, in van Doesburg's cinema–dance hall the support necessarily retained its orthogonality while the oblique was made literal in the dynamic form of van Doesburg's counter-compositions. The ultimate visual and conceptual sources of this interior may be traced back beyond the University Hall ceiling designs and the counter-constructions van Doesburg had made with van Eesteren in 1923 to the Spangen color schemes that Oud had rejected two years earlier. Van Doesburg had conceived of those colors too as oblique-angled planes organized partially in opposition to their architectural setting in order to destroy its presence as a three-dimensional mass.

The Spangen designs can be seen as marking a point midway in the development of van Doesburg's notion of color in architecture. In 1918 he had already been thinking of color and architecture as inherently dissimilar means of expression, but then he believed that "the very fact that they have to fulfill essentially different functions makes possible a harmonious combination." The conflict with Oud over Spangen compelled van Doesburg to consider the conse-

quences of these differences in a new light. He gradually became convinced that it was impossible to reconcile the discordant criteria of color and architecture, just as it was becoming impossible to combine the contributions of colorist and architect in a harmonious yet functional whole. In virtually every instance, one side or the other of this tenuous balance eventually succumbed to the weight against which it was posed. The abstract unity of color could be achieved only in an ideal situation such as the model projects provided in 1923; otherwise, the practical framework in which the architect had to operate militated against the abstract compositional demands of the colorist. In the Aubette, where he had more freedom to develop his ideas, van Doesburg tried to exploit the potential of color to replace architecture as the most important determinant of the viewer's spatial experience. As a colorist he aspired to the position of architect, master of the space he designed. The belligerent tone in which he proclaimed his newest ideas was a verbal counterpart to the embattled forces of color and architecture as he perceived them in 1926, operating against one another to effect an "unbalanced counter-composition."[105]

As van Doesburg described in several essays published in *De Stijl* between 1926 and 1928,[106] the essence of the counter-composition was its opposition to the orthogonal character of the fundamental structural elements found in nature and in architecture. Because architectural construction is subject to the force of gravity, "It makes no essential difference whether architecture uses load-and-carry construction, that based on tension, or no construction at all;" the result will be the same: a horizontal-vertical constellation of contrasts that echoes nature and is subject to its laws. Now that van Doesburg understood the horizontal-vertical relationship as a counterpart or reflection of organic nature, he felt that a true expression of the modern spirit demanded the addition of another dimension to the classical formula of Neo-Plasticism. In other words, he defined the Neo-Plastic principle of balanced relations of opposites as a phenomenon of "physical, real or optical nature" and saw his new manner of painting based on the oblique in contrast to the entire system inherent in orthogonality. He called this new approach Elementarism:

The new manner of painting as a process of spiritual expression is significant only in opposition to and not if homogeneous with organic-natural and architectural structure. This homogeneity expressed itself solely in horizontal-vertically determined painting which functioned within the horizontal-vertically determined construction of architecture. The former reinforced the latter. The development of the colored plane and the line served the same natural, or functional architectural structure. . . . In the case of contrast-painting (the counter-composition) the colored plane and the line develop in opposition to the natural or architectural structure, which is to say they contrast with it.

The very essence of Elementarism was its opposition to all manner of function and construction: "It introduces oblique and discordant planes which are opposed to gravitation and architectural-static construction."

Van Doesburg repeatedly invoked the destructive energy inherent in Elementarism, emphasizing its potential for discord, contrast, and variation, in opposition to the balanced relationship that inflected the Neo-Plastic harmony of equilibrated forms: "The Elementarist is a spiritual rebel, an agitator who sacrifices his own tranquility and who intentionally disturbs the peace, the regularity and routine, of bourgeois life." It is as if in Elementarism van Doesburg finally found a means of joining the disparate foci of his own artistic interests, particularly in Dada and Neo-Plasticism, and he justified his new attitude as the culmination of all previous modern movements: "Because of its new orientation towards former efforts to renovate life and art (which include Futurism, Cubism, Expressionism, Dadaism, Neo-Plasticism and so on) *Elementarism* contains all truly modern elements (which one-sidedly have often been ignored!)."

Although van Doesburg's Elementarism has been understood as an outgrowth of his experiments in architecture dating at least as far back as 1923, the consequences of the introduction of the oblique in his work have usually been discussed in terms of painting, that is, as contributing to the argument that ensued from van Doesburg's rejection of Mondrian's aesthetic principles. This aspect of Elementarism is undoubtedly of great importance, but it is necessary to grasp as well that theoretically Elementarism also involved a rejection of all physical, natural, and practical characteristics fundamental to architectural structure: "The great struggle engendered by Elementarism revolves around the destruction of the old concept of life, which is based upon illusionism in all its aspects (which satiates both nature and art, for example); on the other hand, Elementarism seeks to reconstruct an elementary world of *super-sensible* reality." This profoundly abstract, antimaterialistic, "super-sensible" reality was precisely what van Doesburg wanted to make manifest in the Café Aubette. The cinema–dance hall in particular should therefore be recognized as the ultimate expression of van Doesburg's conflict with the traditionally accepted premises of architecture. All of van Doesburg's previous concepts of the role of color in space coalesced in this one interior. Its function as a dance hall calls to mind van Doesburg's painting of about 1918, *Rhythm of a Russian Dance* (Museum of Modern Art, New York), which grew out of an interest in the complex relationship between music, dance, and abstract art that informed several of Mondrian's paintings as well. The tripartite window in the de Lange Town House, which interpreted—or at least evoked—a Bach fugue in terms of coloristic and compositional contrast, placed this kind of abstraction in an architectural setting. The mathematical precision of Bach's music was explored further in van Doesburg's designs for Drachten, where he established a proportional ratio for the contrasting coloristic elements of his environmental scheme. No longer working with color in fundamentally pictorial terms, he conceived of the musical movement of color through and across space, making analogies not only with the abstract character of music, or with Bach's contrapuntal mode of composition, but also with the sequential experience of music, which develops through time. It was at this point that van Doesburg's interest in a musical conception of color in space coincided with his recognition of the implications of abstract film. As has been mentioned, he was profoundly affected by the work of Hans Richter and Viking Eggeling, and some of his own drawings for Drachten appear to reflect their experiments with scroll drawings that were made to be filmed. Van Doesburg described and reproduced these drawings in *De Stijl*.

It was not until he collaborated with van Eesteren on the model projects exhibited in 1923 that van Doesburg developed a more architectural approach to the synthetic integration of color and space.[107] The abstract counter-constructions he began to make at that juncture incorporated the notions of simultaneity and duration in terms of the fourth dimension of time-space. Here the qualities of music (time) and architecture (space) were harmonized through color for the first time. Furthermore, the counter-constructions provided the springboard for van Doesburg's introduction of diagonal elements in his counter-composition paintings, which in turn bear an obvious visual resemblance to the color scheme he applied to the cinema–dance hall in the Café Aubette. Soon after completing the designs for the cinema–dance hall, he turned his attention once more to film, publishing an important essay on the subject in 1929.[108] It should thus be clear that the conceptual principles and formal arrangement of the cinema–dance hall embodied the synthesis of van Doesburg's cumulative artistic interests in a monumental work that provided an appropriately abstract, dynamic setting where the spectator would find himself in the midst of the plastic arts and, as a dancer, become an active participant in them.

Of all the projects for interiors by artists associated with De Stijl, the Café Aubette was the biggest and the most ambitious. Van Doesburg devoted an entire issue of *De Stijl* to documenting the interiors and related designs that he, Arp, and Taeuber-Arp worked on for one and a half years, and the café has deservedly received a great deal of attention from those interested in De Stijl interior design. The remarkable nature of all the remodeled Aubette interiors is enough to justify their fame. But what makes the Aubette particularly interesting in the context of this discussion is the response it provoked when it opened in 1928. On February 17 of that year, an enormous celebration marked the inauguration of the newly redesigned café. At a banquet attended by the elite of Strasbourg society and several foreign diplomats (including the Dutch consul), speeches were given tracing the history of the Aubette, music was played, and toasts were made to the success of the new establishment. The meal was followed by a tour of the premises, which culminated in the cinema–dance hall, where "to the strains of Sambre-et-Meuse, and to the unanimous acclaim of the enthusiastic and emotional crowd, a film of the entry of French troops into Strasbourg was shown."[109] One might well expect to learn that an abstract film by Richter had been shown, but this expression of nationalistic pride doubtless corresponded far more closely to the taste and mood of the audience, which thus celebrated the new Aubette as a symbol of France's triumph over the Germans a decade earlier.

Upon its completion the Aubette was proclaimed to be a magnificent aesthetic achievement not only by the artists who made it but also by most of those who wrote about it in the Strasbourg press, yet almost immediately thereafter the process of its destruction had already begun. In 1968 Theo Wolters described the paradox of the Aubette, which seems to have been unwittingly dramatized in the cinema–dance hall on opening night:

The circumstances in which the Aubette was produced are at least as surprising as the creation of the work itself. It is, in effect, difficult to understand how, in a provincial city submerged in rigid conservatism, an avant-garde work representative of the quintessence of the great artistic movements of the 1920s could have been realized in a public establishment open to a largely bourgeois clientele. The disparity

between the value of the work and the average taste of the public explains to a large extent the disappearance of this monumental work in the decade that followed its creation.[110]

Exactly how and under what conditions the Aubette was altered after 1928 is open to dispute.[111] It is certain, however, that less than a year after the café opened van Doesburg was already expressing bitter disappointment at the public's reception of this, the embodiment of his aesthetic ideals. He wrote in this vein to Adolf Behne in November 1928:

. . . the aubette in strasbourg has taught me that the time is not yet ripe for an "all-embracing creation." when the aubette was just finished, before its inauguration, it was really good and significant as the first realization of a program which we have cherished for years: the total artistic design [gesamtkunstwerk]. yet as soon as the proprietors heeded the opinion of their customers (who of course considered it cold and uncomfortable) all sorts of things which did not belong were carried into it. the public cannot leave its "brown" world, and it stubbornly rejects the new "white" world. the public wants to live in mire and shall perish in mire. let the architect create for the public. . . . the artist creates beyond the public and demands new conditions diametrically opposed to old conventions, and therefore every work of art contains a destructive power. . . . constant values are only contained by a 100% art. this is now my firm conviction. . . .[112]

Despite his aspiration to design on an environmental scale, and notwithstanding his earlier criticism of Mondrian's concepts for being "too much an ideal image outside of normal life," van Doesburg was finally compelled to acknowledge that what he strove for in the Aubette was also a fundamentally ideal, aesthetic image of the new environment. Precisely because he had not been forced to concede to practical demands, van Doesburg succeeded in creating a series of totally abstract interiors; however, the same refusal to deal with practical demands also resulted in the ultimate failure of his revolutionary intentions. Van Doesburg's remark that he would let the architect fulfill the traditional requirements and expectations of the public while he as an artist created "beyond the public" amounted to a retreat into his own aesthetic domain. It is comparable to the choice Mondrian made after 1926 to concentrate any future environmental design efforts in his own atelier. It also represents van Doesburg's ultimate rejection of the ideal of collaboration between painter and architect upon which the De Stijl artists' design principles and attempts to create a coloristic architecture had originally been based.

Van Doesburg's experience is especially demonstrative of how, as a result of changes in the collaborative relationship between painter and architect, the predominance of the painter had gradually become evident in the abstract environment, which consequently evolved away from and in reaction against the exigencies of mundane, practical concerns. By opting for an abstraction that was uncompromising in the extreme, artists responsible for this kind of environment ensured the disappearance of the work they designed. In contrast, architects who were determined to apply themselves to solving social problems managed to produce work that was experimental and yet suggested ways to fulfill functional requirements. This had been the motivating force behind Le Corbusier's Pavillon de l'Esprit Nouveau (figure 85), which introduced a concept of the

85 Le Corbusier, *Pavillon de l'Esprit Nouveau, Paris*, 1925. Illustrated in W. Boesiger and O. Stonorov, *Le Corbusier et Pierre Jeanneret: Oeuvre complète. 1910–1929* (1974), p. 101.

domestic environment that was entirely new to the French public when it was exhibited in Paris in 1925.

Based on principles of standardization for machine production, the pavilion proposed very unconventional solutions to problems of low-cost, mass-produced housing suited to the needs of all classes. Although Le Corbusier evoked traditions, they were not those of early nineteenth-century France to which the Maison Cubiste had referred in 1912. Instead, Le Corbusier's emphasis on simplicity and geometry resulted in a classicism that accorded with the nascent International Style. The mechanistic notion of the *objet-type*, which governed the pavilion, was based on a supposedly objective, scientific principle meant to counteract the individualism and materialism associated with specially designed, hand-wrought, Art Deco productions such as those included in the Maison Cubiste.

Although Le Corbusier wanted to create a totally harmonious environmental ensemble, his conception of the interior did not proceed from abstract, primarily painterly concerns. Instead of an interior like the cinema–dance hall of the Café Aubette—which the public found "cold and uncomfortable" if not downright oppressive in the machinelike rigidity of its geometric design—Le Corbusier produced an interior that blended a machine aesthetic with comforts that the public seems to have at least some right to expect. The initial premise of the *objet-type* was the same as that upon which Purism was based: a notion of mechanical selection that reinterpreted Darwin in twentieth-century technological terms. It allowed Le Corbusier to justify his use of familiar, mass-produced objects whose value was confirmed in his mind by their familiarity and by the durability of their design—which,

he argued, had ensured their pervasive presence in the first place.

The radical nature of Le Corbusier's interior was not a result of the introduction of anything like Rietveld's Red-Blue Chair, which one might expect to find in a De Stijl interior; rather it resulted from his introduction of typical mass-produced objects, such as Thonet chairs, to a setting in which they were not ordinarily seen: the architect-designed home interior. In effecting this transposition, Le Corbusier's goal was to set a precedent for the kind of interior that would be responsive to the exigencies of the present and not offer itself up as a sacrifice in the name of the ideal environment of some unattainable future, as was so often the case with the colored abstract environments of De Stijl.

The difference between Le Corbusier and De Stijl is further illuminated by a comparison of the French architect's approach to the conjunction of design and mass production with that of Rietveld. Whereas Rietveld's furniture designs were intended to be *prototypes for* machine production, Le Corbusier's were *objet-types of* machine production. The difference is a fundamental one that goes to the heart of the De Stijl enterprise. A moral imperative was inherent in virtually every De Stijl environment: The individual had to adapt to the universal conditions of the modern world—as those were perceived by De Stijl artists. Le Corbusier, on the other hand, tried to find a compromise between the individual and the modern environment. He did not base his conception on an abstract and absolute schema, but rather on a principle of design that was grounded, at least theoretically, in a fundamental respect for the average person and his needs within the contemporary world.

The environmental-design concerns of De Stijl should be distinguished from those of the Bauhaus as well as from those of Le Corbusier. They all shared an interest in modern constructive form and machine production, and all contributed significantly to the development of the International Style in the mid-1920s. The pervasiveness of certain features associated with this style has led to some confusion about the different natures of its various sources. The very fact that it has been called "international" suggests its interweaving of various threads that may be traced to their origins in several countries. If in one sense Le Corbusier's pavilion can be said to have expressed a typically French consideration for the need to adapt modern design to what were essentially traditional, middle-class demands, the Bauhaus was no less a product of a particularly German situation—an assertion borne out by its expressionism in the early postwar years.[113] Whether or not van Doesburg was (as he claimed) responsible for reorienting the Bauhaus toward its later and ultimately more important rationalist course, even after it took that road the products of the Bauhaus were significantly different from those characteristic of De Stijl.

The experimental Haus am Horn (figure 86), designed by Georg Muche and built in time to be shown at the 1923 Bauhaus exhibition, provides a case in point. Intended as the first unit of a Bauhaus housing development, the minimum-circulation house had at its center a relatively large square living room, which was surrounded on all sides by small rectangular rooms, each for a specialized function such as cooking, eating, bathing, or sleeping. The motivating idea was to create a practical structure that would meet the

86 Georg Muche, *Haus am Horn, Weimar,* 1923. Photograph: Bauhaus-Archiv, Berlin.

minimum requirements of a family with limited financial resources while introducing the latest labor-saving devices and modern functional designs.

In its experimental character and its incorporation of machine technology and elements of modern design, the Haus am Horn can be compared in general terms with certain aspects of Rietveld's slightly later Schröder House, or with the designs for the Private House and the House of an Artist that van Eesteren and van Doesburg exhibited, also in 1923. The much greater emphasis on color in the latter designs is an important difference, but it is by no means the only one. In their structures the De Stijl artists were far more concerned to effect an aesthetic awareness of space as a continuity, and they therefore provided for a variety of different interior spatial experiences that were also connected with the surrounding environment. Their facades were presented as a series of receding and protruding planar surfaces that expressed the active integration of interior spaces, in contrast with the Haus am Horn's boxlike appearance and intensive concentration on the functional advantages of the enclosed, central living area.

Although specific elements of this general argument might be subject to dispute, it is clear that the Haus am Horn represents that aspect of the Bauhaus philosophy that was especially concerned with the functional and economic consequences of design and in part reflects the Bauhaus goal of designing for industrial production on a large scale. To be sure, these considerations also had an impact on De Stijl (for example in Oud's Spangen housing in Rotterdam). But, as has been demonstrated, the kind of environment that the De Stijl artists ultimately had in mind was bound up with aesthetic concerns that could not accommodate purely rational demands. It was primarily a painterly vision of a colored, abstract environment that became, in the end, unacceptable even to those architects originally associated with De Stijl. In abandoning that vision, Rietveld, Oud, and others chose to work in a more strictly architectural idiom that they believed was better able to respond to existing social conditions. In this sense, their work of the late 1920s and early 1930s was not dissimilar from that of Le Corbusier or that of such Bauhaus architects as Gropius and Mies van der Rohe. For present purposes, it may indeed be considered as part of an International Style that was no longer concerned with the possibility of integrating color and architecture—which, in the most immediate sense, had given rise to the colored abstract environments of De Stijl. In total opposition to the fundamental nature of the most advanced abstract environment, the temporary demonstration space, architects instead devised exhibitions of permanent, functional environments—living spaces that would eventually be used for public housing.

One example of this phenomenon is the Deutsche Werkbund exhibition of 1927, for which sixteen architects (including Oud) were invited to construct model buildings on property owned by the city of Stuttgart in an area called Weissenhof (figure 87). According to Jürgen Joedicke and Christian Plath: "New construction methods and new materials were used by practically all of the architects for the Weissenhof Colony since one of the central requirements was economy and, along with this, reasonable rent prices for the finished buildings. In addition, special consideration was given to an apartment size suitable for families with restricted incomes.''[114] After the close of the Werkbund exhibition the buildings were used to house residents of Stuttgart, and they still perform that function today.

The Weissenhof Colony was important for many reasons, not the least of which was that it marked the appearance of a self-conscious International Style. Moreover, as an exhibition put to practical use, the Weissenhof Colony represented the architects' response to the breakdown of the collaborative ideal. Insofar as it adhered strictly to issues of rationalization and standardization in an attempt to arrive at a purely architectural solution to problems of housing in modern society, the housing built and exhibited in Stuttgart was an outright rejection of all that the abstract environment had come to represent. Yet here at last was the kind of architecture that De Stijl painters had demanded when they began to consider the application of color to buildings: simple, flat, white, rectangular surfaces ideally suited to abstract coloristic compositions. Ironically, however, there was no longer any question of collaboration. Invoking pragmatic considerations of economy on one hand and demands for artistic license on the other, architects and painters were unwilling to try to bridge the gap that seemed to separate ethical from aesthetic concerns. As artists they all abandoned the ideal of collaboration that had been fundamental to De Stijl in its early years. In doing so they disavowed the generating force behind the creation of the colored abstract environment, which thereafter gradually but unequivocally ceased to be a common goal.

87 J. J. P. Oud, *Housing Block, Weissenhof Colony, Stuttgart*, 1927. Photograph: Nederlands Documentatiecentrum voor de Bouwkunst, Amsterdam.

Conclusion

■ *182*

In view of the emphasis placed on De Stijl's collaborative ideal, it is appropriate to acknowledge the personal, ephemeral qualities that animated the most advanced colored abstract environments produced by artists associated with De Stijl. The individualism that made the work of each artist distinguishable is perhaps especially evident in designs intended to express absolute or universal principles. This individualism was the inevitable counterpart of the artist's personality, a characteristic cherished even by those who tried to integrate their own contributions in cooperative efforts aimed at a higher goal. Historians cannot help but recognize that the personalities of artists play a crucial role in determining the nature of their works. It is necessary to appreciate this fundamental point in order to assess the position of De Stijl in the context of European art during the 1920s.

Time and again it has been shown that the dynamic character of De Stijl was a direct reflection of individual artistic temperaments. With Theo van Doesburg its peripatetic center, De Stijl was active in a wide range of media and commanded the attention of a large number of artists whose backgrounds and interests were similarly widespread. But in spite of all his efforts to camouflage his importance in keeping his magazine alive and championing its ideals, van Doesburg's personality was indelibly stamped on the character of De Stijl. He was the one primarily responsible for establishing international contacts and for corresponding with artists throughout Europe. Whenever he moved to a different city, the editorial office of the magazine went with him. When he died in 1931, no one came forward to continue his crusade; the last number of *De Stijl* was a tribute to the artist who had created and breathed life into the magazine as well as the ''movement'' that shared its name.

Always anxious to promote the group as a whole, van Doesburg was never really willing or able to subordinate himself to any artist or artistic credo. He subscribed to the collaborative ideal but was not the kind of person who would make the compromises required to bring it about. Although his aggressive propensity for domination accounted for many of De Stijl's successes, it also resulted in some notable failures. The fairly continuous publication of *De Stijl* between 1917 and 1928 was primarily his own achievement, and it was perhaps the most important reason why De Stijl's impact could be felt by every major artistic movement in Europe. The pages of the magazine attest to van Doesburg's ability to enlist the support of many great artists, but he eventually alienated at least an equal number.

Van Doesburg's relationship with the Bauhaus reveals a good deal about his complex nature. When he was first introduced to Gropius and invited to visit the Bauhaus, he was obviously impressed with everything he encountered. By the same token, the comparatively well-established Bauhaus seems to have aroused tremendous jealousy in him. With only his little magazine as a forum for his ideas, van Doesburg could not hope to compete with the pedagogical resources and economic potential of the Bauhaus, which, although always embattled and constantly threatened with closure, had nonetheless received a degree of support from government and industry. Whether or not he was officially ...ed to do so, van Doesburg chose to infiltrate the forces ... ould not defeat. The acrimonious battle that ensued, ... van Doesburg on one side and Gropius and several

Bauhaus masters on the other, was very similar to the struggles going on at about the same time within the ranks of De Stijl: Van Doesburg became the center of a controversy that threatened to destroy what the group as a whole had achieved. The Bauhaus painter Lionel Feininger described the situation in a letter written to his wife on September 7, 1922:

. . . Kandinsky says that Doesburg is leaving soon, in fall, to go to Berlin, Weimar being too restrictive for his activities. Tell me, honestly, how many are there in the Bauhaus who really know what they want to achieve, or who are strong enough to make something of themselves through painstaking work? For most of them the unsentimental—if also completely uninspired—Doesburg is something of a pillar among all the heated and conflicting points of view, something definite and clear, which they can hold on to. . . . Why, how is it that there are so many voluntary submissions to the tyranny of van Doesburg and this mulish noncompliance against all requests or even suggestions put forth by the Bauhaus? I don't believe one can do much about it. Either the ideology of the Bauhaus is strong enough to overcome opposition from within and without or it will break down, because there are so few nowadays who unequivocally and with conscious judgment are willing to adhere to the cause. We proceed from suspicion to suspicion, from danger to danger. . . . We are obliged to do that, for the Bauhaus places one under an obligation, whilst van Doesburgism implies nothing of the sort; one can come and go, it is a completely voluntary submission, from which one, as everyone has learned, can soon be made free again. Of course, it is crass sabotage against everything the Bauhaus stands for. But one must always go through something like this before a balance is found. If Doesburg were a master at the Bauhaus, it would not harm the work in general, it could even be useful, for he would be a counterattraction to that rampant romanticism that is haunting us. Only I don't suppose he would be capable of keeping within his own bounds but would, like Itten, soon want to assume command over the whole works. . . . [1]

Feininger clearly articulated the fundamental problem faced by any group when one individual chooses not to subordinate his own aims to the success or, in this case, the survival of the whole. Van Doesburg must have supported the overall goals of the Bauhaus, which were in many respects similar to those of De Stijl; had he not done so he would never have transferred his activities to Weimar. At the same time, however, he was also strongly opposed to some aspects of what was being taught at the Bauhaus. Realizing that he could not dominate the system, he chose to subvert it rather than work from within for the changes he desired. Since he could not play God he became the devil's advocate instead, setting himself up in a studio in Weimar where he taught classes attended mostly by Bauhaus students, whom he tried to convert to his own artistic credo. As far as the Bauhaus was concerned, this particular dilemma was solved when van Doesburg left Weimar in 1922. But the whole episode illuminates the differences between the communal atmosphere and practical orientation of the Bauhaus and the highly individualistic, abstract elements of De Stijl, which van Doesburg personified.

Within his own group, van Doesburg's aggressive tactics produced much the same result. He was in control of the *De Stijl* magazine from the outset, and without consulting van der Leck he allowed architects to become contributors. Exit van der Leck. Later he refused to compromise with Oud when the architect criticized his color schemes for Spangen.

By enlisting the aid of van Eesteren he even managed to capitalize on the consequences of his split with Oud, heretofore the most important architect associated with De Stijl. Van Doesburg also quarreled with Mondrian (certainly a very reticent individual), for whom he seems to have retained a high degree of respect. Nevertheless Mondrian too felt compelled to sever ties with van Doesburg. Similar circumstances affected his involvements with other artists, including Lissitzky and eventually van Eesteren. The problems that arose were not confined to the sphere of aesthetic considerations; they were intimately bound up with van Doesburg's temperament, which, in view of his three marriages, must also have contributed to substantial conflicts in his personal life.

If aggressiveness and conflict are keys to understanding van Doesburg's relations with those around him, they are no less accurate as descriptions of his work as an artist. Given his volatile personality, it is not surprising that van Doesburg refused to confine his artistic output to a single style, particularly one as restrictive as Neo-Plasticism. Several years before he first encountered paintings by Mondrian, van Doesburg had been attracted to the work of Kandinsky, and the expressive qualities for which he appreciated the Russian artist continued to be of major importance to him even after his conversion to Neo-Plasticism. While on one level he more or less adhered to the strict purity of the Neo-Plastic aesthetic, on another he channeled the expressive energies that could not find an outlet within such narrowly defined limits. Undoubtedly van Doesburg was acutely aware of the risks inherent in his own eclecticism. Apart from making one Dada tour of Holland in the company of Kurt Schwitters, he chose not to admit to his activities as a Dada artist. Perhaps he felt that acknowledging them would endanger what he was trying to achieve within the context of De Stijl. For whatever reason, he felt compelled to provide himself with two additional personae, ''I. K. Bonset'' and ''Aldo Camini,'' which he used to distinguish his Dada attitudes from the De Stijl and Constructivist activities he carried out as van Doesburg. Indeed, the decision to keep his pseudonyms secret amounted to a Dada gesture that was discovered only after his death.

Of all the De Stijl artists van Doesburg was certainly the most eclectic, but around 1920 Mondrian also wrote Dada prose, and for a short time Wils managed to juggle aesthetic commitments to De Stijl and to the Dutch Expressionists associated with a magazine called *Wendingen*. The various threads of interest pursued by so many artists in the 1920s weave a complex fabric whose texture reveals the dynamic character of art in the post–World War I period. Nothing illustrates this more clearly than the two poles of Dada and Constructivism between which the work of such artists as Arp, Schwitters, and van Doesburg was situated. All these men dedicated themselves simultaneously to Dada's destruction of traditional artistic values and, as Constructivists, to the establishment of aesthetic criteria that would correspond with the new society they saw taking shape around them.

Historians are not alone responsible for the distinction between Dada and Constructivism that has obscured a proper perspective on how these trends were integrated during the 1920s. Even artists active in both arenas were for the most part unable to convince others of the validity of their two-pronged approach. Van Doesburg's secrecy about the real

identity of Bonset and Camini is one case in point. Another arose when van Doesburg played host to an international congress of artists in Weimar in October 1922. Moholy-Nagy later described his surprise and disappointment upon discovering that the Constructivist meeting he expected to find there was also a Dada event:

The constructivists living in Germany (Theo van Doesburg, El Lissitzki, Max Burchartz, Cornelius van Eesteren, Alfred Kemeny, Hans Richter, and myself) called a congress in October of 1922, in Weimar. Arriving there, to our great amazement we found also the Dadaists, Hans Arp and Tristan Tzara. This caused a rebellion against the host, Doesburg, because at that time we felt in dadaism a destructive and obsolete force in comparison with the new outlook of the constructivists. Doesburg, a powerful personality, quieted the storm and the guests were accepted to the dismay of the younger, purist members who slowly withdrew and let the congress turn into a dadaistic performance. At that time, we did not realize that Doesburg himself was both a constructivist and dadaist writing Dada poems under the pen name of I. K. Bonset.[2]

It is not difficult to understand why Moholy-Nagy was perplexed by this situation. In the Dadaists at Weimar he confronted a group of artists who were engaged in an often outrageous and always highly individualistic kind of activity that was nonetheless dedicated to destroying the individualism associated with the past. Many of these same artists were also Constructivists who published magazines and wrote manifestos declaring their allegiance to shared social and stylistic principles. How can the dichotomy that characterized their aesthetic expression be resolved? Stephen Bann offers one possibility: ''Richter's suggestion that constructivism was the 'counterpart' to 'the law of change that Dada had discovered' helps to explain the fruitful, though curious, juxtaposition of the two strains in the period under review. . . . This suggestion that dadaism was the unspoken, or normally unspoken premise of constructivism makes it easier to understand the complex role of van Doesburg himself. . . . ''[3]

One might also see Dada as an outlet for artists whose temperaments and creative sensibilities could not find adequate expression within the rigorously defined boundaries of Constructivist-oriented tendencies such as De Stijl. But, as pointed out earlier, even the work of art that adheres most closely to the supposedly rigid formula of De Stijl always seems to betray the hand and mind of the artist responsible for it. The same holds true for the fruits of a collaborative endeavor: The work, whether an easel painting or an environment, reflects both the historical moment and the process of its creation. How else can one account for the facts that, in spite of its apparent simplicity, Mondrian's style eludes successful forgery and restorers find it difficult to repair damages to the pristine surfaces of his mature paintings? Indeed, the individuality and temperament of Mondrian also require examination in order to understand the nature of De Stijl's contribution to the artistic climate of the 1920s and especially its legacy thereafter.

While van Doesburg was primarily responsible for promoting the ideas of De Stijl, it was Mondrian, through his writing and his artistic production, who defined their shape. Although the hermeticism of his personal life has often been overemphasized, it is true that in comparison with van Doesburg (or any other De Stijl artist) he was far more reserved. In his determination to merge his art with his life, Mondrian mirrored the restraint and inaccessibility of his paintings as well as the environment in which he lived and worked. In a certain sense the totality of his commitment and the way he expressed it in every aspect of his person makes Mondrian comparable to a Dada artist—for example, Schwitters, who also lived his life as a gesture of defiance against bourgeois social values. In spite of this, Mondrian was unquestionably the most influential artist associated with De Stijl, and it is with his Neo-Plastic paintings that De Stijl is most often and closely identified. Although his environmentally related work was largely restricted to his own ateliers, in this sphere too the legacy of De Stijl is profoundly indebted to Mondrian. This is due in part to circumstances beyond the artist's control. Like van Doesburg, though for very different reasons, he too became a peripatetic artist. In order to escape the Second World War, Mondrian was forced to flee the intimate world he had created for himself in Paris—first to England and finally to the United States. Partly as a result of his residence in London and New York, at the end of his life Mondrian's work came to the attention of an international audience. He wrote essays in English and in 1942 he had a one-man show in New York. While living there he was at the center of a small but important group of American abstract artists upon whom his work had a very strong impact. The isolated cultural situation of certain abstract artists working in New York in the 1930s made them particularly responsive to Mondrian's message. Of all the European painters who spent the war years in America, Mondrian seems to have inspired the most direct following, and the broader, more long-term legacy of De Stijl is also bound up with the attention he received on this side of the Atlantic.

Before discussing Mondrian's contribution to the climate of art in America in the 1940s, it is appropriate to summarize the situation he left behind in Europe, particularly as far as De Stijl and the colored abstract environment were concerned. As has been noted, only one number of *De Stijl* was published after van Doesburg's death in 1931. Well before that time, the original notion of De Stijl as a group of like-minded artists had ceased to have any real significance. To a substantial degree the history of the colored abstract environment runs parallel to that of De Stijl. Interest and activity in environmental design was sustained at a high level through 1923, the year of the De Stijl exhibition in Paris; thereafter the number of projects by De Stijl artists declined significantly. A last burst of energy came around 1926, when several artists were inspired by Mondrian to produce designs directly indebted to what they had seen in his studio.[4] The year 1923 thus marks a turning point in the development of both De Stijl and the abstract environment. Ironically, although it was originally intended to establish De Stijl at the forefront of modern architectural and related artistic activities, Léonce Rosenberg's exhibition actually intensified the conflicts contributing to the dissolution of the group. In 1925, Mondrian joined van der Leck, Oud, Wils, and van 't Hoff, who had already severed ties with *De Stijl* and its editor. In the following years, of all the contributors, it was really only van Doesburg who enlisted the cooperation of other artists to keep the magazine going or share in the design of interiors, such as the Café Aubette. Even in that project van Doesburg was bitterly disappointed when the public failed to accept the austerity his designs imposed.

During the 1930s, Huszar, van der Leck, and Zwart were engaged in activities only tangentially related to their earlier abstract environmental work: Huszar had already begun to concentrate on advertising, van der Leck continued to paint while also making some designs for commercially produced carpets, and Zwart was devoting his time to a variety of typographical and industrial design endeavors. Only Mondrian was still involved with a colored abstract environment like those he and the other De Stijl artists had envisioned several years earlier. He alone had a temperament suited to the severity that made everyone else so uncomfortable in that kind of space.

The general public was unable to tolerate the austere, inaccessible qualities inherent in such works of art and never accepted the challenge implied by their merging of moral and aesthetic ideals. Nevertheless, many aspects of the contemporary environment reflect the impact of geometric abstraction. The artistic language of De Stijl in particular has been assimilated by designers of almost every imaginable kind of object, from clothing to billboards and advertising copy. Yet many people still seem unable to grasp or respond to the message De Stijl artists meant their work to convey. The stark simplicity of much of that work was easily integrated into the modern environment, but in the process a great deal of the meaning with which it was originally so richly endowed has been stripped away. We are usually left with gigantic wall graphics providing a colored environment that has some of the look of De Stijl but very little of its content. Alternatively we may be presented with large-scale murals inspired by Neo-Plasticism, like the one by Fritz Glarner in the Time-Life Building in New York. But no matter how vast their size, such paintings have little effect on how we experience our environment, since they most often function something like Léger's murals: as decorative backdrops bearing scant relation to what goes on around them.

This situation represents a return to a far more traditional concept of color in architecture. The collaborative relationship between painter and architect is once again very close to that described by Richard Norman Shaw in 1904: The role of the painter is merely to "ennoble" a given architectural surface "with color, interest, and art."[5] A prominent example in the 1930s was the series of abstract murals commissioned from twelve American artists in 1936 for the Williamsburg Housing Project in Brooklyn, New York. Painted on canvas, which was supposed to be attached to the walls at a later date, these murals were neither conceived nor carried out with respect to a collaborative ideal. Several of them were completely nonfigurative and all involved some consideration for their intended architectural setting, but in the final analysis they bore little resemblance to a total abstract interior because for the most part they never overcame their status as wall-size easel paintings on canvas. In spite of the original intention to give the twelve commissioned artists a "unique opportunity to collaborate in solving technical problems, to experiment with new media, and to redefine their approach to painting,"[6] the artists worked on their murals in isolation from one another and had little or no contact with the architect who was responsible for designing the housing project. The whole notion of commissioning abstract murals for Williamsburg had little to do with the ideals that had motivated the De Stijl environment. Rather it was a pragmatic response to the desperate situation of advanced

artists, whose work was otherwise difficult if not impossible to place in the publicly funded context of virtually every artistic undertaking in America during the 1930s.

The neglect and abuse that eventually led to the destruction of almost all of the Williamsburg murals illustrates the dilemma faced by young American painters who were attempting to make abstract art that reflected their social awareness. In the decade before Mondrian's arrival in America a number of these modernists had been grappling with the structural and spatial problems of late Cubism and the issues of abstraction and content in nonfigurative painting. Their stylistic investigations were played out against the background of the Depression, which affected them both economically and politically. As committed leftists, many of them supported the same ideals as Social Realist artists, but they vehemently rejected the chauvinism inherent in regional styles and paintings of the "American scene." Their attitude toward art was thus conditioned by their interest in European modernism and by a felt need to respond to the social realities of the period.[7]

It was largely because of this climate of conflicting allegiances and confusion about aesthetic criteria that Mondrian became so important to a small group of American painters. In his work they found a moral message couched in aesthetic terms they could accept. Even before his arrival in New York in 1940 Mondrian's paintings were well known to American modernists, including Ilya Bolotowsky, Burgoyne Diller, Harry Holtzman, and Carl Holty. Wealthy artist-patrons such as Katherine Dreier and Albert Eugene Gallatin had visited Mondrian in Paris in the 1920s. They purchased examples of his work, which they later exhibited in New

York. American artists could read about Mondrian in publications such as the French journal *Cahiers d'Art*, and several participated along with Mondrian in activities of the Paris-based group Abstraction-Création. But Mondrian's presence in New York was undoubtedly the most important factor contributing directly to his influence on American art. Conversely, the environment of New York and the support Mondrian received from a growing audience there had a profound impact on his artistic development.

The transformation Mondrian's easel painting style underwent during his three and a half years in New York was reflected in his work and living space. Throughout this period Mondrian continued to use his studio as a forum for the exploration of his environmental concerns, which he seems to have felt were more appropriate to the modern urban setting of New York than they had been to Paris. In 1941 Sidney Janis reported that Mondrian even envisioned a "complete living interior for the American home" based on his own ideas.[8]

As had been the case when he lived on the rue du Départ in Paris, once again Mondrian's studio functioned as something more than a simple background. It was both a material and a conceptual space, contributing to and yet at the same time also growing out of the artist's other work. Indeed this interior epitomizes the dichotomies of De Stijl's colored abstract environment. At once a climax and an endpoint of developments that had begun almost two decades earlier, it was ephemeral yet enduring in impact, highly personal while directed toward universal aims.

Although only a few artists and friends visited him there, Mondrian's last apartment in New York (figure 88) has become a familiar image of the colored abstract environment. Located on the top floor of a now-destroyed building at 15 East 59th Street, the apartment consisted of a kitchen, a bathroom, a small bedroom, and a large studio space. Mondrian himself made many of the furnishings, including tables, stools, and shelves, which he fashioned out of wooden fruit and packing crates reinforced with thin strips of wood and painted white. The walls as well as the furniture were white, and to them Mondrian pinned rectangular pieces of red, yellow, and blue pasteboard in compositional clusters that he studied continually and often rearranged. He used much the same process in planning his last paintings, employing strips of colored tape and pinning little rectangles of color paper to the surface of each canvas and constantly shifting the elements until he arrived at the definitive composition.

After Mondrian died on February 1, 1944, his friend Harry Holtzman filmed and photographed the entire apartment with the help of Fritz Glarner and made tracings of the walls to document how the colors applied to them had been arranged. Cognizant of the importance of the studio in its own right, Holtzman kept it open for more than a month, inviting anyone interested to see the environment Mondrian had created as an extension of his other work. While the studio was open, Mondrian's last unfinished painting, *Victory Boogie-Woogie* (Museum of Modern Art, New York), was placed on an easel that "stood like an altar, alone at the end of the almost barren room."[9] The effect was much like a temple of pure art to which visitors were making a final pilgrimage.

88 Piet Mondrian, *Studio of the Artist, New York*, 1944. Photograph: collection of Harry Holtzman, Lyme, Connecticut.

The real and lasting tribute to Mondrian came after the studio was closed, when Bolotowsky, Diller, Glarner, Holtzman, and many other artists produced Neo-Plastic works attesting to Mondrian's continuing influence on American art. Indeed, the salient characteristics of Mondrian's style—straight lines and rectangular planes of primary color and noncolor—became so pervasive, and his relational mode of composition assumed so much authority, that in the 1960s Barnett Newman felt compelled to declare his independence from this tradition at the same time that he paid homage to its power in a series of monumental paintings entitled *Who's Afraid of Red, Yellow and Blue?*. Yet none of Mondrian's American followers attempted to create colored abstract interiors such as the one they might have seen in the artist's studio. Like so many earlier environments, that space too was locked in its historical moment and fell victim to its temporary status. Yet the studio survives as an inspiration if not as a physical entity, because in it Mondrian merged his art with his life, forging both into expressions of ethical as well as aesthetic values. These same values shaped the ideals and the images that are the lasting heritage of De Stijl.

■ 192

Key to Abbreviations of Principal Sources
of Visual Documentation

BW	*Bouwkundig Weekblad*
Brown	Brown, Theodore. *The Work of G. Rietveld, Architect.* Utrecht: A. W. Bruna & Zoon, 1958.
CMU	Centraal Museum, Utrecht
DIL'EN	*Documents Internationaux de L'Esprit Nouveau*
DS	*De Stijl*
EGM	*Elseviers Geïllustreerd Maandschrift*
E-FL	Van Eesteren–Fluck & Van Lohuizen Foundation, Amsterdam

FH-A	Fondation Hagenbach-Arp, Meudon
GMH	Gemeentemuseum, The Hague
INP	Fondation Custodia, Institut Néerlandais, Paris
L'AV	*L'Architecture Vivante*
L'EM	*Bulletin de ''L'Effort Moderne''*
LK	*Levende Kunst*
MIB	Museum It Bleekerhûs, Drachten
MNAM	Musée National d'Art Moderne, Centre National d'Art et de Culture Georges Pompidou, Paris

NDB	Nederlands Documentatiecentrum voor de Bouwkunst, Amsterdam
RK-M	Rijksmuseum Kröller-Müller, Otterlo
SKD	Staatliche Kunstsammlungen, Dresden
SMA	Stedelijk Museum, Amsterdam
VAE	Stedelijk Van Abbemuseum, Eindhoven
VDA	Van Doesburg Archive, Dienst Verspreide Rijkskollekties, The Hague

Year	Colorist	Architect	Project	Source
1916	Theo van Doesburg	J. J. P. Oud	De Geus house, Broek in Waterland	*In situ*
1916–17	Bart van der Leck	H. P. Berlage	Art Room, Kröller house, Groot Haesebroek, Wassenaar	Design RK-M
1917	Theo van Doesburg	J. J. P. Oud	Trousselot house, Villa Allegonda, Katwijk aan Zee	Photos VDA
1917	Theo van Doesburg	Jan Wils	De Lange town house, Alkmaar	Window; wall design VDA
1917–18	Theo van Doesburg, H. H. Kamerlingh Onnes	J. J. P. Oud	De Vonk, Noordwijkerhout	*In situ*
1918	Theo van Doesburg	Rob van 't Hoff	De Ligt house, Lage Vuursche	
1918	Vilmos Huszar		Bruynzeel stand, Annual Industrial Fair, Utrecht	Photos *LK* 1919
1918	Bart van der Leck		Interior, de Leeuw house, De Leeuwerik, Laren	Design Staatsgalerie, Stuttgart
1918	Piet Zwart		Interior, Henny house, The Hague	Design GMH
1918	Piet Zwart		Interior, Applied and Folk Art Exhibition, Rotterdam	
1918–19	Theo van Doesburg	Jan Wils	Café De Dubbele Sleutel, Woerden	Furniture design; photos NDB
1918–19	Vilmos Huszar	P. J. C. Klaarhamer	Bedroom, Bruynzeel house, De Arendshoeve, Voorburg	Furniture GMH; photos NDB
1919	Theo van Doesburg	Furniture Gerrit Rietveld	Interior, De Ligt house, Katwijk	Design VDA; photo *De Stijl* 1920
1919	Vilmos Huszar		Stairwell, Bruynzeel house, De Arendshoeve, Voorburg	Design *LK* 1919
1919	Vilmos Huszar	Jan Wils	Sitting room, location unknown	Photos of designs NDB

Year	Colorist	Architect	Project	Source
1919	Bart van der Leck	P. J. C. Klaarhamer	Bruynzeel stand, Annual Industrial Fair, Utrecht	Photo *EGM*, 1919
1919	Bart van der Leck	H. P. Berlage	Kröller hunting lodge, St. Hubertus, Hoenderloo	*In situ*
1919	Bart van der Leck		Studio, Blaricum	
1919	Piet Mondrian		Studio, 5 rue du Coulmiers, Paris	
1919	Piet Zwart		Interior, Aesthetically Made Utensils Exhibition, Rotterdam	
1920	Chris Beekman	Rob van 't Hoff	Interior, location unknown	Design CMU
1920	Theo van Doesburg	J. J. P. Oud (furniture Gerrit Rietveld)	Spangen I and V, Rotterdam	Design coll. A. Oud-Dinaux, Wassenaar
1920	Vilmos Huszar	Jan Wils? (furniture Piet Zwart)	Conversation room, women's residence, The Hague?	Photos of designs GMH
1920	Vilmos Huszar	Kees van Moorsel	Bedroom, location unknown	Photos of designs coll. G. Oorthuys, Amsterdam
1920–21	Theo van Doesburg		Evert Rinsema house, Drachten	
1920–21	Vilmos Huszar		Plastic theater	Design *DS* 1921
1920–21	Vilmos Huszar	Jan Wils	Atelier Berssenbrugge, The Hague	Photos NDB
1920–21	Piet Zwart	Jan Wils	Dans Instituut Gaillard-Jorissen, The Hague	Designs NDB
1920–1922	Gerrit Rietveld	Gerrit Rietveld	Shop interior and facade, Amsterdam	Photos *BW* 1922; Brown cat. no. 16
1921	Max Burchartz		Study for color division in three dimensions	Photo *DS* 1922
1921	Theo van Doesburg	C. R. de Boer	Agricultural school, Drachten	Designs MIB

Year	Colorist	Architect	Project	Source
1921	Theo van Doesburg	C. R. de Boer	Middle-class housing, Drachten	Designs MIB
1921	Theo van Doesburg	J. J. P. Oud	Spangen VIII and IX, Rotterdam	Designs INP
1921	Vilmos Huszar		Dining room, location unknown	Design *DS* 1922
1921	Vilmos Huszar	Jan Wils	Stairwell, town house, Alkmaar	Photos of designs SMA
1921	Vilmos Huszar	Furniture Piet Zwart	Interiors, Bruynzeel house, De Storm Hoek, Zaandam	Photos GMH
1921	Peter Röhl		Residenz Theater, Weimar	
1921	Piet Zwart	Furniture Piet Zwart	Cramer house, The Hague	Designs; photos GMH
1921	Piet Zwart	Piet Zwart	Celluloid firm stand, Annual Industrial Fair, Utrecht	Design GMH
1921–1936	Piet Mondrian		Studio, 26 rue du Départ, Paris	Photos GMH
1922	Max Burchartz		Studio, Weimar?	Design private coll., Cologne
1922?	Vilmos Huszar		Music room, location unknown	Model *Vouloir* 1927
1922	Willem van Leusden	Willem van Leusden	Tram-stop shelter with transformer and flower kiosk, location unknown	Model *DS* 1923
1922	Willem van Leusden	Willem van Leusden	Public urinal, location unknown	Model *L'AV* 1925
1922	Willem van Leusden	Willem van Leusden	Public transport shelter, location unknown	Model *L'AV* 1925
1922?	Willem van Leusden	Willem van Leusden	Garage with boutique	
1922	Gerrit Rietveld	Furniture Gerrit Rietveld	Consultation room for Dr. A. M. Hartog, Maarssen	Desk GMH, Brown cat. no. 13
1922	Thijs Rinsema		Interior, Thijs Rinsema house, Drachten	Furniture GMH

Year	Colorist	Architect	Project	Source
1923	Theo van Doesburg	Cornelis van Eesteren	University hall, Amsterdam	Designs E-FL
1923	Theo van Doesburg	Cornelis van Eesteren	Private house, Alblasserdam	Photo; designs *L'AV* 1924, 1925
1923	Theo van Doesburg	Cornelis van Eesteren	Private house, Paris	Designs; photos of model VDA
1923	Theo van Doesburg	Cornelis van Eesteren	House of an artist, Paris	Designs; photos of model VDA
1923	Vilmos Huszar	Furniture Gerrit Rietveld	Spatial color composition for an exhibition, (Juryfreie Kunstschau?), Berlin	Photos *L'AV* 1924
1923	El Lissitzky		Proun Space, Grosse Berliner Kunstausstellung	Photo *G* 1923
1923	J. J. P. Oud		Superintendent's shed, Oud-Mathenesse	Photos; designs *L'AV* 1924
1923 or 1924	Piet Zwart		Hotel Pomona, Utrecht	
1923–24	Gerrit Rietveld	Gerrit Rietveld	Shop interior and facade, Utrecht	Photo *DS* 1924; Brown cat. no. 25
1924	Vilmos Huszar		Music room, Brugman house, The Hague	Photos NDB; SMA
1924	Willem van Leusden	Willem van Leusden	Teahouse in a city park, location unknown	Model *DS* 1927
1924	Gerrit Rietveld	Gerrit Rietveld	Schröder house, Utrecht	*In situ*
1924–25	Theo van Doesburg	Rob Mallet-Stevens	De Noailles villa, Hyères	Design VAE
1925	Theo van Doesburg	Cornelis van Eesteren	Shopping arcade and café-restaurant, The Hague	Designs E-FL
1925	J. J. P. Oud	J. J. P. Oud	Workers' housing with shops, Hoek van Holland	Design NDB

Year	Colorist	Architect	Project	Source
1925	J. J. P. Oud	J. J. P. Oud	Café de Unie, Rotterdam	Design private coll., Paris
1926	Cesar Domela		Interior, Müller-Lehning house, Amsterdam	Photo coll. C. Domela, Paris
1926	Piet Mondrian		Study, Bienert house, Dresden	Designs SKD
1926	Piet Mondrian		Stage design for *L'Ephémère est éternel*	Photo *DIL'EN* 1927
1926	Georges Vantongerloo		Dining room, location unknown	Designs estate of the artist, Zurich
1926	Piet Zwart		Restaurant, Bij Leo Faust, Paris	Photos GMH
1926	Félix Del Marle	Furniture Félix Del Marle	Living room, Del Marle house, Lille	Furniture formerly coll. R. Walker, Paris
1926	Félix Del Marle		Shop interior and facade, Lille	Design Galleria Milano, Milan
1926–1928	Jean Arp, Theo van Doesburg, Sophie Taeuber-Arp	Paul Horn	Interior, Café Aubette, Strasbourg	Designs and photos VDA; *DS* 1928
1926–1928	Jean Arp? Sophie Taeuber-Arp		Bar Hannong, Strasbourg	Photos FH-A
1926–1928	Jean Arp, Sophie Taeuber-Arp		Heimendinger house, Strasbourg	Photos FH-A
1926–1928	Theo van Doesburg, Sophie Taeuber-Arp		Interior, Horn apartment, Strasbourg	Photos *Binnenhuis* 1930
1926–1928	Jean Gorin		Studio, Nort-sur-Erdre	Photos coll. S. Gorin, Nort-sur-Erdre
1927?	Max Burchartz	A. Fisher	Sachs house, Gelsenkirchen	Photo *DS* 1927
1927	Félix Del Marle	Furniture Félix Del Marle	Interior, Rosenberg house, Paris	Photo *L'EM* 1927

Year	Colorist	Architect	Project	Source
1927	Félix Del Marle		Interior, Wimereux	Photo *L'EM* 1927
1927	Cesar Domela		Domela apartment, Berlin	Photos coll. C. Domela, Paris
1927	Jean Gorin	Jean Gorin	Study of a minimum house, location unknown	Design MNAM
1927	Jean Gorin		Interior, location unknown	Design MNAM
1928	Jean Gorin		Interior, location unknown	Design MNAM
1930	Jean Gorin	Furniture Jean Gorin	Interior, Nort-sur-Erdre	Design MNAM
1930–31	Theo van Doesburg	Theo van Doesburg, A. Elzas	Van Doesburg house, Meudon	*In situ*
1932	Jean Gorin	Jean Gorin	Neo-Plastic house, location unknown	Design MNAM

Appendix B

■ *200*

ROOM I

C. VAN EESTEREN AND THEO VAN DOESBURG. PARIS.
Private villa
1 Ground floor
2 First floor
3 Second floor
4 Model. Made by G. Rietveld. Utrecht.
House of an artist
5 Ground floor
6 First floor
7 Second floor
8 Third floor
9 Model

J. J. P. OUD. ROTTERDAM.
10 Houses on a seaside boulevard
11 Country house
12 Factory

ROOM II

C. VAN EESTEREN AND THEO VAN DOESBURG. PARIS.
Development of an architecture demonstrated by a private house
13 Ground floor
14 First floor
15 Second floor
16 Diagram of the architecture
17 Diagram of the architecture
18 Diagram of the architecture
19 Diagram of the architecture
20 Analysis of the architecture (counter-construction)
21 Construction of the color
22 Construction of the color
23 Construction of the color
24 Determination of the different planes of the architecture by means of color
25 Architecture (seen from below)
26 Architecture (seen from below)

27 Architecture (seen from above)
28 Model

ROOM III

V. HUSZAR. THE HAGUE.
29 Composition of colors in space
30 Composition of colors in space
Bedroom
31–31ᴬ Composition of colors in space
Studio of a photographer. Executed.

J. J. P. OUD. ROTTERDAM.
32 Courtyard of workers' housing. Rotterdam.
33 Workers' housing. Rotterdam.
34 Workers' housing. Rotterdam.
35 Small semipermanent house. Rotterdam.
⎫ Executed

J. WILS. THE HAGUE.
36 Housing complex. "Daal en Berg." The Hague.
37 Housing complex. "Daal en Berg." The Hague.
38 Housing complex. "Daal en Berg." The Hague.
Executed

G. RIETVELD. UTRECHT.
39 Model of a jewelry shop
(Executed in Amsterdam)

MIES VAN DE [sic] ROHE
40 Skyscraper

W. VAN LEUSDEN. MAARSEN [sic].
41 Tram-stop shelter with transformer and flower kiosk
42 Garage with boutique

ROOMS IV AND V

Project for a hall of a university, Amsterdam
ARCHITECTURAL CONSTRUCTION. C. VAN EESTEREN. PARIS.
CONSTRUCTION OF THE COLOR. THEO VAN DOESBURG. PARIS.

 43 Ground floor of the university
 44 Sections [of the university]
 45 Two sides [of the university]
 46 View of the hall as a whole
 47 Ceiling of the hall (in glass brick and reinforced concrete)
 48 Sketch of the ceiling of the gallery of the hall and a part of the corridors
 49 Floor of the hall and a part of the corridors, in rubber
 50 Ceiling of the gallery and a part of the corridors
 51 Bird's eye view of the university
 52 Model of a public urinal by W. van Leusden. Maarsen [sic].

EXPLANATORY NOTES

Original manuscript in Department of Applied Arts, Stedelijk Museum, Amsterdam.

 1–3: 1922–23. Plans. Not executed.
  4: Figure 51 [This and subsequent figure citations refer to the present volume.]
 5–8: 1923. Plans. Not executed.
  9: Figure 55
  10: 1917. Scheveningen. Not executed.
  11: 1921–22. Kallenback House, Berlin. Not executed.
  12: 1919. Purmerend. Not executed.
 13–15: 1923. Plans. Not executed.
 16–19: Line drawings of the elevation of each side of the house
  20: An axonometric line drawing—possibly by van Doesburg, who would have made it by tracing on paper laid down over a design by van Eesteren. (See figure 52.)
 21–23: Drawings by van Doesburg in which color was added to the kind of axonometric drawing exhibited as no. 20. (See figure 53.)

  24: Four drawings by van Doesburg in which color was added to the same kind of elevations exhibited as nos. 16–19.
 25–27: Probably axonometric line drawings, although versions shaded in black and gray were also made.
  28: Figure 54
  29: 1920. Two designs for the interior of a conversation room in a residence for women. Not executed. Huszar was responsible for the color only; Piet Zwart was responsible for the "form," which may refer to the interior architecture as well as the furniture in the room. However, the designs may have been associated with an unrealized residence for unmarried women in The Hague, designed by Jan Wils at this time.
  30: 1918. Bedroom, Bruynzeel House, Voorburg. (See figures 15–17, 19.)
 31–31^: 1920–21. Studio of Henri Berssenbrugge, The Hague. Photographs were exhibited. (See figure 81.)
 32–35: Probably photographs
  32: 1920–1923. Tusschendijken.
  35: 1923. Superintendent's shed, Oud-Mathenesse.
 36–38: 1920
  39: 1920–1922. Goud- en Zilversmids Compagnie, Amsterdam.
  40: 1920–21. Not executed.
  41: 1922. Not executed.
  42: Probably 1922. Not executed.
  43: Plan. Not executed.
 44–45: Drawings by van Eesteren with color indications by van Doesburg.
  46: Figure 46.
  47: A variation of figure 45
  49: Figure 47. Photographs of the installation show that this design was laid out on the floor of the gallery.
  52: 1922. Not executed.

Notes

Introduction

1. Hans L. C. Jaffé, *De Stijl, 1917–1931: The Dutch Contribution to Modern Art* (Amsterdam: J. M. Meulenhoff, 1956), p. 10. Jaffé's book was the first comprehensive study devoted to De Stijl and established the context in which the subject has since been considered.

2. Writing in German in 1929, van Doesburg described the word *Gestaltung* (in Dutch it is *beelding*; in English it is best translated as *plasticism*) as involving a "sense of creative achievement." He continued: "The word 'Gestaltung' had been revalued; it meant for us [the De Stijl artists] the superrational, the a-logical and inexplicable, the depth coming to the surface, the balance of interior and exterior, the spoils of the creative battle we fought against ourselves. A new terminology came into existence by means of which we expressed the collective idea, the moving spring of our common action. All art, acoustic or visual, sprang from one idea: Creation (Gestaltung)." ["Der Kampf um den neuen Stil," *Neue Schweizer Rundschau* (1929), quoted in translation in Jaffé, *De Stijl, 1917–1931*, p. 55.] Jaffé discusses the various sources and the meaning of Neo-Plasticism as a term and as a philosophy on pp. 53–62.

3. A common yearning for the union of the arts in the modern environment seems to have brought Taut and van Doesburg together in 1920–21. It was in Taut's Berlin home that van Doesburg was introduced to Walter Gropius; that meeting led to van Doesburg's encounter with the Bauhaus in 1921. While in Weimar in October of that year, van Doesburg was asked, but apparently did not agree, to submit an article to Taut's review, *Frühlicht*. See Claudine Humblet, *Le Bauhaus* (Lausanne: Editions l'Age d'Homme, 1980), p. 189.

4. Adolf Loos, "The Story of a Poor Rich Man," tr. Harold Meek in Ludwig Münz and Gustav Künstler, *Adolf Loos: Pioneer of Modern Architecture* (New York: Praeger, 1966), pp. 223–225.

5. Muthesius, quoted in translation in Marcel Franciscono, *Walter Gropius and the Creation of the Bauhaus in Weimar* (Urbana: University of Illinois Press, 1971), p. 94.

6. See Marie-Noëlle Pradel, "La Maison Cubiste en 1912," *Art de France* 1 (1961): 177–186.

1. In addition to van Doesburg, those who contributed to the first number of *De Stijl* were Vilmos Huszar (who designed the cover), Anthony Kok, Bart van der Leck, Piet Mondrian, and J. J. P. Oud. In the tenth-anniversary issue [*De Stijl* VII, 79–84 (1927): pp. 59–60; facsimile reprint (Amsterdam: Athenaeum and Polak & Van Gennep; The Hague: Bert Bakker, 1968), vol. II, p. 558] van Doesburg omitted van der Leck from his list of those who had originated the review; this is significant in light of the differences that in the meantime had developed between him and van der Leck, who certainly deserved inclusion. Hereafter, references to the facsimile reprint will follow references to the original edition, giving volume and page numbers only, in parentheses.

2. See Louis Gans, *Nieuwe Kunst: De Nederlandse bijdrage tot de "Art Nouveau"* (Utrecht: Libertas, 1960), and Joop Joosten, "Henry van de Velde en Nederland, 1892–1902: De Belgische Art Nouveau en de Nederlandse Nieuwe Kunst," *Cahiers Henry van de Velde* 12–13 (1974): 28–32.

3. Here and in the ensuing pages the discussion of van der Leck is indebted to Rudolf W. D. Oxenaar, Bart van der Leck: Een Primitief van de nieuwe tijd, Ph.D. diss., Rijksuniversiteit te Utrecht, 1976.

4. Bart van der Leck, "Klaarhamer's meubelen," *Onze Kunst* 3 (1904): 76. This and subsequent translations are by the author unless otherwise noted.

5. Theodore M. Brown, *The Work of G. Rietveld, Architect* (Utrecht: A. W. Bruna & Zoon, 1958), p. 23.

6. Auke van der Woud, "Variaties op een thema: 20 jaar belangstelling voor Frank Lloyd Wright," in *Americana: Nederlandse architectuur 1880–1930* (Otterlo: Rijksmuseum Kröller-Müller, 1975), p. 34.

7. Bart van der Leck, letter to H. P. Bremmer, January 1914, quoted in Oxenaar, pp. 76–77.

8. Oxenaar, pp. 29–32.

9. S. van Deventer, *Kröller-Müller: De Geschiedenis van een cultureel levenswerk* (Haarlem: Tjeenk Willink, 1956), pp. 44–45.

10. On the history of this problem-riddled commission, for which both Behrens and Mies van der Rohe constructed full-scale wood and canvas models of their designs on the actual site, see Fritz Hoeber, *Peter Behrens* (Munich: Georg Müller und Eugen Rentsch, 1913), pp. 200–202, and Arthur Drexler, *Ludwig Mies van der Rohe* (New York: George Braziller, 1960), figures 2–4. The designs of 1911–1913 were not realized, but they formed the basis for Henry van de Velde's remodeling of the Kröller house (Groot Haesebroek, in Wassenaar) between 1921 and 1926. See Klaus Jürgen Sembach, "Van de Velde's nalatenschap," *Museum-journaal* 8 (1962): 8–14, and Oxenaar, pp. 100–101.

11. Oxenaar, pp. 98–99.

12. Oxenaar, p. 100.

13. The series of paintings *Composition 1917 (Donkey Riders)* was based on a figurative painting of 1915, entitled *Arabs* (Rijksmuseum Kröller-Müller, Otterlo); number 6 of the 1917 series was reproduced in *De Stijl* I, 1 (1917), plate 1 (I: 15).

14. Oxenaar, p. 118.

15. Oxenaar, p. 118.

16. Bart van der Leck, letter to Helene Kröller, December 18, 1916, quoted in Oxenaar, p. 114.

17. Bart van der Leck, "De Plaats van het moderne schilderen in de architectuur," *De Stijl* I, 1 (1917); and "Over schilderen en bouwen," *De Stijl* I, 4 (1918); both translated in *Bart van der Leck* (Otterlo: Rijksmuseum Kröller-Müller, 1976).

18. Quoted in translation in Michel Seuphor, *Piet Mondrian: Life and Work* (New York: Harry N. Abrams, 1956), p. 138. Van der Leck's second essay on painting and architecture was already in preparation; it was published in *De Stijl* several months later. Cees

Hilhorst notes that van der Leck's break with van Doesburg and departure from the De Stijl group was the result of several other disagreements as well. See his essay on van der Leck (especially pp. 181–183) in Carel Blotkamp et al., *De Beginjaren van De Stijl 1917–1922* (Utrecht: Reflex, 1982). This volume of essays (which appeared when the present book was in publication) contains a great deal of valuable information gleaned from correspondence recently made available in the Van Doesburg Archive, Dienst Verspreide Rijkskollekties, The Hague.

19. Robert P. Welsh, "Theo van Doesburg and Geometric Abstraction," in F. Bulhof, ed., *Nijhoff, Van Ostaijen, "De Stijl"* (The Hague: Martinus Nijhoff, 1976), p. 83.

20. M. de Meijer-van der Waerden, *Zoekt een ster niet te ver* (Amsterdam: Fonds voor het Honderdste Geboortejaar van Emilie Charlotte Knappert, 1960), p. 64 and passim. See also Jane Beckett, " 'De Vonk,' Noordwijk: An Example of Early De Stijl Co-operation," *Art History* 3 (1980): 202–217.

21. Jan Gratama, "Vakantiehuis te Noordwijkerhout," *Klei* 12 (1920): 13.

22. Gunther Stamm, "Het Jeugdwerk van de architekt J. J. P. Oud 1906–1917," *Museumjournaal* 22 (1977): 263.

23. Theo van Doesburg, letter to J. J. P. Oud, June 1, 1916, inv. no. 1972-A.502[(2)], Fondation Custodia, Institut Néerlandais (hereafter referred to as IN), Paris.

24. Jaffé, *De Stijl, 1917–1931*, p. 15.

25. Theo van Doesburg, "Aanteekeningen over monumentale kunst," *De Stijl* II, 2 (1918), tr. R. R. Symonds in *De Stijl*, ed. Hans L. C. Jaffé (London: Thames and Hudson, 1970), p. 99.

26. Theo van Doesburg, *Drie voordrachten over de nieuwe beeldende kunst* (Amsterdam: Maatschappij voor Goede en Goedkoope Lectuur, 1919), p. 102.

27. Van Doesburg, "Monumentale kunst," pp. 102–103.

28. J. J. P. Oud, "Het Monumentale stadsbeeld," *De Stijl* I, 1 (1917), tr. R. R. Symonds, in *De Stijl*, ed. Jaffé, p. 95.

29. Van Doesburg, "Monumentale kunst," p. 102.

30. J. J. P. Oud, "Glas-in-lood van Theo van Doesburg," *Bouwkundig Weekblad* 39 (1918): 201.

31. N. Troy, interview (November 1977) with the present owner of the building (which, long after Oud's renovation of 1927, was extensively remodeled; it is now the Hotel-Panorama-Restaurant Savoy).

32. J. J. P. Oud, "Verbouwing huize 'Allegonda' Katwijk aan Zee," *Bouwkundig Weekblad* 29 (1918): 29.

33. Oud, "Glas-in-lood," p. 202. Carel Blotkamp interprets Oud's comments so as to distinguish between the "motif" and the "aesthetic idea which forms the basis of the piece." He identifies the motif as a sitting nude figure. See Blotkamp et al., *De Beginjaren van De Stijl*, p. 26.

34. The present location of the window is not known, and it is presumed to have been destroyed. Only black and white photographs of it survive, but the colors are described by Alfred Roth in *Begegnung mit Pionieren*, Institut für Geschichte und Theorie der Architektur, Eidgenössische Technische Hochschule, 8 (Zurich and Stuttgart: Birkhauser, 1973), p. 128.

35. Joop P. Joosten, "Abstraction and Compositional Innovation," *Artforum* XI, 8 (1973): 57; Welsh, "Theo van Doesburg and Geometric Abstraction," pp. 87–88. Welsh also argues (pp. 90–91) that after circa 1920, when Mondrian ceased to employ mathematical grid composition, van Doesburg continued to incorporate "either a full or partial modular grid," and that this practice can be seen in paintings van Doesburg made throughout the remainder of his career. Van Doesburg's interest in mathematical relationships of form can, as will be shown, also be discerned in the ratio he developed in 1921 to determine the application of color to certain

architectural structures. The interest of van Doesburg and Mondrian in complex notions of the fourth dimension of time-space evidences a further development of their concern for mathematics during the late teens and the twenties.

36. Theo van Doesburg, letter to Anthony Kok, September 9, 1917, quoted in Jean Leering, "De Architectuur en Van Doesburg," in *Theo van Doesburg 1881–1931* (Eindhoven: Stedelijk Van Abbemuseum, 1968–1969), p. 20.

37. In an interview (N. Troy, November 8, 1977), Jean Leering stated that *Composition IV* was composed according to a Bach fugue. Leering's statement figured significantly in the discussion of this window in Nancy J. Troy, "Theo van Doesburg: From Music into Space," *Arts Magazine* LVI, 6 (1982): 92–101. Responding to that article in a letter to the author (April 11, 1982), Carel Blotkamp argued that van Doesburg appealed to Bach's music only as an analogy. The window, he believes, could not have been based on a specific fugal theme because in it (Blotkamp rightly notes) van Doesburg used formal configurations close to those that appear in *Composition II*, the Villa Allegonda window with the rising-surf theme. Although Blotkamp's argument is convincing, it is not entirely conclusive: Van Doesburg could have reorganized the same basic elements in a different coloristic system to arrive at an image that corresponded to music by Bach. This sequence of events would also accommodate Oud's description (cited above) of the Villa Allegonda window as having been based on the "aesthetic idea [of] 'the rhythmic, upward-rising movement of sea surf. . . .'"

The radical character of van Doesburg's conception of music becomes clear in light of the sarcastic reaction it provoked from Willem Brouwer: "He eliminates all the HEART. Bach . . . is beautiful only because it is arranged so scientifically. Does he listen like a butcher with a carving knife? All emotion is old-fashioned, or so it seems." [Letter to J. J. P. Oud, January 15, 1920; Oud Archive, Nederlands Documentatiecentrum voor de Bouwkunst (hereafter referred to as NDB), Amsterdam.]

38. Theo van Doesburg, *Klassiek–Barok–Modern* (Antwerp: De Sikkel, 1920), p. 25.

39. Theo van Doesburg, "Lijstenaesthetiek," *De Stijl* III, 11 (1920): 95 (I: 617).

40. Seuphor, *Piet Mondrian*, classified catalog nos. 285–289.

41. In the *Composition with Color Planes* series, Mondrian may also have been concerned with environmental issues. As Welsh has pointed out, "the series anticipates the appearance of Mondrian's subsequent Paris, London and New York studios, in which unbounded color rectangles seem to have always been placed on the walls" [*Piet Mondrian 1872–1944* (Art Gallery of Toronto, 1966), p. 164]. Similarly, it may have been partly as a result of his desire to imply compositional extension that Mondrian rarely used prominent frames, which would have set his mature, Neo-Plastic paintings too much apart from the walls on which they were hung. Like van Doesburg, he seems in this way to have avoided the sense of enclosure a traditional frame produces, making the viewer feel as though he is looking through a window in the wall to a space he cannot experience directly. However, in an article devoted to Mondrian's frames, Joosten has pointed out that Mondrian did not develop his simple white frame, in front of which the canvas itself projected forward slightly, until the 1920s. For the *Composition with Colored Planes* series, Mondrian employed a more traditional frame, which extended protectively around the edges of the canvas surface, limiting the sense of lateral movement of the painted forms and thus creating tension between the individual painting and its immediate environment. [Joop P. Joosten, "Grenzen van Mondriaan," *Openbaar Kunstbezit* (1977): 185.]

42. Van Doesburg, *Drie voordrachten*, pp. 63–64.

43. Van Doesburg, *Drie voordrachten*, p. 90.

44. De Leeuw was director of Metz & Co., the Dutch branch of Liberty & Co., from whom in the following years van der Leck was to receive several other commissions to apply color in interior design.

45. One might well speculate on the relationship between van der Leck's use of this shape and that of Mondrian, who produced his first paintings in a diamond format during the same year.

46. The design on the curtain in the doorway compares closely with *Composition*, 1918 (Stedelijk Van Abbemuseum, Eindhoven), although in the painting each of the three black squares has been broken up into four smaller units. The tablecloth in the bottom right corner of the drawing has a design identical to *Composition No. 3*, also of 1918 (collection of Mrs. A. R. W. Nieuwenhuizen Segaar-Aarse, The Hague), and the tablecloth in the upper right bears the same configuration as van der Leck's gouache and pencil *Study* (McCrory Corporation collection, New York). The dating to ca. 1916–17 of this latter drawing by Willy Rotzler in *Constructive Concepts* (Zurich: ABC, 1977), catalog no. 319, should be reexamined in light of its close relation to other works by van der Leck that are securely dated 1918.

47. "Even at a young age he [Bruynzeel] had been interested in anything connected with machines and new inventions. Old-fashioned handwork was antipathetic to him. He was attracted by the idea of using machines to make a product that was needed, especially one that would be well made yet inexpensive." [*Bruynzeel's fabrieken, Zaandam: Gedenkboek* (privately printed, n.d. [1931]), p. 7.]

48. Vilmos Huszar, "Over de organisatie in de ambachts-kunst," *Bouwkundig Weekblad* 41 (1920): 183.

49. Vilmos Huszar, "Iets over de Farbenfibel van W. Ostwald," *De Stijl* I, 10 (1918): 113–118 (I: 169–174). Huszar's interest in color theory can already be discerned in his paintings of about 1910. Like those of several other Dutch artists at that time, including Mondrian, these were in a luminist style influenced primarily by the work of French Post-Impressionists and older Dutch artists, particularly Jan Toorop. See Mariette Josephus Jitta, "Achtergronden," in *Licht door kleur: Nederlandse luministen* (The Hague: Gemeentemuseum, 1976–77), pp. 3–31. After a trip to The Netherlands in 1905, Huszar had returned to his native Budapest via Dusseldorf in 1906. In October of that year he was again in Holland, where he came into contact with H. P. Bremmer, who may have suggested that he visit Paris. In the catalog of the 1906 Salon d'Automne, where he showed two paintings, Huszar's address was indicated as "chez M. Caselhucho. 14 *bis*, rue de la Grande-Chaumière." It is unlikely that Huszar was actually in Paris at that time, but it is known that he spent six months there in 1907–08. See Sjarel Ex's exceptionally informative essay on Huszar (especially pp. 86–87) in Blotkamp et al., *De Beginjaren van De Stijl*. For a thorough discussion of the influence of French painting on Dutch artists in the period 1900–1910, see A. B. Loosjes-Terpstra, *Moderne kunst in Nederland 1900–1914* (Utrecht: Haentjens Dekker & Gumbert, 1959), pp. 32–107. Robert Welsh has pointed out that Mondrian, Huszar, and other De Stijl artists were influenced by Ostwald's color theory around 1918. Apparently, Welsh states, Ostwald's "works (e.g., *Die Farbenfibel*, 1917) were standard reading for the group." According to Welsh, "Ostwald believed that his theory of three measurable elements of color—hue, white and black—was closer to nature than the theories of his predecessors, Chevreul and Helmholtz, who derived their spectrum from refracted light" [in *Piet Mondrian* (Toronto, 1966), p. 166]. Thus Ostwald's color theory represented an advance beyond those that had influenced the earlier, French-derived, luminist styles of Huszar and Mondrian, for example.

50. Ro van Oven, "Moderne glasschilderkunst in Holland, I: Vilmos Huszar," *Levende Kunst* 2 (1919): 53.

51. The stairwell design, which Oxenaar (p. 138) identifies as having been intended for Bruynzeel's house, was dated 1919 when it was published in *Levende Kunst* 2 (1919), alongside Huszar's drawings for the bedroom, dated 1918–19 in the same publication. When a photograph of the bedroom was reproduced in the tenth-anniversary issue of *De Stijl* [79–84 (1927): 28 (II: 542)] it was dated 1917, but in Huszar's own discussion of the interior ["Over de moderne toegepaste kunsten," *Bouwkundig Weekblad* 43 (1922): 75–76] he assigned it to 1918. Photographs of the realized interior published with the article were dated "1918–19," which suggests that execution of the design was not completed until 1919.

52. G. Rietveld, filmed interview with Piet van Mook, 1963, quoted in translation in *G. Rietveld, Architect* (Amsterdam: Stedelijk Museum, 1971–72), catalog nos. 11 and 12.

Chapter 2

53. Huszar, "Over de moderne toegepaste kunsten," pp. 75–76.

54. In a design for a dining room published in *De Stijl* in January 1922 [V, no. 1: 15 (II: 166)], Huszar did employ both large, single-colored planes and enclosed compositions that resemble paintings framed even more strictly than van Doesburg's Alkmaar wall pattern. Huszar's dining-room design was dated 1921, and although the conception of the coloristic applications seems less advanced than that of the Bruynzeel bedroom there is no reason to doubt that the somewhat conservative design was produced in that year. Two chairs in the room recall those Jan Wils provided for the photographic atelier of Henri Berssenbrugge in 1921 (figure 81), and the table in the center is similar to furniture Piet Zwart designed for the Bruynzeel family in the same year [reproduced in *Piet Zwart* (The Hague: Gemeentemuseum, 1973), catalog no. 42]; Huszar had collaborated as colorist on both of these projects.

55. Joost Baljeu and Oxenaar date the design to 1918 [Joost Baljeu, *Theo van Doesburg* (New York: Macmillan, 1974), p. 32; Oxenaar, p. 138]. Oxenaar states that van Doesburg's color scheme was designed for the Lage Vuursche home of Bart de Ligt, but, as Blotkamp demonstrates on the basis of van Doesburg's correspondence with Anthony Kok, the room in question was in a residence in Katwijk to which De Ligt moved in 1919. De Ligt's 1918 proposal that van 't Hoff renovate his previous home in Lage Vuursche, for which van Doesburg apparently designed color schemes for a corridor and six rooms, was never carried out. See Blotkamp et al., *De Beginjaren van De Stijl*, pp. 43–44.

56. Theo van Doesburg, "Aanteekening bij de bijlage," *De Stijl* III, 12 (1920): 103 (I: 633). The same photograph, with primary colors added, was reproduced in *L'Architecture Vivante* (autumn 1925), pl. 12. In February 1920, Rietveld wrote to Oud: ". . . I have sent on the furniture for de Ligt in Katwijk—I have seen the little room in Katwijk (not long enough). The impression I have of the coloristic solution is very good! The room itself is really very unrestful and rather sloppy." (Gerrit Rietveld, letter to J. J. P Oud, February 26, 1920, Oud Archive, NDB, Amsterdam.)

1. Several surviving photographs of the redesigned interior, as well as one of the room before it was altered, and a photograph of Huszar's preliminary design (all in the Wils Archive, NDB, Amsterdam) are dated 1918. Annotations on the backs of two other photographs (Rietveld file, Department of Applied Arts, Stedelijk Museum, Amsterdam) indicate that the Music Room was a composition in gray executed in 1924, a date that seems more convincing. The complexity of Huszar's paint applications—particularly in one corner of the room—supports a later dating, as does the fact that a table designed by Rietveld in 1923 is visible in two of the photographs (though not in the preliminary design). Jaffé, however, dates the design to 1922, stating that in the same year van Doesburg and Schwitters also painted one room each in the Brugman apartment, where a "fourth room was left white—it housed a painting by Mondrian" (*De Stijl, 1917–1932*, p. 22). Jaffé cites no evidence to support his dating, nor does he illustrate any of these interiors. The room by Huszar can be identified as one of those Jaffé mentions on the basis of a photograph taken between 1926 and 1928, when it was used as a studio by Hannah Höch, who was living with Brugman in The Hague. See Götz Adriani, ed., *Hannah Höch* (Cologne: DuMont, 1980), p. 36.

2. See Aloys Fischer, "Das Musikzimmer," *Kunstgewerbeblatt* 22 (1911): 186.

3. Conversely, Moholy-Nagy was familiar with Huszar's work at least as early as 1922, when he wrote Oud asking for a photograph of an interior by Huszar (Laszlo Moholy-Nagy, letter to J. J. P. Oud, May 9, 1922, Oud Archive, NDB, Amsterdam).

4. Van Doesburg, "Aanteekeningen over monumentale kunst," p. 101.

5. See Kees Broos, in *Piet Zwart* (The Hague: Gemeentemuseum, 1973), p. 10. The ensuing discussion of Zwart is indebted to Broos's catalog text.

6. Piet Zwart, "Kunst op de Jaarbeurs," *Elsevier's Geïllustreerd Maandschrift* 29 (1919): 319.

7. Theo van Doesburg, "Rondblik: Holland," *De Stijl* II, 12 (1919): 144 (I: 456).

8. Broos, p. 14.

9. Broos, p. 16.

10. Zwart, pp. 316–317.

11. Zwart, p. 317.

12. Broos, p. 22.

13. Axonometry can be traced back several centuries to its origins in Oriental drafting techniques. It was used extensively at the turn of the century by Auguste Choisy, who chose it because it enabled him to render an architectural plan simultaneously with its section and elevation. Axonometric projection is one of several types of metric projection that, like traditional diminishing perspective views, give an illusion of actual spatial appearance, but axonometrics are unique in that they also allow for the measurement of proper scale relationships in three dimensions. When axonometry is used, surfaces that meet at 90° angles in three-dimensional depth are very often projected on paper at 45° angles with respect to the vertical representation of elevational height, and therefore also with respect to the rectangular edges of the page on which they are drawn. Reyner Banham has noted the abstract character of axonometric drawings such as those by Choisy, which, he remarks, was precisely the quality "that endeared these illustrations to the generation born in the Eighteen-eighties, the generation which, outside architecture though never out of touch with it, also perfected Abstract art" [*Theory and Design in the First Machine Age*, second edition (New York: Praeger, 1967), p. 25]. I am grateful to Yve-Alain Bois, whose book on the history of axonometry is in preparation, for sharing his knowledge of this subject with me.

14. The de Noailles villa, built at Hyères in the south of France by Robert Mallet-Stevens in 1924, was decorated throughout with contemporary furnishings. It inspired and provided the location for Man Ray's 1929 film *Les Mystères du Château du Dés*. The Comte and Comtesse de Noailles were patrons of modern art whose collection included paintings by Picasso, Braque, Gris, Léger, and many others. But as Léon Deshairs described in 1928,

The canvases . . . have been removed to the wardrobes. They are taken out when one wishes to see them, like the kakemonos in Japanese houses. Not that they are judged to be too anecdotal: the names of their authors guarantee us that they do not involve the sin of petty realism. But paintings that are hung disturb the surfaces of the walls and collect dust. Removal of the canvases is doubtless an extreme consequence of the cult of hygiene and the intoxication with cleanliness which reigns throughout the villa in Hyères. The only ornaments which one tolerates here, or rather, which one likes, are flowers. A special small room has been arranged by Van Doesburg for cutting stems and grouping arums or roses in vases of limpid crystal. ["Une Villa moderne à Hyères," *Art et Décoration* 54 (1928): 8.]

15. In preparation for the van Doesburg retrospective he organized in 1968, Jean Leering examined the Flower Room and came to the following conclusion: ". . . in fact the room was realized incorrectly as a result of the complicated type of drawing van Doesburg had employed. All the walls were actually done in reverse with respect to his original intention. . . ." In explanation, Leering suggests that in 1924–25 van Doesburg had not yet mastered the complexities of axonometry and other architectural drafting techniques and was therefore unable to indicate his intentions clearly to the workmen, who in his absence carried out the design incorrectly ("De Architectuur en Van Doesburg," p. 24). Leering commissioned a full-scale "corrected" version of the Flower Room (Stedelijk Van Abbemuseum, Eindhoven) for the 1968 exhibition (N. Troy, interview with Jean Leering, November 8, 1977).

16. Piet Mondrian, "De Realiseering van het Neo-Plasticisme in verre toekomst en in de huidige architectuur," *De Stijl* V, 3 (1922), tr. R. R. Symonds in *De Stijl*, ed. Jaffé, p. 169.

17. Mondrian, ''De Realiseering,'' p. 169.

18. Piet Mondrian, ''Natuurlijke en abstacte realiteit,'' *De Stijl* II, 8–III, 10 (1919–20), tr. in Seuphor, *Piet Mondrian*, p. 339.

19. Albert Gleizes and Jean Metzinger, *Du ''Cubisme,''* English translation (London: Unwin, 1913); reprinted in *Modern Artists on Art*, ed. Robert L. Herbert (Englewood Cliffs, N.J.: Prentice-Hall, 1964), p. 6. Although Mondrian always worked in a distinctive style, he did go through what has been called a Cubist phase. While living in Paris in 1912 and 1913, he was in contact with Gleizes and Metzinger, as well as with Robert Delaunay, Fernand Léger, and Henri Le Fauconnier (the Montparnasse Cubists to whom he had been introduced by Conrad Kikkert and Lodewijk Schelfhout, two Dutch painters also working in Paris at that time). See Loosjes-Terpstra, *Moderne kunst in Nederland*, pp. 152–153, and Adriaan Venema, *Nederlandse schilders in Parijs 1900–1940* (Baarn: Het Wereldvenster, 1980), pp. 133–141.

20. Piet Mondrian, *Le Néo-Plasticisme: Principe générale de l'équivalence plastique* (Paris: Editions de l'Effort Moderne, 1920), p. 5. The essay did not appear in print until January 1921. See Carel Blotkamp, ''Mondriaan als literator,'' *Maatstaf* XXVI, 4 (1978): 16.

21. ''Bij Piet Mondriaan,'' *De Telegraaf*, September 12, 1926 (clipping). Sources of this and subsequently cited clippings are indicated in the bibliography.

22. Mondrian, ''De Realiseering,'' p. 171.

23. Piet Mondrian, letter to Theo van Doesburg, February 13, 1917, quoted in translation in Jaffé, *De Stijl, 1917–1931*, p. 13.

24. Gleizes and Metzinger, *Du ''Cubisme''*, p. 5.

25. Mondrian, ''Realiteit,'' p. 339.

26. Piet Mondrian, letter to Theo van Doesburg, December 4, 1919, Van Doesburg Archive, Dienst Verspreide Rijkskollekties, The

Hague. I am grateful to Yve-Alain Bois for bringing this letter to my attention.

27. Mondrian, ''Realiteit,'' p. 335.

28. Nelly van Doesburg, ''Some Memories of Mondrian,'' in *Piet Mondrian 1872–1944 Centennial Exhibition* (New York: Solomon R. Guggenheim Museum, 1971), p. 68.

29. ''Een Bezoek bij Piet Mondriaan,'' *Het Vaderland*, July 9, 1920 (clipping). See also Herbert Henkels, ''Mondrian in his Studio,'' in *Mondrian: Zeichnungen, Aquarelle, New Yorker Bilder* (Stuttgart: Staatsgalerie, 1980–81), pp. 257–281.

30. Mondrian, ''Realiteit,'' p. 335.

31. Mondrian, ''Realiteit,'' p. 334.

32. The studio belonged to another Dutchman named de Stieltjen, who allowed Mondrian to use it temporarily while he and his wife were in The Netherlands (Piet Mondrian, letter to Salomon Slijper, October 19, 1921, Documentation Archive, Gemeentemuseum, The Hague; I am grateful to Herbert Henkels for bringing this letter to my attention). Within several months Mondrian was able to take over the studio permanently, and on February 25, 1922, he wrote to Oud that the studio was registered in his name (Piet Mondrian, letter to J. J. P. Oud, February 25, 1922, inv. no. 1972-A.397, IN, Paris).

33. Mondrian, ''Realiteit,'' p. 341.

34. ''Bij Piet Mondriaan,'' *Nieuwe Rotterdamse Courant*, March 22, 1922 (clipping).

35. M. van Domselar-Middelkoop, ''Herinneringen aan Piet Mondriaan,'' *Maatstaf* VII, 5 (1959): 290.

36. Seuphor, *Piet Mondrian*, p. 158. Although Seuphor first visited Mondrian in 1923, his description incorporates changes that oc-

curred in the studio over the course of the ensuing years. For instance, in photographs taken there in 1926, the easel in front of the long rear wall was still black; the earliest existing photograph of the atelier showing the same easel painted white was not taken until 1929.

37. N. Troy, interview with Michel Seuphor, November 23, 1977. Seuphor stated that toward the end of 1921, while en route to their home in Menton in the south of France, Vantongerloo and his wife had visited Mondrian in Paris. In order to thank him for his hospitality on that occasion, Vantongerloo did most of the physical work involved in painting the studio for Mondrian. Apparently it was only in 1920 that Gino Severini had introduced Mondrian to Vantongerloo, who often stopped in Paris, evidently staying with Mondrian, on his way between Belgium and Menton [Maurits Bilcke, "Pionier zonder weerklank in Vlaanderen: Georges Vantongerloo is eenzaam begraven," *De Standaard*, October 19, 1965, 8 (clipping)].

38. In an interview (N. Troy, November 29, 1978), Herbert Henkels pointed out that the temporary character of the studio's interior design and Mondrian's reluctance to paint colors directly on the walls may originally have been due to the fact that, during his first months there in 1921–22, Mondrian had only borrowed the rue du Départ studio from a friend.

39. The first visit is documented in Gerrit Rietveld's letter to J. J. P. Oud of February 26, 1920 (Oud Archive, NDB, Amsterdam), and the second in Theo van Doesburg's letter to Evert Rinsema of June 23, 1921 [in K. Schippers, *Holland Dada* (Amsterdam: Querido, 1974), p. 174].

40. Theo van Doesburg, letter to J. J. P. Oud, September 12, 1921, inv. no. 1972-A.555[4], IN, Paris.

41. Piet Mondrian, letter to J. J. P. Oud, August 30, 1921, inv. no. 1972-A.391, IN, Paris.

42. Piet Mondrian, letter to Theo van Doesburg, 1923, quoted in translation in Jaffé, *De Stijl, 1917–1931*, p. 162.

1. Willem C. Brouwer, letter to J. J. P. Oud, January 15, 1920, Oud Archive, NDB, Amsterdam.

2. J. J. P. Oud, "Gemeentelijke volkswoningen, Polder 'Spangen,' Rotterdam," *Bouwkundig Weekblad* 41 (1920): 219–220.

3. See Piergiorgio Dragone, "Le Vicende dell'edilizia di massa (1913–1920)," in *Olanda 1870–1940: Città, casa, architettura*, ed. Maristella Casciato et al. (Milan: Electa Editrice, 1980), p. 58.

4. J. J. P. Oud, "Bouwkunst en normalisatie bij den massabouw," *De Stijl* I, 7 (1918), tr. in *Lotus International* 16 (1977): 53–54.

5. Theo van Doesburg, "Der Wille zum Stil," *De Stijl* V, 2 (1922), tr. Mary Whitall in *De Stijl*, ed. Jaffé, p. 161.

6. Theo van Doesburg, letter to J. J. P. Oud, October 1, 1920, inv. no. 1972-A.531[6], IN, Paris.

7. Theo van Doesburg, letter to J. J. P. Oud, postmarked October 19, 1920, inv. no. 1972-A.532, IN, Paris.

8. Humblet, *Le Bauhaus*, p. 167.

9. Wulf Herzogenrath, "Die holländische und russische Avantgarde in Deutschland," in *Malewitsch-Mondrian: Konstruktion als Konzept* (Hanover: Kunstverein, 1977), p. 167.

10. Van Doesburg's use of the term *monument* suggests that he meant his *Monument for Leeuwarden*, a design he had made for a competition sponsored by Leeuwarden (the capital city of the province of Friesland) in 1918. The competition involved redesigning the square in front of the train station and called for an architectural solution of the station that would take into account the traffic patterns in the square, where a fountain or sculpture was to be located. Jan Wils and van Doesburg collaborated on a design with the motto "klein in groot vierkant" (small square in large square), for which they won second prize. However, van Doesburg's contribution was severely criticized: "The fountain, or rather the monu-

ment, is not positioned well and it lacks expression" ["Juryrapport, prijsvraag tot verfraaiing Stationsplein te Leeuwarden," *Bouwkundig Weekblad* 39 (1918): 94, 97–99]. According to Nelly van Doesburg's inscription on a photograph of the model for the *Monument* (Van Doesburg Archive, Dienst Verspreide Rijkskollekties, The Hague), van Doesburg made his *Monument* design at about the same time that he wrote a commentary on van 't Hoff's very similar *Ruimte-Plastische Binnenhuisarchitectuur (Trappaal)* [spatial plastic interior architecture (stepped column)], published in *De Stijl* I, 6 (1918): 70–72 (I: 106–108). Apparently van 't Hoff was infuriated by van Doesburg's *Monument*, which bordered on plagiarism of his own work; the argument that ensued contributed to the break between van Doesburg and van 't Hoff. See also *L'Architecture Vivante* (autumn 1925), plate 13: four *Plastiques du Jardin* by van Doesburg, there dated 1919. The object illustrated at upper left was van Doesburg's reworking of his *Monument for Leeuwarden* into a garden sculpture, such as he evidently felt would be appropriate for Rosenberg's house.

11. Theo van Doesburg, letter to J. J. P. Oud, n.d. [April 1921], inv. no. 1972-A.541[(2)], IN, Paris.

12. In an exhibition of De Stijl architecture and related arts held in Rosenberg's gallery. See appendix B.

13. Piet Mondrian, letter to J. J. P. Oud, April 9, 1921, inv. no. 1972-A.387, IN, Paris.

14. Theo van Doesburg, "Data en feiten (betreffende de invloedsontwikkeling van 'DE STIJL' in 't buitenland) die voor zich spreken," *De Stijl* VII, 79–84 (1927): 55–56 (II: 556).

15. Piet Mondrian, letter to J. J. P. Oud, April 9, 1921, inv. no. 1972-A.387, IN, Paris.

16. Theo van Doesburg, letter to Evert Rinsema, June 23, 1921, in Schippers, *Holland Dada*, p. 175.

17. Léonce Rosenberg, letter to J. J. P. Oud, September 1, 1921, inv. no. 1972-A.471, IN, Paris.

18. Jaffé, *De Stijl, 1917–1931*, p. 166.

19. J. J. P. Oud, *Mein Weg in "De Stijl"*, tr. Kees and Erica de Wit (The Hague and Rotterdam: Nijgh en Van Ditmar, n.d.), p. 19.

20. Theo van Doesburg, letter to J. J. P. Oud, September 12, 1921, inv. no. 1972-A.555[(4)], IN, Paris.

21. Theo van Doesburg, letter to J. J. P. Oud, September 12, 1921, inv. no. 1972-A.555[(4)], IN, Paris.

22. Theo van Doesburg, letter to J. J. P. Oud, n.d. [September–October 1921], inv. no., 1972-A.579[(2)], IN. Paris.

23. Theo van Doesburg, letter to J. J. P. Oud, postmarked October 3, 1921, inv. no. 1972-A.557, IN, Paris.

24. Theo van Doesburg, letter to J. J. P. Oud, November 3, 1921, inv. no. 1972-A.564, IN, Paris.

25. Brief statements by Oud were included in the fifth- and tenth-anniversary numbers of *De Stijl*, and his work was included in the exhibition at Rosenberg's gallery, although the bitterness between van Doesburg and Oud persisted long after they stopped working together. In a letter to Oud of June 10, 1928, Jean Badovici, the editor of *L'Architecture Vivante*, who by this time shared Oud's negative attitude toward van Doesburg, described some of the problems he had encountered in producing the autumn 1925 issue of *L'Architecture Vivante* (which was devoted to De Stijl):

Doesburg wanted a volume in which the largest part (the part of the *Lion de la Fable*) referred to him. He clearly wanted to eliminate most of your works, particularly those, my dear Oud, [which he criticized as] being too decorative and consequently foreign to the spirit of the group. He wanted an absolutely abstract volume, an impossible thing to make its first appearance in France in 1923. Because I had to deal with the interests of the publisher and with public opinion, it was necessary to arrive at a compromise. Question of tactics. "You will ruin us," the publisher said to me. "You betray us sir," Doesburg cried in attacking me. . . . So, I neglected Doesburg better to convince the publisher. The mistakes in the editing of the issue were a result of this. . . . Today, after three years, Doesburg is the first person to be vain about and to take credit for publishing [such a volume] for the first time in France, where no one wanted it. . . ." (Jean Badovici, letter to J. J. P. Oud, June 10, 1928, Oud Archive, NDB, Amsterdam.)

Thus Badovici defended the mistakes contained in the De Stijl number of *L'Architecture Vivante* by blaming van Doesburg's egotism and desire to exclude Oud's work, such as the Superintendent's Shed or Café de Unie, which Van Doesburg condemned in part for what he described as the decorative quality of Oud's coloristic treatment.

26. J. J. P. Oud, "Over de toekomstige bouwkunst en hare architectonische mogelijkheden," *Bouwkundig Weekblad* 42 (1921): 159–160.

27. Banham, *Theory and Design in the First Machine Age*, pp. 161–162.

28. Van Doesburg's article, "Van de esthetiek naar het materiaal," was first published in *Bouwkundig Weekblad* 43 (1922): 372–375. The translation in Baljeu, *Theo van Doesburg*, pp. 127–131, entitled "The New Aesthetics and its Realization," quoted here, is from the German version of the article published in *De Stijl* VI, 1 (1923): 10–14 (II: 333–335).

29. "Van de esthetiek," tr. in Baljeu, p. 130.

30. J. J. P. Oud, letter to Bruno Zevi, quoted in Bruno Zevi, *Poetica dell'architettura Neoplastica* (Milan: Politecnica Tamburini, 1953), p. 161, and tr. H. J. Landry in Leonardo Benevolo, *History of Modern Architecture* (Cambridge, Mass.: MIT Press, 1971), vol. II, pp. 410–411.

31. For a discussion of van Doesburg's activities in Drachten see Schippers, *Holland Dada*, pp. 104–112. Schippers's book also contains correspondence that sheds light on van Doesburg's several other applied design schemes in Drachten.

32. Inscribed by van Doesburg on his drawing *Color Design for Exterior of Middle-Class Housing, Drachten*, 1921 (figure 41). The drawing is reproduced in *Trotwaer* [special "Dada in Drachten" number] 9–10 (1971); van Doesburg's inscription is transcribed there.

33. Inscribed by van Doesburg on his drawing *Diagram of Color Scheme, Agricultural School, Drachten* (figure 43).

34. See Karin von Maur, "Mondrian and Music," in *Mondrian: Zeichnungen* (Stuttgart: Staatsgalerie, 1980–1981), pp. 287–311.

35. Seuphor, *Piet Mondrian*, classified catalog nos. 228–232, 237–239.

36. Mondrian, *Le Néo-Plasticisme*, p. 11.

37. Piet Mondrian, "De 'Bruiteurs Futuristes Italiens' en 'het' nieuwe in de muziek," *De Stijl* IV, 8–9 (1921): 114–118, 130–136 (II: 95–97, 107–110); "Het Neo-Plasticisme (De Nieuwe Beelding) en zijn (hare) realiseering in de muziek," *De Stijl* V, 1–2 (1922): 1–7, 17–23 (II: 159–162, 171–174); "Le Néo-Plasticisme, sa réalisation dans la musique et le théâtre future," *La Vie des Lettres et des Arts* (1922); "De Jazz en de Neo-Plastiek," *i10* I (1927) [reprinted: Nendeln-Lichtenstein: Kraus, 1979], pp. 421–427].

38. Mondrian, "De 'Bruiteurs Futuristes Italiens,'" 134–135 (II: 109–110).

39. "Een Bezoek bij Piet Mondriaan," 1920 (clipping).

40. Mondrian, "Het Neo-Plasticisme . . . in de muziek," pp. 23–24 (II: 173–174). Mondrian's idea sounds remarkably similar to Lud-

wig Hirschfeld-Mack's "Reflected Light Compositions," involving projections of colored light accompanied by music and dance, which the Bauhaus artist began to develop in 1921–22, but which were not performed publicly before 1924. See Basil Gilbert, "The Reflected Light Compositions of Ludwig Hirschfeld-Mack," *Form 2* (1966): 10–14, and Hans M. Wingler, *Bauhaus: Weimar, Dessau, Berlin, Chicago* (Cambridge, Mass.: MIT Press, 1969), pp. 370–371.

41. It is also worth noting the musical terms in which two other artists, Amedée Ozenfant and Charles-Édouard Jeanneret (better known as Le Corbusier) discussed color in their principal essay on Purism published in *L'Esprit Nouveau* in 1920 [tr. in Herbert (ed.), *Modern Artists on Art: Ten Unabridged Essays* (Englewood Cliffs, N.J.: Prentice-Hall, 1964)]. Like those of Mondrian and van Doesburg, their color theories were associated not only with music but with architecture as well. Beginning with the notion that "when one says painting, inevitably he says color," Ozenfant and Le Corbusier proceeded to state that "painting is a question of architecture, and therefore volume is its means." They recognized that color is intimately associated with architecture because of its ability to modify the viewer's perception of volume and hence of space. Having thus established a connection between color and architecture, they then went on to discuss color in terms of music, describing how the three scales of color, "the major scale," "the dynamic scale," and "the transitional scale," each possess different properties which affect the architectural construction of any work of art. Taking Cézanne as an example of an artist "who practiced the obstinate and maniacal search for volume with all the confusion and trouble which animated his being," they compared him as a painter to "an orchestra leader . . . who tries to make violin music with an English horn, and bassoon sounds with a violin." Although they retained the vocabulary and the analogy of music in describing their color theory, like van Doesburg, ultimately Ozenfant and Le Corbusier also opted for an architectural understanding of color, limiting their palette to "the major scale," which, they asserted, was composed of the essentially constructive colors: "ochre yellows, reds, earths,

white, black, ultramarine blue, and, of course, certain of their derivatives. . . . " In establishing these as the colors most appropriate to an architectural aesthetic, Ozenfant and Le Corbusier referred to "certain purely rational investigations which add reassuring certitudes based upon our visual functions, our experience, and our habits." Their color theory, though couched in the language of experimental science, involved a lingering element of subjectivity that was antipathetic to Mondrian's and van Doesburg's supposedly more objective emphasis on the primary colors, their color opposites, and the noncolors—a similarly limited range, but one that was based on the investigations of scientists (e.g., Wilhelm Ostwald). Unlike the Purist colors such as forest green and earth brown, which Le Corbusier also applied directly to architecture (e.g. in his 1925 housing at Pessac), Mondrian's and van Doesburg's color schemes avoided all evocations of nature. They would never have accepted Le Corbusier's association of the pale green walls at Pessac with "the foliage of gardens and of the forest" [Le Corbusier, "Pessac," *L'Architecture Vivante* (autumn and winter 1927): 30]. That kind of associative naturalism was of course contrary to Mondrian's entire enterprise, and it was diametrically opposed to the conception of consonant and dissonant, contrasting colors that van Doesburg wanted to apply to the buildings designed by de Boer in Drachten.

42. In 1917 van Doesburg made a pair of stained glass windows on the theme of a dancing figure. One is composed of primary colors; its companion contains the secondaries. (*Dance I* and *Dance II*, Dienst Verspreide Rijkskollekties, The Hague.)

43. Van Doesburg's lecture, "De kleur van onze woning" (the color of our housing), was summarized in the *Dragster Courant* of December 23, 1921. The same newspaper had published an article by H. Martin on the housing block: "De Middenstandswoningen" (October 11, 1921). Martin's article was followed by the publication of letters to the editor from van Doesburg's friend Evert Rinsema and from de Boer himself on October 14, 1921. In response to the growing controversy, Martin then wrote a series of articles (entitled "Moderne kunst") dealing with issues raised by

van Doesburg's color schemes for de Boer's buildings. These were published in four weekly installments between October 21 and November 11, 1921 (photocopies: Museum It Bleekerhûs, Drachten).

44. Martin, "Moderne kunst," part III, *Dragster Courant*, November 4, 1921 (photocopy: Museum It Bleekerhûs, Drachten).

45. Van Doesburg, "Van de esthetiek," p. 129.

46. Reinder Blijstra, *C. van Eesteren*, tr. Roy Edwards (Amsterdam: Meulenhoff, 1971), p. 5.

47. Blijstra, pp. 5–6.

48. In 1924, when van Doesburg submitted photographs of his color designs for the University Hall for publication in *Nederlandsche ambachts- en nijverheidskunst jaarboek 1923*, he informed the editor that the designs were made in Paris in the summer of 1923 (ms. collection Kees Broos, The Hague). Therefore the date 1922 attached to the University Hall designs when they were reproduced in *L'Architecture Vivante* (autumn 1925, pls. 11 and 12) is incorrect. Willy Rotzler's dating to 1922 of van Doesburg's *Study for a Composition* (figure 45), a design for the ceiling of the hall, is also mistaken. Van Doesburg himself dated this design 1923, but a correct reading of the year is difficult because a framing mat partially obscures the last digit, making it look like a 2 instead of a 3. See Rotzler, catalog no. 138.

49. Oud, *Mein Weg in "De Stijl"*, p. 23.

50. *De Stijl* VI, 9 (1925) (II: 421).

51. As seen in a photograph taken there in 1923, reproduced in *Theo van Doesburg 1881–1931* (Eindhoven: 1968–1969), p. 18.

52. Van Doesburg twice mentioned the possibility of using enameled plaques in the captions for photographs of the University Hall designs he submitted to the editor of *Nederlandsche ambachts- en nijverheidskunst jaarboek 1923* (mss. collection Kees Broos, The Hague).

53. Because of problems concerning authorship that later developed between van Doesburg and van Eesteren, it is noteworthy that when two perspective designs of the hall interior—one with and one without van Doesburg's color indications—were reproduced alongside the ceiling and floor color designs in the autumn 1925 issue of *L'Architecture Vivante*, only van Doesburg's name and not that of van Eesteren accompanied the illustrations. No mention was made that van Eesteren was responsible for the architectural plan and for both perspective drawings, one of which served as the basis for van Doesburg's color scheme (figure 46). According to a comment made later by van Eesteren, "Van Doesburg studied color in architecture on and in my architectural designs. He had this work, which was entirely designed by me, published under his name with the note: C. van Eesteren, associate." (Quoted in Blijstra, *C. van Eesteren*, p. 8.) A black and white version of the University Hall exploded box plan also demonstrates how ambiguities concerning the authorship of van Doesburg's and van Eesteren's collaborative projects have arisen. This version, in which the rectangles where color was to be applied were left blank and only the black areas were filled in, was reproduced over van Doesburg's name only on page 24 of the autumn–winter 1926 issue of *L'Architecture Vivante*, where it was called *Peinture murale*. Why the drawing (Dienst Verspreide Rijkskollekties, The Hague) was given this title is not clear, but the fact remains that in this instance no mention was made of the University Hall or of the architect responsible for its design.

54. Quoted in A. Elzas, "Theo van Doesburg," *De 8 en Opbouw* 6 (1935): 174.

55. Baljeu, *Theo van Doesburg*, p. 58. Rietveld eventually did participate by building the model of the villa, but he had no part in its design.

56. Blijstra, *C. van Eesteren*, p. 7.

57. The house, for which van Doesburg designed interior and exterior color schemes, was completed in 1924. The designs and a photograph of the finished structure were reproduced in *L'Architecture Vivante* in 1924 and 1925.

58. N. Troy, interview with C. van Eesteren, November 2, 1978.

59. Leering, "De Architectuur en Van Doesburg," p. 21.

60. Leering, "De Architectuur en Van Doesburg," p. 23; Baljeu, *Theo van Doesburg*, pp. 58–60.

61. Theo van Doesburg, letter to Gerrit Rietveld, August 10, 1923, tr. in Brown, *Rietveld*, p. 31.

62. Baljeu, *Theo van Doesburg*, p. 60.

63. N. Troy, interview with C. van Eesteren, November 2, 1978.

64. Leering, "De Architectuur en Van Doesburg," p. 21.

65. See Theo van Doesburg, "Tot een beeldende architectuur," *De Stijl* VI, 6–7 (1924): 81 (II: 389). On van Doesburg's interest in the fourth dimension see Joost Baljeu, "The Fourth Dimension in Neoplasticism," *Form* 9 (1969): 6–14, and Linda Dalrymple Henderson, The Artist, The Fourth Dimension, and Non-Euclidean Geometry 1900–1930: A Romance of Many Dimensions, Ph.D. diss., Yale University, 1975, pp. 424–443.

66. Leering, "De Architectuur en Van Doesburg," p. 22.

67. Mondrian, "De Realiseering," pp. 168–169.

68. Mondrian, "Realiteit," p. 349.

69. See appendix B. The exhibition, entitled Les Architectes du Groupe "de Stijl" (Hollande), was installed by van Doesburg and van Eesteren in five rooms on the ground floor of Rosenberg's gallery at 19 rue de la Baume, Paris. A photograph of the installation was reproduced in *De Stijl* [VI, 6–7 (1924) (II: 393)], where it was accompanied by photographs of many of the designs van Doesburg and van Eesteren contributed to the exhibition. In 1924 the De Stijl exhibition was reassembled in the École Spéciale d'Architecture in Paris, where it formed part of a larger, student-organized exhibition entitled Architecture et les arts qui s'y rattachent (architecture and the related arts). In 1926 a modified version of the exhibition was reconstituted in a museum in Nancy.

70. Theo van Doesburg and C. van Eesteren, "Vers une construction collective," *De Stijl* VI, 6–7 (1924), tr. R. R. Symonds in *De Stijl*, ed. Jaffé, p. 191.

71. *L'Architecture Vivante* (autumn 1925), plates 2–5, 7–9.

72. Baljeu, *Theo van Doesburg*, p. 62.

73. Theo van Doesburg, letter to Gerrit Rietveld, August 10, 1923, tr. in Brown, *Rietveld*, p. 31. The exhibition involved was the Internationale Architekturausstellung at the Staatliche Bauhaus in Weimar, August 15–September 30, 1923. According to Marijke Küper (in Blotkamp et al., *De Beginjaren van De Stijl*, p. 284), Rietveld finally decided not to contribute to the exhibition after all.

74. See Walter Gropius's letter of November 3, 1952, tr. in Zevi, p. 161. Van Doesburg's own account is contained in "Data en feiten (betreffende de invloedsontwikkeling van 'DE STIJL' in het buitenland) die voor zich spreken," *De Stijl* VII, 79–84 (1927): 54–55 (II: 55–56). See also Lothar Schreyer, *Erinnerungen an Sturm und Bauhaus* (Munich: Albert Langen–Georg Mueller, 1956), p. 237, and "Documentatie," in *Theo van Doesburg 1881–1931* (Eindhoven, 1968–1969), pp. 45–48, which includes memoirs of Fred Forbat, two letters from van Doesburg dated 1921, and a text by Werner Graeff. Humblet (*Le Bauhaus*, pp. 167–207) closely examines the relationship between the Bauhaus and van Doesburg, and other De Stijl artists.

75. Theo van Doesburg, "De Beteekenis van de kleur in binnen- en buitenarchitectuur," *Bouwkundig Weekblad* 44 (1923), tr. in Baljeu, *Theo van Doesburg*, pp. 137–140.

76. Van Doesburg, "Tot een beeldende architectuur," tr. in Baljeu, p. 147.

Chapter 4

■ *216*

77. N. Troy, interview with Mrs. Truus Schröder, September 10, 1977.

78. Carel Blotkamp, "Rietveld en De Stijl," in *Rietveld Schröder Huis 1925–1975*, ed. Bertus Mulder and Gerrit Jan de Rook (Utrecht and Antwerp: A. W. Bruna & Zoon, 1975), p. 14.

79. Brown, *Rietveld*, pp. 62–64.

80. N. Troy, interview with Mrs. Truus Schröder, September 10, 1977.

81. Cornelis van Eesteren, letter to Theo van Doesburg, August 25, 1924, Van Doesburg Archive, Dienst Verspreide Rijkskollekties, The Hague.

82. Baljeu (p. 66) states that "Vers une construction collective" and "− □ + = R₄" were "both written by van Doesburg but published with van Eestern listed as co-author."

83. Theo van Doesburg and C. van Eesteren, "− □ + = R₄," *De Stijl* VI, 6–7 (1924), tr. R. R. Symonds in *De Stijl*, ed. Jaffé, p. 192.

84. Alan Birnholz, El Lissitzky, Ph.D. diss., Yale University, 1973, pp. 141–142.

85. Theo van Doesburg, "Rechenschaft der Stijlgruppe," *De Stijl* V, 4 (1922), tr. Mary Whitall in *De Stijl*, ed. Jaffé, p. 172.

86. Theo van Doesburg, El Lissitzky, and Hans Richter, "Erklärung," *De Stijl* V, 4 (1922), tr. Mary Whitall, in *De Stijl*, ed. Jaffé, p. 177.

1. Marie-Noëlle Pradel, "La Maison Cubiste en 1912," *Art de France* 1 (1961): 177–186.

2. W[illem] Kromhout, "Interieur-kunst op den Haagse Kunstkring," *Architectura* 15 (1907): 306.

3. Theo van Doesburg, "De Onafhankelijken," *De Eenheid* 318 (1916).

4. Birnholz, El Lissitzky, p. 158.

5. Alan C. Birnholz, "El Lissitzky and the Jewish Tradition," *Studio International* CLXXXVI, 959 (1973): 134.

6. Alan C. Birnholz, review of M. Tafuri (ed.), *Socialismo, città, architettura URSS 1917–1937*, Art Bulletin 54 (1972): 369.

7. Birnholz, El Lissitzky, p. 168.

8. El Lissitzky, "Proun," *De Stijl* V, 6 (1922): 82 (II: 223).

9. El Lissitzky, "Prounen Raum," *G* 1 (1923), tr. Helene Aldwinckle in Sophie Lissitzky-Küppers, *El Lisstzky: Life, Letters, Texts* (London: Thames and Hudson, 1968), p. 365.

10. Kenneth Frampton, "The Work and Influence of El Lissitzky," *Architects' Year Book* 12 (1968): 263.

11. El Lissitzky, letter to J. J. P. Oud, June 30, 1924, in Sophie Lissitzky-Küppers and Jen Lissitzky (eds.), *El Lissitzky, Proun und Wolkenbugel* (Dresden: VEB Verlag der Kunst, 1977), pp. 125–126.

12. Jean Leering, "Lissitsky's Importance Today," in *El Lissitzky* (Cologne: Galerie Gmurzynska, 1976), p. 35.

13. John Bowlt, "Concepts of Color and the Soviet Avant-Garde," *The Structurist* 13–14 (1973–1974): 27–28.

14. Camilla Gray, *The Great Experiment: Russian Art, 1863–1922* (New York: Harry N. Abrams, 1962), p. 216. Photographs of the café interior, such as one published in *Bulletin de ''L'Effort Moderne''* 17 (1925), indicate that the space must have been quite large, not a ''tiny interior'' as Gray suggests.

15. *Grosse Berliner Kunstausstellung* (Berlin: Lehrter Bahnhof, 1923), catalog nos. 1144–1148, 1228 and 1408.

16. Birnholz, El Lissitzky, p. 169. Lissitzky was the only one of all these artists who definitely exhibited a demonstration space; see *Grosse Berliner Kunstausstellung*, catalog no. 1253. Unlike Lissitzky's *Proun Space*, the entries of Baumeister, Buchholz, and Huszar were listed in the catalog as shown in rooms where many other objects were also displayed, not in spaces of their own. Confusion about this issue seems to have been generated by Lissitzky's statement in ''Prounen Raum'' (note 9 above) that several independent spaces were set aside in the exhibition: ''Various rooms have been built like boxes into the exhibition hall at the Lehrter Bahnhof. One of these boxes has been kindly put at my disposal.''

17. See *Erich Buchholz* (Berlin: Galerie Dedalus, 1971), and ''Berliner Ausstellungen,'' *Der Cicerone* 15 (1923): 1056.

18. It has not been possible to locate a catalog of the Juryfreie Kunstschau of 1923 (if indeed one was ever produced) or to find mention of any abstract interiors in contemporary reviews of the exhibition. Thus one cannot be certain that Huszar's and Rietveld's design was realized for that exhibition. The fact that Buchholz's interior was not built lends weight to the supposition that their design never progressed beyond model form. On the other hand, one of two photographs formerly belonging to Rietveld (collection of Mrs. Truus Schröder, Utrecht) shows an inscription on one wall of Huszar's and Rietveld's design stating that it was realized in an exhibition in Berlin in October 1923 (''Uitgevoerd te Berlijn, Oct. 1923''). This corresponds to the timing of the Juryfreie Kunstschau. A note written in pencil under the two mounted photographs indicates that the room was 9 × 9 meters in size.

19. I am grateful to Hans L. C. Jaffé for making this slide available to me.

20. ''In the earliest texts published in *De Stijl*, he [Rietveld] mainly discusses the manner in which his furniture was constructed. He speaks from the point of view of practicality.'' [Blotkamp, ''Rietveld en De Stijl,'' In Bertus Mulder and Gerrit Jan de Rook, eds., *Rietveld Schröder Huis* (Utrecht: A. W. Bruna & Zoon, 1975), p. 14.]

21. Christopher Green, ''Painting for the Corbusian Home: Fernand Léger's Architectural Paintings, 1924–26,'' *Studio International* CXC, 977 (1975): 106.

22. Vilmos Huszar, ''Aesthetische beschouwingen III,'' *De Stijl* I, 5 (1918): 55 (I: 85).

23. Bertus Mulder, ''Rietveld Schröder Huis 1924–1975,'' in *Rietveld Schröder Huis*, ed. Mulder and de Rook, p. 32. Brown disagrees: ''There is no evidence that Rietveld and Mrs. Schröder studied the functional requirements—in this case the needs of a family with three children—and then formulated the architectural program from strictly functional factors. Rather, they arbitrarily established a variety of different kinds of volumes—closed on the ground floor, open above—which could be adjusted and adapted to the needs of *any* inhabitant.'' (*The Work of G. Rietveld, Architect*, p. 51.)

24. Gerrit Rietveld, ''On De Stijl and Bauhaus,'' tr. in *G. Rietveld, Architect* (Amsterdam: Stedelijk Museum, 1971–72).

25. Brown has noted the following about the Berlin interior: ''This work was assigned to Huszar in the Stedelijk Museum catalogue no. 81, 1951, on the occasion of the *De Stijl* exhibition. There is no doubt, however, that Huszar did only the color and that Rietveld did the furniture and spatial design.'' (*The Work of G. Rietveld, Architect*, p. 154, note 16.) (The fact that Rietveld worked closely with the organizers of the Stedelijk Museum exhibition, which he installed himself, raises the question of why he did not in-

form those responsible for the catalog of his role in determining the spatial form of the Berlin interior.) Although Brown's statement accords well with the role Huszar at one time envisioned for himself as color consultant in a collaborative effort directed toward the design of a totally integrated interior, a number of circumstances seem to contradict this apparently logical attribution. Most important is the fact that, although Rietveld was indeed responsible for the furniture in the interior, he sent his contribution to Berlin; only Huszar and not Rietveld went to Berlin in October 1923, presumably in order to be present for the installation of the interior and the opening of the exhibition. Huszar's trip is indicated in two letters he wrote to J. J. P. Oud (September 1923 and October 24, 1923; Oud Archive, NDB, Amsterdam). G. A. van de Groenekan, Rietveld's assistant at the time of the Berlin exhibition, stated in an interview (N. Troy, March 24, 1978) that Rietveld did not go to Berlin. This was confirmed by Mrs. Truus Schröder in telephone interviews (N. Troy, September 1978).

26. Jean Badovici, "Entretiens sur l'architecture vivante: Intérieur par V. Huszar," *L'Architecture Vivante* (summer 1924): 14–15. *L'Architecture Vivante* is not always a reliable documentary source. Badovici was forced to acknowledge that numerous errors appeared in the special issue he devoted to De Stijl in the autumn of 1925. That issue, which had taken almost two years to assemble, provoked a furious argument between Badovici and van Doesburg (see note 25 to chapter 3, above), who was still bitter about it in 1927 when he wrote in *De Stijl* of Badovici's "arbitrary, careless alteration of titles, the jumbling together of names and information concerning the buildings in question, the omission and modification of articles, and so on" [van Doesburg, "Data en feiten," p. 57 (II: 557)]. Nevertheless, the wealth of information suggesting Huszar as principal author of the Berlin interior supports such a reading of Badovici's 1924 text.

27. "Korte inhoud van de voordracht door Vilmos Huszar over het wandvlakprobleem in de beeldende kunst," mimeographed typescript in "Jaarboek, Haagse Kunstkring," 1922, p. 146 (ms. in Gemeentearchief, The Hague).

28. Katherine S. Dreier and Constantin Aladjalov, *Modern Art* (New York: Société Anonyme—Museum of Modern Art, 1926), p. 49.

29. Max Bill, "*Composition I with Blue and Yellow*, 1925, by Piet Mondrian," tr. Marion Wolf in *Piet Mondrian 1872–1944 Centennial Exhibition* (New York: Solomon R. Guggenheim Museum, 1971), pp. 74–75.

30. For a brief discussion of this issue see Angelica Zander Rudenstine, *The Guggenheim Museum Collection: Paintings 1880–1945* (New York: Solomon R. Guggenheim Museum, 1976), vol. II, p. 585. More recently, E. A. Carmean, Jr., has made an extensive study of Mondrian's diamond pictures in *Mondrian: The Diamond Compositions* (Washington, D.C.: National Gallery of Art, 1979).

31. "Bij Piet Mondriaan," 1926 (clipping).

32. Fernand Léger, "The Machine Aesthetic: Geometric Order and Truth," tr. Alexandra Anderson, in Fernand Léger, *Functions of Painting*, ed. Edward F. Fry (New York: Viking, 1973), p. 63.

33. For example, *Peinture murale*, 1924, Musée National Fernand Léger, Biot. Other examples are mentioned in Green, "Painting for the Corbusian Home," p. 106.

34. Green, pp. 106–107.

35. Loosjes-Terpstra, *Moderne kunst in Nederland*, p. 160.

36. Mondrian, "Realiteit," p. 339.

37. Mondrian, "Realiteit," p. 336.

38. Michel Seuphor, *Diaphragme intérieur et un drapeau* (Paris: Les Ecrivains Réunis, 1926). The text of Seuphor's play is reprinted alongside color photographs of a reconstructed version of Mondrian's model (Stedelijk Van Abbemuseum, Eindhoven) in Herbert Henkels (ed.), *Seuphor* (Antwerp: Mercator Fonds; The Hague:

Gemeentemusum, 1976), pp. 53–60. In a 1978 conversation with the author, Herbert Henkels suggested this interpretation of the photograph shown here as figure 67.

39. Michel Seuphor, "le jeu de je," in Henkels (ed.), *Seuphor*, p. 312.

40. Piet Mondrian, letter to J. J. P. Oud, December 20, 1926, inv. no. 1972-A.428⁽²⁾, IN, Paris.

41. As reported in "Bij Piet Mondriaan," 1926 (clipping).

42. Nevertheless, Mondrian's designs were not entirely unknown in Paris around 1926–27. In his letter to Oud of December 20, 1926 (see note 40) Mondrian mentioned that when Vantongerloo was in Paris—he left early in September 1926—he had read that the French architect Rob Mallet-Stevens was planning to deliver a lecture concerning the theater. Vantongerloo wrote Mallet-Stevens, asking if he was aware that Mondrian was also engaged in theater design. As Mondrian recounted to Oud: "Two weeks later, after Vantong[erloo] left, he shows up, is very pleasant (just like van Doesb[urg] at first) has a good look around and wants to have photos of the theatrical model made as slides for his lecture. I've done that. Of course others will pinch a part [of my ideas] but it's possible that I will have a chance to realize it myself so I don't worry about that. . . ." Furthermore, photographs of the model with the three interchangeable decors were published in *Documents Internationaux de l'Esprit Nouveau* 1 (1927), the first and only issue of a review coedited by Seuphor (reprinted: Paris: Jean-Michel Place, 1977).

43. See Will Grohmann, *Die Sammlung Ida Bienert, Dresden* (Potsdam: Müller und I. Kiepenheuer, 1933).

44. The exhibition, arranged by Küppers, also included works by Man Ray. See Will Grohmann, "Dresdener Ausstellungen," *Der Cicerone* 17 (1925): 1007.

45. Lissitzky-Küppers, *El Lissitzky*, pp. 61–62.

46. German translations of five essays by Mondrian were published in 1925 as *Neue Gestaltung*, the fifth Bauhaus Book [reprint: Hans Wingler, ed. (Mainz and Berlin: Florian Kupferberg, 1974)].

47. Fritz Löffler, "Ida Bienert und ihre Sammlung," *Literatur und Kunst der Gegenwart* 71–72 (1971): 192. I am grateful to Dr. Löffler for making a photocopy of this text available to me.

48. El Lissitzky, letter to Sophie Küppers, October 18, 1925, tr. Helene Aldwinckle in Lissitzky-Küppers, *El Lissitzky*, p. 69.

49. Hannah Höch's recollection of a visit to Bienert's house in 1931 is the only documentation suggesting that Mondrian realized a design for the reception hall: "In 1931 Til Brugman and I stayed with Bienert. Mondrian had already completed the entrance." [Quoted in Heinz Ohff, *Hannah Höch* (Berlin: Gebr. Mann, 1968), p. 29.]

50. Piet Mondrian, letter to J. J. P. Oud, n.d. [early 1926], inv. no. 1972-A.424, IN, Paris.

51. These four unattributed drawings, formerly in the Bienert family collection, were acquired by the Staatliche Kunstsammlungen, Dresden, together with those by Mondrian described below.

52. Piet Mondrian, letter to Alfred Roth, June 28, 1937, published in Roth, *Begegnung met Pionieren*, p. 176.

53. Claude Bragdon, *The Frozen Fountain: Being an Essay on Architecture and the Art of Decorative Design in Space* (New York: Knopf, 1932), pp. 61–62.

54. Piet Mondrian, letter to Félix Del Marle, December 16, 1926. This and subsequently cited Del Marle correspondence is in the collection of the Ex Libris gallery in New York.

55. Herzogenrath even states [in *Malewitsch-Mondrian* (Cologne, 1976), p. 180] that van Doesburg taught his De Stijl course in Burchartz's Weimar studio. According to an announcement of the

course signed by van Doesburg and dated "Weimar, February 20, 1922," the classes were to meet in the studio of Peter Röhl. See "Documentatie," in *Theo van Doesburg 1881–1931* (Eindhoven, 1968–1969), p. 46.

56. Seuphor, *Piet Mondrian*, p. 192.

57. Mondrian wrote Oud that Vantongerloo would leave Paris on September 7 (September 6, 1925, inv. no. 1972-A.417, IN, Paris).

58. Dreier and Aladjalov, *Modern Art*, p. 51.

59. *Vouloir* 25 (1927).

60. This is shown by two letters from El Lissitzky to Sophie Lissitzky-Küppers (January 30 and March 2, 1926, published in Lissitzky-Küppers, *El Lissitzky*, pp. 72, 74). All three Dresden drawings are signed "PM '26."

61. As proposed by Lissitzky-Küppers, *El Lissitzky*, pp. 61–62.

62. In response to a question whether Mondrian visited van Doesburg when the latter was in Weimar, Nelly van Doesburg stated: "Not Mondrian, he stayed calmly in Paris. He would have nothing to do with Germany and Germans. You could never send him a postcard from Germany, he found that horrid." [Carel Blotkamp, "Nelly van Doesburg: 'De Sikkenprijs komt veertig jaar te laat,' " *Vrij Nederland* XXIX, 14 (1968): 11.] It seems unlikely that Mondrian would still have harbored such a negative attitude in 1926, since it was in Germany that he had first received a significant amount of recognition. Already in 1923, he had written to Oud that he was pleased to hear what "Lisitzky [sic] and Moholy-Nagy said about my work in Berlin." "I've also heard," he continued, "that among a small circle of people it is very highly valued. . . ." He went on to state that he had sold a small canvas to a man in Weimar, and that a large work was going to be reproduced in color. The German critic Adolf Behne would thereafter try to sell the latter painting to a Scandinavian museum. Furthermore, Mondrian said that in the July number of *Der Sturm* Moholy-Nagy had written about his ideas concerning the new music (Piet Mondrian,

letter to J. J. P. Oud, November 12, 1923, inv. no. 1972-A.408, IN, Paris). The first public gallery to purchase one of his paintings was the Hanover Landesmuseum, and, having acquired several of his works by 1926, Ida Bienert (a German) was among Mondrian's most important patrons. Indeed, as Seuphor has noted (*Piet Mondrian*, p. 163), it was in Germany that Mondrian had his first real success as a result of the appearance of *Neue Gestaltung* in 1925: "The publication of this work consolidated his influence, especially with the Bauhaus circles, where Doesburg had smoothed the way." The Bauhaus connection might be particularly relevant to the Bienert commission. Bienert's daughter Ise was a student at the Bauhaus, and Ida Bienert herself was a close friend of Walter Gropius. When Mondrian was unable to execute his designs for the interior, the commission may have been passed along to Gropius, to his associate Adolf Meyer, or to one of Gropius's students. This is suggested by the four other drawings for the same interior in Bienert's house (Staatliche Kunstsammlungen, Dresden). The desk and bookcases incorporated in those designs are similar to the furniture in Gropius's office in the Weimar Bauhaus.

63. Piet Mondrian, letter to J. J. P. Oud, May 22, 1926, inv. no. 1972-A.426, IN, Paris. In his undated letter to Oud of early 1926 (inv. no. 1972-A.424, IN, Paris), Mondrian had written that the fee for the Bienert designs was only 150 marks.

64. El Lissitzky, letter to Sophie Küppers, March 2, 1926, tr. Helene Aldwinckle in Lissitzky-Küppers, *El Lissitzky*, p. 74.

65. Piet Mondrian, "Le Home—la rue—la cité," tr. Martin James and Harry Holtzman in *Mondrian: The Process Works* (New York: Pace Gallery, 1970), pp. 11, 13.

66. As Mondrian wrote to Oud of the Bienert designs, "Without the preparatory study of my own interior, I wouldn't have been able to do it." (Undated letter [early 1926], inv. no. 1972-A.424, IN, Paris.)

67. Harry Holtzman, "Piet Mondrian, 1872–1944. Some Notes on Mondrian's Method: The Late Drawings," in *Mondrian: The Process Works*, p. 3.

68. Mondrian, "Le Home," p. 14.

69. Mondrian, "Le Home," p. 11.

70. Quoted in "Eleven Europeans in America," *Museum of Modern Art Bulletin* XIII, 4–5 (1946): 35.

71. Exactly when van Doesburg decided on the definitive orientation of *Counter-Composition V* is not known. There is substantial evidence, including a drawing made after the painting (Yale University Art Gallery, New Haven), that the painting was originally intended to be a diamond with an internal compositional format like that of Mondrian's paintings and like some of van Doesburg's own paintings in the counter-composition series.

72. Piet Mondrian, letter to J. J. P. Oud, n.d. [early 1926], inv. no. 1972-A.424, IN, Paris.

73. Piet Mondrian, letter to Félix Del Marle, August 26, 1927.

74. Some of this might have occurred in 1925. Around September–October of that year Mondrian wrote Oud that since the beginning of September "I have been busy fixing up the atelier. You won't recognize it, I have painted everything over." On November 10, 1925, he wrote, "I've now gotten the house somewhat in order; I still have to paint the chairs. It seems completely different now." (Inv. nos. 1972-A.418 and 1972-A.422[2], IN, Paris.)

75. Alexander Calder, *Calder: An Autobiography with Pictures* (New York: Pantheon, 1966), p. 113.

76. Quoted in John Summerson, *Ben Nicholson* (West Drayton, Middlesex: Penguin, 1948), pp. 12–13.

77. On Peeters's relationship with De Stijl artists see Phil Maertens, " 'Het Overzicht' en de plaats van de Vlaamse kunst in het Europa van de jaren twintig," *Bulletin des Musées Royaux des Beaux-Arts de Belgique* 13 (1964): 74–76; Robert Melders, *Jozef Peeters (1895–1960)* (Antwerp and Amsterdam: Nederlandsche Boekhandel, 1978), pp. 39–40, 83–86; Serge Goyens de Heusch, "*7

Arts*" *Bruxelles 1922–1929* (Ministère de la Culture Française de Belgique, 1976), p. 25; and Herbert Henkels (ed.), *Seuphor*, pp. 9–10. This discussion is also indebted to the text by Flor Bex in *Jozef Peeters (1895–1960)* (Antwerp: International Cultureel Centrum, 1978).

78. Jozef Peeters, "Over Kunstenaarsraden," *Vlaamsche Arbeid* 12 (1922), quoted in Bex, p. 15.

79. The apartment and its furnishings, also designed by Peeters, are described in detail by Edmond Devoghelaere, "Abstrakt Jozef Peeters schilderde eigen huis," *Gazet van Antwerpen*, July 15, 1970, p. 10 (clipping).

80. As stated by Anne Dary in *Félix Del Marle: Disegni dal 1912 al 1949* (Milan: Galleria Milano, 1976), p. 5.

81. Van Doesburg, "Data en feiten," p. 58 (II: 557).

82. Mondrian was not altogether pleased by this. In a letter to Del Marle dated January 7, 1927, he wrote, "I see in No. 24 of Vouloir: monthly review of the Neo-Plastic aesthetic. I am flattered because it was I who discovered the word neo-plasticism, but wouldn't it be better to put <u>new</u> aesthetic, e.g., because it would be difficult to follow neo-plastic ideas completely, especially in literature! I think it is better for a review not to limit itself too much!"

83. Before March 2, 1926, as evidenced by a letter of that date from Mondrian to Del Marle.

84. Piet Mondrian, letter to Félix Del Marle, December 30, 1926.

85. N. Troy, interview with Mrs. Lucy Del Marle-Leyden, November 23, 1977.

86. Piet Mondrian, "Neo-Plasticisme: De Woning—de straat—de stad," *i10* 1, 1 (1927): 12–16.

87. Quoted in Kees Broos, "Schilderijen en reliëfs 1923–1980," in *Domela* (The Hague: Gemeentemuseum, 1980), p. 11.

88. Quoted in Betty van Garrel, "Cesar Domela, de laaste over-levende van de Stijlgroep," *Haagse Post*, May 21, 1973, p. 57 (clipping).

89. N. Troy, interview with Cesar Domela, November 18, 1977.

90. See "Biographie" in *Dessins de Jean Gorin* (Paris: Centre National d'Art et de Culture Georges Pompidou, Musée National d'Art Moderne, 1977).

91. Laura Miner, Abstract Art in Paris, M.A. report, Courtauld Institute of Art, University of London, p. 7 in chapter on Gorin.

92. R. W. D. Oxenaar, in *Bart van der Leck* (Otterlo, 1976).

93. On Berssenbrugge, see H. J. Scheffer, *Portret van een fotograaf: Henri Berssenbrugge, 1873–1959* (Leiden: A. W. Sijthoff, 1967). Clippings of reviews dating from June and July 1921 may be found in the Kunsthistorisch Instituut van de Rijksuniversiteit, Leiden; I am grateful to Chris Rehorst for making photocopies available to me.

94. "Verkoop-tentoonstelling van beeldende- en nijverheidskunst," dated December 17, 1921, mimeographed typescript in "Jaarboek, Haagse Kunstkring," 1921, p. 77 (ms. in Gemeentearchief, The Hague).

95. J. S. Gibson, "Artistic Houses," *The Studio* (1893); reprinted in *The Birth of the Studio 1893–1895* (Woodbridge, Suffolk: Antique Collectors Club, 1976), p. 39.

96. Mark Girouard, *The Victorian Country House*, revised edition (New Haven: Yale University Press, 1979), p. 68.

97. Theo van Doesburg, "L'Élémentarisme et son origine," *De Stijl* 87–89 (1928), tr. in Baljeu, *Theo van Doesburg*, p. 175.

98. Théo Wolters speculates on how this might have happened in the context of a discussion of other interior designs that Taeuber-Arp executed in Strasbourg during the same period. See Théo Wolters, "Décorations d'intérieurs créées et réalisées à Strasbourg par Sophie Taüber [sic] et Jean Arp," *L'Information de l'Histoire de l'Art* XV, 2 (1970): 79–80.

99. See van Doesburg's enumeration of the different spaces and their locations in "Notices sur l'Aubette à Strasbourg," *De Stijl* 87–89 (1928), tr. R. R. Symonds in *De Stijl*, ed. Jaffé, p. 234.

100. Although Arp worked in a "premorphist" or biomorphic style in the caveau-dancing and the adjacent bar américain, his other contributions to the Aubette, such as the tile floor in the passageway and the colors in the stairwell, were geometric and as such intended to work directly with the architecture. Van Doesburg described how the latter designs were inspired by the direction in which people would be moving in these areas of the Aubette: The lateral extension of the color design in the passageway emphasized horizontality while the colors in the stairwell were oriented vertically to suggest ascension. Even Arp's premorphist style sometimes corresponded to architectural features. For example, the rounded forms of his work in the bar américain were based on the shape of a previously existing round pillar that had been retained in the renovation. See van Doesburg, "Notices sur l'Aubette," p. 237.

101. Van Doesburg, "Notices sur l'Aubette," p. 234.

102. Van Doesburg, "Notices sur l'Aubette," p. 235.

103. Theo van Doesburg, "Farben im Raum und Zeit," *De Stijl* 87–89 (1928), tr. in Baljeu, *Theo van Doesburg*, p. 175.

104. Van Doesburg, "Notices sur l'Aubette," p. 236.

105. Theo van Doesburg, "Schilderkunst en plastiek. Élémentarisme (Manifest-fragment)," *De Stijl* VII [78] (1926–1927), tr. in Baljeu, p. 164.

106. In addition to that cited in note 105, articles from which quotations are cited in the following discussion are: "Schilderkunst. Van komposititie tot contra-kompositie," *De Stijl* VII, 73–74 (1926), tr.

Conclusion

in Baljeu, pp. 151–156; ''Schilderkunst en plastiek. Over contra-compositie en contra-plastiek. Élémentarisme,'' *De Stijl* VII, 75–76 (1926), tr. in Baljeu, pp. 156–161.

107. Van Doesburg's remark to Oud in a letter of April 1921 (inv. no. 1972-A.541$^{(2)}$, IN, Paris) that Rosenberg's initial idea for his Private Villa lacked a music-dance room also gains significance in light of van Doesburg's Aubette designs.

108. Theo van Doesburg, ''Film als reine Gestaltung,'' *Die Form* 5 (1929): 214–248.

109. ''Ouverture de l'Aubette'' (clipping).

110. Théo Wolters, ''L'Aubette de Strasbourg (1928): Monument disparu d'art concret,'' *L'Information de l'Histoire de l'Art* 13 (1968): 144.

111. Edmée de Lillers states [''Histoire de l'Aubette,'' in *Theo van Doesburg: Projets pour l'Aubette* (Paris: Centre National d'Art et de Culture Georges Pompidou, Musée National d'Art Moderne, 1977), p. 9] that the café was not altered until 1938. Baljeu (p. 85) says that the changes were made shortly after World War II. Wolters (p. 144) suggests that its destruction was gradual, taking place over the decade following its completion.

112. Theo van Doesburg, letter to Adolf Behne, November 7, 1928, quoted in translation in Ulrich Conrads and Hans G. Sperlich, *The Architecture of Fantasy*, ed. George R. Collins (New York: Praeger, 1963), p. 155.

113. Franciscono has shown that the expressionist period was only an interlude, bracketed by the more rational work of Gropius before the war and after 1922. He also demonstrates that much of the expressionist output of the immediate postwar period was a direct result of the lack of funds and materials in Germany at that time.

114. Jürgen Joedicke and Christian Plath, English-language summary in *Die Weissenhofsiedlung* (Stuttgart: Karl Krämer, 1977), p. 76.

1. Lionel Feininger, letter to Julia Feininger, September 7, 1922, tr. Wolfgang Jabs and Basil Gilbert in Wingler, *Bauhaus*, p. 56.

2. Laszlo Moholy-Nagy, *Vision in Motion* (Chicago: Paul Theobald, 1947), p. 315.

3. Stephen Bann (ed.), *The Tradition of Constructivism* (New York: Viking, 1974), p. xxxvi.

4. See appendix A.

5. R. N. Shaw, ''The Home and its Dwelling Rooms,'' in *The British Home Today*, ed. W. Shaw (New York: A. C. Armstrong & Son, 1904), p. civ.

6. Burgoyne Diller, ''Abstract Murals,'' in *Art for the Millions: Essays from the 1930s by Artists and Administrators of the WPA Federal Art Project*, ed. Francis V. O'Connor (Boston: New York Graphic Society, 1975), p. 70.

7. See Nancy J. Troy, The Williamsburg Housing Project Murals and the Polemic of Abstraction in American Painting of the 1930s, M.A. thesis, Yale University, 1976.

8. Sidney Janis, ''School of Paris Comes to U.S.,'' *Decision* II, 5–6 (1941): 90.

9. Harriet Janis, ''Notes on Piet Mondrian,'' *Arts & Architecture* LXII, 1 (1945): 49.

Bibliography

Original editions of articles that have been reprinted or translated in books, catalogs, or anthologies are not cited separately.

References to the original edition of *De Stijl* are followed by references to volume and page numbers in the two-volume facsimile reprint (Amsterdam: Athenaeum and Polak & Van Gennep; The Hague: Bert Bakker, 1968).

Exhibition catalogs are listed under the names of the cities in which the exhibitions originated.

The bibliography is divided as follows:

I. General works, and publications on issues of international scope
II. The house, the interior, decoration, and color theory
III. Correspondences between the arts
IV. International Art Nouveau
V. The Netherlands
  A. The pre–De Stijl period
  B. Hendrik Petrus Berlage
  C. Dutch arts and architecture during the De Stijl period
  D. De Stijl
    1. Principal archival resources
    2. General works, and publications about more than one artist
    3. Theo van Doesburg
    4. Cesar Domela
    5. Cornelis van Eesteren
    6. Robert van 't Hoff
    7. Vilmos Huszar
    8. Bart van der Leck
    9. Piet Mondrian
    10. Jacobus Johannes Pieter Oud
    11. Gerrit Rietveld
    12. Georges Vantongerloo
    13. Jan Wils
  E. Piet Zwart

VI. Belgium
  A. General works
  B. Jozef Peeters
  C. Henry van de Velde

VII. France
  A. General works
  B. The Maison Cubiste
  C. Félix Del Marle
  D. Jean Gorin
  E. Le Corbusier
  F. Fernand Léger

VIII. Austria, Germany, and Switzerland
  A. General works
  B. The Bauhaus
  C. Walter Gropius
  D. Adolf Loos
  E. Sophie Taeuber-Arp

IX. Russia
  A. General works
  B. El Lissitzky

I. General works, and publications on issues of international scope

Baljeu, Joost. "The Problem of Reality with Suprematism, Constructivism, Proun, Neoplasticism, and Elementarism." *Lugano Review* 1 (1965): 105–124.

Banham, Reyner. *Theory and Design in the First Machine Age*, second edition. New York: Praeger, 1967.

Bann, Stephen, ed. *The Tradition of Constructivism*. New York: Viking, 1974.

Benevolo, Leonardo. *History of Modern Architecture*. Two volumes. Tr. H. J. Landry. Cambridge, Mass.: MIT Press, 1971.

Berlin: Lehrter Bahnhof. *Grosse Berliner Kunstausstellung*. May 19–September 17, 1923.

Berlin: Neue Nationalgalerie; Akademie der Kunste; Grosse Orangerie im Schloss Charlottenburg. *Tendenzen der Zwanziger Jahre*. 15. Europäische Kunstausstellung. August 14–October 16, 1977.

Birnholz, Alan C. Review of *Socialism, città, architettura URSS 1917–1937. Il contributo degli architetti europei* [Manfredo Tafuri, editor; Collana di Architettura, III. (Rome: Officina Edizioni, 1971)]. *Art Bulletin* 54 (1972): 368–369.

Bois, Yve-Alain. "Metamorphosis of Axonometry." *Daidalos* 1 (1981): 41–58.

Bragdon, Claude. *The Frozen Fountain: Being an Essay on Architecture and the Art of Design in Space*. New York: Knopf, 1932.

Brooklyn Museum. *International Exhibition of Modern Art Assembled by Société Anonyme*. November 19, 1926–January 1, 1927.

Cologne: Kunstverein. *Malewitsch—Mondrian und ihre Kreise: Aus der Sammlung Wilhelm Hack*. May 26–August 1, 1976.

Conrads, Ulrich, and Hans G. Sperlich. *The Architecture of Fantasy: Utopian Building and Planning in Modern Times*. Translated, edited, and expanded by Christine Craseman Collins and George R. Collins. New York: Praeger, 1962.

Dreier, Katherine, and Constantin Aladjalov. *Modern Art*. New York: Société Anonyme–Museum of Modern Art, 1926.

Frampton, Kenneth. *Modern Architecture: A Critical History*. London: Thames and Hudson, 1980.

Hanover: Kunstverein. *Malewitsch—Mondrian: Konstruktion als Konzept. Alexander Dorner Gewidmet*. March 27–May 1, 1977.

Harmsen, Ger. "Nederlandse en russische kunstenaars tijdens de revolutiejaren." *De Nieuwe stem* 22 (1967): 309–321.

Henderson, Linda Dalrymple. The Artist, "The Fourth Dimension," and Non-Euclidian Geometry 1900–1930: A Romance of Many Dimensions. Ph.D. diss., Yale University, 1975.

Herbert, Robert L., ed. *Modern Artists on Art: Ten Unabridged Essays*. Englewood Cliffs, N.J.: Prentice-Hall, 1964.

Herzogenrath, Wulf. *Oskar Schlemmer: Die Wandgestaltung der neuen Architektur*. Munich: Prestel, 1973.

Hitchcock, Henry-Russell, and Philip Johnson. *The International Style*. 1932. Revised edition: New York: Norton, 1966.

Lawder, Standish P. *The Cubist Cinema*. New York University Press, 1975.

Rischbieter, Henning. *Art and the Stage in the 20th Century: Painters and Sculptors Work for the Theater*. Tr. Michael Bullock. Greenwich, Conn.: New York Graphic Society, 1970.

Rotzler, Willy. *Constructive Concepts: A History of Constructive Art from Cubism to the Present*. Zurich: ABC Edition, 1977.

Zurich: Kunstgewerbemuseum. *Die Zwanziger Jahre: Konstraste eines Jahrzehnts*. May–September, 1973.

II. The house, the interior, decoration, and color theory

■ *226*

Aslin, Elizabeth. *The Aesthetic Movement: Prelude to Art Nouveau.* New York: Praeger, 1969.

Badovici, Jean. *La Maison d'aujourd'hui.* Paris: Albert Morancé, 1925.

Baillie Scott, M. H. "An Artist's House." *The Studio* 9 (1896–1897): 28–37.

Banham, Reyner. "Ateliers d'artistes." *Architectural Review* CXX, 715 (1956): 75–83.

Becker, Eugene Matthew. Whistler and the Aesthetic Movement. Ph.D. diss., Princeton University, 1959.

Bibb, Burnley, "Fritz Erler, I: Decorations for a Music-Room." *The Studio* XVII, 75 (1899): 25–32.

Celant, Germano. *Ambiente/Arte: Dal Futurismo alla Body Art.* Venice: Edizioni La Biennale di Venezia, 1977.

Celant, Germano. "Artspaces." *Studio International* CXC, 977 (1975): 115–123.

Clarijs, Petra. *Een eeuw Nederlandse woning.* Amsterdam: Querido, 1941.

Crane, Walter. *The Claims of Decorative Art.* London: Houghton, Mifflin, 1892. Dutch tr. Jan Veth, *Kunst en Samenleving* (Amsterdam: Scheltema & Holkema, 1894).

Farmer, Albert John. *Le Mouvement esthétique et décadent en Angleterre (1873–1900).* Paris: Champion, 1931.

Ferriday, Peter. "The Peacock Room." *Architectural Review* 125 (1959): 407–414.

Fischer, Aloys. "Das Musikzimmer." *Kunstgewerbeblatt* 22 (1911): 181–191.

Gibson, J. S. "Artistic House." *The Studio* 1 (1893). Reprinted in *The Birth of the Studio 1893–1895* (Woodbridge, Suffolk: Antique Collectors Club, 1976), pp. 38–49.

Girouard, Mark. "The Victorian Artist at Home, I: The Holland Park Houses; II: Chelsea's Bohemian Studio Houses." *Country Life* 152 (1972): 1278–1281, 1370–1374.

Girouard, Mark. *The Victorian Country House*, revised edition. New Haven: Yale University Press, 1979.

Godwin, Edward. "Painted Decorations: The Duty of the Painter in Relation to the Architect." *Building News* 15 (January 3, 1868): 6–8.

Günther, Sonja. *Interieurs um 1900: Bernhard Pankok, Bruno Paul und Richard Riemerschmid als Mitarbeiter Vereinigten Werkstätten für Kunst im Handwerk.* Munich: Wilhelm Fink, 1971.

Hanks, David A. *The Decorative Designs of Frank Lloyd Wright.* New York: Dutton, 1979.

Haweis, Mrs. H. R. *The Art of Decoration.* London: Chatto & Windus, 1881.

Haweis, Mrs. H. R. *Beautiful Houses: Being a Description of Certain Well-Known Artistic Houses.* London: S. Low, Marston, Searle & Rivington, 1882.

Kornwolf, James D. *M. H. Baillie Scott and the Arts and Crafts Movement.* Baltimore: Johns Hopkins University Press, 1972.

Kossatz, Horst-Herbert. "The Vienna Secession and its Early Relations with Great Britain." *Studio International* CLXXXI, 929 (1971): 9–20.

Masheck, Joseph. "The Carpet Paradigm: Critical Prolegomena to a Theory of Flatness." *Arts Magazine* LI, 1 (1976): 82–109.

Maus, Octave. "Propos sur l'art décoratif moderne." *L'Art Moderne* 30 (1910): 297–299.

Naylor, Gillian. *The Arts and Crafts Movement: A Study of its Sources, Ideals and Influence on Design Theory.* London: Studio Vista, 1971.

Ostwald, Wilhelm. *Die Farbenfibel.* Leipzig: Unesma, 1917.

Ostwald, Wilhelm. "Die Harmonie der Farben." 1919. Reprinted in *De Stijl* III, 7 (1920): 60–62 (I: 560–562).

Pennell, E. R., and J. Pennell. *The Life of James McNeill Whistler.* Two volumes. London: W. Heinemann, 1908.

Pennell, E. R., and J. Pennell. "Whistler as Decorator." 1912. Reprinted in E. R. Pennell and J. Pennell, *The Whistler Journal* (Philadelphia: Lippincott, 1921).

Rykwert, Joseph. "Ornament is No Crime." *Studio International* CXC, 977 (1975): 91–97.

Shaw, R. N. "The Home and its Dwelling Rooms." In *The British Home of To-day,* edited by W. Shaw Sparrow (New York: A. C. Armstrong & Son, 1904), pp. ci–cvi.

Sluys, Corn. van der. *Binnenhuiskunst: Over de ontwikkeling der vormen van meubels, metaalwerken, sierkunst, aardewerk, kunstnaaldwerk, weefsel, enz.* Two volumes. Amsterdam: Maatschappij voor goede en goedkoope lectuur, 1921.

Thompson, E. P. *William Morris: Romantic to Revolutionary.* London: Merlin, 1955.

Venice: Biennale d'Arte, Section of Visual Arts and Architecture. *Ambient/Art.* General Catalogue, volume I. 1976.

Watson, Rosamund Marriott. *The Art of the House.* London and New York: George Bell & Sons, 1897.

Bowlt, John E. "The Spirit of Music." In *The Isms of Art in Russia 1907–30* (Cologne: Galerie Gmurzynska, 1977) pp. 5–17.

Dresden, Sem. "Muziek—een bouwkunst." In *Nederlandsche ambachts- en nijverheidskunst jaarboek* (Rotterdam: W. L. & J. Brusse, 1920), pp. 14–27.

Greer, Thomas Harry, Music and its Relation to Futurism, Cubism, Dadaism and Surrealism 1905–1950. Ph.D. diss., North Texas State University, 1969.

Hoeber, Fritz. "Das Musikalische in der Architektur." *Der Sturm* 4 (1913): 108, 110.

Karsten, C. J. F. "Integratie of synthese van de architectuur en beeldende kunst." *Bouwkundig Weekblad* 75 (1957):549–552.

Lockspeiser, Edward. *Music and Painting: A Study in Comparative Ideas from Turner to Schoenberg.* New York: Icon Editions, Harper & Row, 1973.

Meyer, Leonard. *Music, The Arts, and Ideas: Patterns and Predictions in Twentieth-Century Culture.* University of Chicago Press, 1967.

Rimington, A. Wallace. *Colour-Music: The Art of Mobile Colour.* New York: Frederick A. Stokes, 1912.

Stahley, Allen. "The Condition of Music." *The Academy. Art News Annual* 33 (1967): 81–87.

Billcliffe, Roger. *Charles Rennie Mackintosh: The Complete Furniture, Furniture Drawings & Interior Designs.* New York: Taplinger, 1979.

Bing, S. "L'Art Nouveau." Tr. Irene Sargent. 1903. Reprinted in *Artistic America, Tiffany Glass, and Art Noveau,* edited by Robert Koch (Cambridge, Mass.: MIT Press, 1970), pp. 237–246.

Champier, Victor. "Les Expositions de l'"Art Nouveau.' " *Revue des Arts Décoratifs* 16 (1896):1–6.

Darmstadt: Mathildenhöhe. *Darmstadt: Ein Dokument deutscher Kunst 1901–1976.* October 22, 1976–January 30, 1977.

Fred, W. "The Artist's Colony at Darmstadt." *The Studio* 24 (1901): 22–30.

Howarth, Thomas. *Charles Rennie Mackintosh and the Modern Movement.* New York: George Wittenborn, 1953.

Jacobus, John. Review of Stephan Tschudi Madsen, *Sources of Art Nouveau,* tr. Ragnar Christophersen [Oslo: H. Aschehoug & Co. (W. Nygaard), 1956]. *Art Bulletin* 40 (1958): 364–373.

Jullian, Phillipe. *The Triumph of Art Nouveau: Paris Exhibition 1900.* Tr. Stephen Hardman. New York: Larousse, 1974.

■ *228*

Koch, Robert. "Art Noveau Bing." *Gazette des Beaux-Arts* 53 (1959): 179–190.

Mourey, Gabriel. "Round the Exhibition I: The House of the 'Art Nouveau Bing.'" *The Studio* 20 (1900): 164–180.

Mourey, Gabriel. "Studio Talk: Paris." *The Studio* 7 (1896): 51–52.

Schmutzler, Robert. *Art Nouveau.* Tr. Edouard Roditi. New York: Harry N. Abrams, 1964.

Schmutzler, Robert. "The English Origins of Art Nouveau." *Architectural Review* CXVII, 698 (1955): 108–117.

A. The pre–De Stijl period

Amsterdam: Architectuur Museum. *Architectura 1893–1918.* September 6–November 16, 1975.

"Belangrijke onderwerpen: Arts and Crafts." *De Hollandsche Revue* (1902): 210–214. [Clipping in Gemeenetearchief, The Hague.]

Blijstra, Reinder. "Art Nouveau in 's-Gravenhage." *Maandblad der Gemeente 's-Gravenhage* XX, 12 (special number) (1967).

Gans, L. *Nieuwe Kunst: De Nederlandse bijdrage tot de "Art Nouveau."* Utrecht: Libertas, 1960.

The Hague: Gemeentemuseum. *Licht door kleur: Nederlandse luministen.* December 18, 1976–February 27, 1977.

Hoff, August. *Johann Thorn Prikker.* Recklinghausen: Aurel Bongers, 1958.

Joosten, Joop. "Documentatie: Thorn Prikker." *Museumjournaal* 11 (1966): 236–242.

Kalf, Jan. "Het Binnenhuis." *De Kroniek* 6 (1900): 309–310.

"Kijkjes in het atelier voor dekoratieve kunst 'Het Huis.' " *Het Huis Oud & Nieuw* 3 (1905): 161–175.

Loosjes-Terpstra, A. B. *Moderne kunst in Nederland 1900–1914.* Utrecht: Haentjens Dekker & Gumbert, 1959.

Simons, L. " 't Binnenhuis." 1915. Reprinted in *Moderne Hollandsche interieurs, 3e aflevering: 't Binnenhuis* (Bussum: Het Hollandsche Interieur, 1918).

Veldheer, J. G. "Das Neue Künstlerhaus genannt 'Het Binnenhuis' (Das Hausinnere) in Amsterdam." *Dekorative Kunst* 4 (1900): 197–203.

Vogelsang, W. "Hollandsche Gebruikskunst: 't Binnenhuis, de Woning, Arts and Crafts." *Onze Kunst* 3 (1903): 19–32.

Wember, Paul. *Johann Thorn Prikker: Glasfenster, Wandbilder, Ornamente 1891–1932.* Krefeld: Scherpe, 1966.

B. Hendrik Petrus Berlage

Berlage, Hendrik Petrus. *Gedanken über Stil in der Baukunst.* Leipzig: J. Zeitler, 1905.

Berlage, Hendrik Petrus. *Grundlagen und Entwicklung der Architektur.* Berlin: J. Bard, 1908.

Berlage, Hendrik Petrus. *Over Stijl in bouw- en meubelkunst,* second edition. Rotterdam: W. L. & J. Brusse, 1908.

Berlage, Hendrik Petrus. *Studies over bouwkunst, stijl en samenleving.* Rotterdam: W. L. & J. Brusse, 1910.

Boot, Marjan. "Carel Henny en zijn huis: Een Demonstratie van 'goed wonen' rond de eeuwwisseling." *Nederlands Kunsthistorisch Jaarboek* 25 (1974): 91–131.

The Hague: Gemeentemuseum. *H. P. Berlage, bouwmeester 1856–1934*. August 30–November 16, 1975.

Singelenberg, Pieter. *H. P. Berlage: Idea and Style, The Quest for Modern Architecture*. Utrecht: Haentjens Dekker & Gumbert, 1972.

C. Dutch arts and architecture during the De Stijl period

Amsterdam: Stedelijk Museum. *Amsterdamse School 1910–1930*. September 13–November 9, 1975.

Behne, Adolf. "Holländsche Baukunst in der Gegenwart." *Wasmuth's Monatshefte für Baukunst* 6 (1921–22): 1–37.

Casciato, Maristella, Franco Panzini, and Sergio Polano, eds. *Olanda 1870–1940: Città, casa, architettura*. Milan: Electa, 1980.

Eindhoven: Stedelijk Van Abbemuseum. *Bouwen '20–'40: De Nederlandse bijdrage aan het Nieuwe Bouwen*. September 17–November 7, 1971.

Fanelli, Giovanni. *Architettura edilizia urbanistica Olanda 1917–1940*. Florence: Francesco Papafava, 1978.

Fanelli, Giovanni. *Architettura moderna in Olanda: 1900–1940*. Florence: Marchi & Bertolli, 1968. Translated and updated as *Moderne architectuur in Nederland 1900–1940*, edited by Wim de Wit (Cahiers van het Nederlands Documentatiecentrum voor de Bouwkunst, II; The Hague: Staatsuitgeverij, 1978).

Gouwe. W. F. *Glas in lood*. Rotterdam: W. L. & J. Brusse, 1932.

Gouwe, W. F., ed. *Ruimte, Werk, Vorm*. Jaarboeken van Nederlandsche Ambachts- en Nijverheidskunst 9–11, 1929–1931.

Grinberg, Donald I. *Housing in the Netherlands 1900–1940*. Delft University Press, 1977.

The Hague: Haagse Kunstkring. *Wandschildering tentoonstelling*. October 15–November 13, 1921.

The Hague: Pulchri Studio. *Haagse Kunstkring: Werk verzameld*. 1977.

Hoogendoorn, Matsya. "Nederlanders in Parijs." *Museumjournaal* 17 (1972): 247–253.

Jong, Jo de. *De Nieuwe richting in de kunstnijverheid in Nederland: Schets eener geschiedenis der Nederlandsche kunstnijverheidsbeweging*. Rotterdam: W. L. & J. Brusse, 1929.

Kromhout, W[illem]. "Interieur-kunst op den Haagse Kunstkring." *Architectura* 15 (1907): 305–309.

Luns, Frank. "Toneel- en nijverheidskunst." *Nederlandsche Ambachts- en Nijverheidskunst Jaarboek*. Rotterdam: W. L. & J. Brusse, 1920.

Oorthuys, Gerrit. "Architetti olandesi e avanguardie russe 1919–1934." In *Socialismo, città, architettura URSS 1917–1937. Il contributo degli architetti europei*, edited by Manfredo Tafuri (Collana di architettura, III; Rome: Officina, 1971), pp. 311–321.

Otterlo: Rijksmuseum Kröller-Müller. *Americana: Nederlandse architectuur, 1880–1930*. August 24–October 26, 1975.

Redeker, Hans. *Willem van Leusden*. Utrecht and Antwerp: Spectrum, 1974.

Schippers, K. *Holland Dada*. Amsterdam: Querido, 1974.

Utrecht: Centraal Museum. *Het Nieuwe wereldbeeld: Het Begin van de abstrakte kunst in Nederland 1910–1925*. January 19–February 28, 1973.

D. De Stijl

1. Principal archival resources

Dienst Verspreide Rijkskollekties (Van Doesburg Archive), The Hague.

Fondation Custodia, Institut Néerlandais, Paris.

Gemeentemuseum (Documentation Archive), The Hague.

Nederlands Documentatiecentrum voor de Bouwkunst, Amsterdam.

Rijksbureau voor Kunsthistorische Documentatie, The Hague.

Stedelijk Museum (Department of Applied Arts), Amsterdam.

2. General works, and publications about more than one artist

Amsterdam: Stedelijk Museum. *De Stijl*. July 6–September 25, 1951.

Badovici, Jean. "Entretiens sur l'architecture vivante: A propos d'une Exposition." *L'Architecture Vivante* (spring and summer 1924): 32–33.

Beckett, Jane. " 'De Vonk,' Noordwijk: An Example of Early De Stijl Cooperation." *Art History* 3 (1980): 202–217.

Blotkamp, Carel, et al. *De Beginjaren van De Stijl 1917–1922*. Utrecht: Reflex, 1982.

Brown, Theodore M. "Mondrian and Rietveld: The Divining Rod and the Compass." *Nederlands Kunsthistorisch Jaarboek* 19 (1968): 205–214.

Cimaise XVII, 99 [special De Stijl number] (1970).

Cologne: Galerie Gmurzynska. *De Stijl, Cercle et Carré: Entwicklungen des Konstruktivismus in Europa ab 1917*. March–May, 1974.

Friedman, Mildred, ed. *De Stijl: 1917–1931. Visions of Utopia*. New York: Abbeville, 1982.

Goudsmit, Sam. "Vier schilders van het vlak." *Groot Nederland* 25 (1927): 182–189.

Internationale Revue i10. 1927–1929. Reprinted: Nendeln-Liechtenstein: Kraus, 1979.

Jaffé, Hans L. C. "The Diagonal Principle in the Works of Van Doesburg and Mondrian." *The Structurist* 9 (1969): 15–21.

Jaffé, Hans L. C. "Die niederländische Stijl-Gruppe und ihre soziale Utopie." In *Stil und Überlieferung in der Kunst des Abendlandes* (Berlin: Gebr. Mann, 1977), pp. 46–52.

Jaffé, Hans L. C., ed. *De Stijl*. Tr. R. R. Symonds and Mary Whitall. London: Thames and Hudson, 1970.

Jaffé, Hans L. C. "The De Stijl Concept of Space." *The Structurist* 8 (1968): 8–11.

Jaffé, Hans. L. C. *De Stijl, 1917–1931: The Dutch Contribution to Modern Art*. Amsterdam: J. M. Meulenhoff, 1956.

Jongh, Ankie de. "De Stijl." *Museumjournaal* 17 (1972): 262–282.

Kahn, Gustave. "L'Exposition de l'Amicale de l'École Spéciale d'Architecture." *Le Quotidien*, April 18, 1924. [Clipping in Van Doesburg Archive, Dienst Verspreide Rijkskollekties, The Hague.]

Maarssen: Gemeentelijk Administratiekantoor. *Willem van Leusden—Gerrit Rietveld*. May 2–14, 1977.

Merz 1 ["Holland Dada" number] (1923).

"Naar een nieuwen bouwstijl." *Nieuwe Rotterdamsche Courant*, March 28, 1924, Avondblad B: 1.

Naylor, Gillian. "De Stijl: Abstraction or Architecture." *Studio International* CXC, 977 (1976): 98–102.

"Nederlandse architecten te Parijs." *De Telegraaf*, November 15, 1923. [Clipping, courtesy Joop Joosten, Stedelijk Museum, Amsterdam.]

Overy, Paul. *De Stijl*. New York: Dutton, 1969.

"Op de tentoonstelling van moderne architectuur te Parijs. . . ." *Nieuwe Rotterdamsche Courant*, March 17, 1924, Avondblad C: 2.

De Stijl, I–VIII and "Dernier numéro." 1917–1928, 1932. Reprinted: Amsterdam: Athenaeum and Polak & Van Gennep; The Hague: Bert Bakker, 1968.

"De Stijl 1917–1928." *Museum of Modern Art Bulletin* XX, 2 (1952–1953).

Sujo Volsby, Glenn R. New Approaches to Environmental Design: Piet Mondrian—Theo van Doesburg. M.A. report, Courtauld Institute of Art, University of London, 1976.

Veissière, Gabriel. "Les Architectes du groupe 'Styl.' " *L'Architecture* 34 (1923): 370.

Venema, Adriaan. *Nederlandse schilders in Parijs 1900–1940*. Baarn: Wereldvenster, 1980.

Vouloir 25 [special "Ambiance" number] (1927).

Weaver, Mike, ed. "Great Little Magazines, No. 6: 'De Stijl.' " *Form* 6 (1967), 29–32; 7 (1968): 25–32.

Weyergraf, Clara. *Piet Mondrian und Theo van Doesburg: Deutung von Werk und Theorie*. Munich: Wilhelm Fink, 1979.

Wijk, Kees van. *Internationale Revue i10*. Utrecht: Reflex, 1980.

Zevi, Bruno. *Poetica dell'architettura neoplastica*. Milan: Politecnica Tamburini, 1953.

3. *Theo van Doesburg*

Badovici, Jean. "Entretiens sur l'architecture vivante: La Couleur dans la nouvelle architecture." *L'Architecture Vivante* (spring and summer 1924): 17–18.

Baljeu, Joost. "The Fourth Dimension in Neoplasticism." *Form* 9 (1969): 6–14.

Baljeu, Joost. *Theo van Doesburg*. New York: Macmillan, 1974.

Baljeu, Joost. "Theo van Doesburg en de oprichting van De Stijl." *Coubouw* June 16, 1967. [Clipping in Rijksbureau voor Kunsthistorische Documentatie, The Hague.]

Beckett, Jane. "Van Doesburg and *De Stijl*." In *Dada: Studies of a Movement*, edited by Richard Sheppard (Chalfont St. Giles, Buckinghamshire: Alpha Academic, 1980), pp. 1–25.

Blok, Cor. "Theo van Doesburg." *Art International* XIII, 4 (1969): 21–23.

Blotkamp, Carel. "Nelly van Doesburg: 'De Sikkenprijs komt veertig jaar te laat.' " *Vrij Nederland* XXIX, 14 (1968): 11.

Bonset, I. K. *Nieuwe Woordbeeldingen: De Gedichten van Theo van Doesburg*. Amsterdam: Querido, 1975.

Deshairs, Léon. "Une villa moderne á Hyères." *Art et Décoration* 54 (1928): 1–24.

Doesburg, Theo van. "Aanteekening over de nieuwe muziek." *De Stijl* III, 1 (1919): 5–8 (I: 467–470).

Doesburg, Theo van. "Architectuurvernieuwingen in het buitenland: De ombeelding van de Aubette in Straatsburg." *Bouwbedrijf* 6 (1929): 116–122.

Doesburg, Theo van. "De Beelding van het interieur," *Binnenhuis* 10 (1928): 279–283, 345–351; 11 (1929): 29–31, 39–42, 54–56, 67–70, 111–114,
145–148, 181–184, 205–208, 241–243; 12 (1930): 97–101, 157–161, 181–184.

Doesburg, Theo van. "Data en feiten (betreffende de invloedsontwikkeling van 'DE STIJL' in 't buitenland) die voor zich spreken." *De Stijl* VII, 79–84 (1927): 53–74 (II: 555–564).

Doesburg, Theo van. *Drie voordrachten over de nieuwe beeldende kunst: Haar ontwikkeling, aesthetisch beginsel en toekomstigen stijl*. Amsterdam: Maatschappij voor Goede en Goedkoope Lectuur, 1919.

Doesburg, Theo van. "L'Evolution de l'architecture moderne en Hollande." *L'Architecture Vivante* (autumn and winter 1925): 14–20.

Doesburg, Theo van. "Film as Pure Form." 1929. Tr. Standish D. Lawder, *Form*, 1 (1966): 5–11.

Doesburg, Theo van. *Grundbegriffe der neuen gestaltenden Kunst*. 1925. Reprint: Mainz: Florian Kupferberg, 1966.

Doesburg, Theo van. "Interieurbeelding." *Binnenhuis* 12 (1930): 287–290.

Doesburg, Theo van. "De invloed van de Stijlbeweging in Duitsland." *Bouwkundig Weekblad* 44 (1923): 80–83.

Doesburg, Theo van. *Klassiek–Barok–Modern*. Antwerp: De Sikkel, 1920.

Doesburg, Theo van. "Lijstenaesthetiek." *De Stijl* III, 11 (1920): 92–95 (I: 614–617).

Doesburg, Theo van. "Moderne tuinplastiek (bloemenvaas)." *Bouwkundig Weekblad* 40 (1919): 313.

Doesburg, Theo van. "Die neue Architektur und ihre Folgen." *Wasmuths Monatscheft für Baukunst* 9 (1925): 502–518.

Doesburg, Theo van. "De Nieuwe architectuur." *Bouwkundig Weekblad* 45 (1924): 200–204.

Doesburg, Theo van. *De Nieuwe beweging in de schilderkunst.* Delft: Technische Boekhandel en Drukkerij, 1917.

Doesburg, Theo van. "De Onafhankelijken (Indrukken van een bezoeker)." *De Eenheid* 318 (1916).

Doesburg, Theo van. "Réponse à notre enquête: 'Où va la peinture moderne?'" *Bulletin de l'Effort Moderne* 3 (1924): 7–8.

Doesburg, Theo van. "Ruimte-plastische binnenarchitectuur." *De Stijl* I, 6 (1918): 71–72 (I: 107–108).

Doesburg, Theo van. "De Taak der nieuwe architectuur." *Bouwkundig Weekblad* 41 (1920): 278–280, 281–285; 42 (1921): 8–10.

Doesburg, Theo van. "Vers un art élémentaire." *Vouloir* 19 (1926).

Doesburg, Theo van. *Wat is Dada?* 1923. Reprinted: Leeuwarden: N. Miedema, 1971.

Eindhoven: Stedelijk Van Abbemuseum. *Theo van Doesburg 1881–1931.* December 13, 1968–January 26, 1969.

Elzas, A. "Theo van Doesburg." *De 8 en Opbouw* 6 (1935): 174–182.

Faure, Jean-Louis. "L'Aubette et ses créateurs." *Plaisir de France* XXXVIII, 394 (1971): 22–27.

Franeker: 't Coopmanshuis. *Dada in Drachten.* November 20, 1971–January 2, 1972.

Gerstner, J. "Die Aubette als Beispiel integrierter Kunst." *Werk* 47 (1960): 375–380.

Henkels, Herbert. "Theo van Doesburg en het masker van de dogmatische profeet." *Haagse Post*, April 12, 1974: 44–47. [Clipping in Rijksbureau voor Kunsthistorische Documentatie, The Hague.]

Leering, Jean. "Van Doesburg: Stijl and All." *Art News* LXVIII, 1 (1969): 38–41, 57.

Leeuwarden: Fries Museum. *Thijs Rinsema 1877–1947.* 1980.

"Lijsten-Aesthetiek." *De Hollandsche Revue* 25 (1920): 625–628.

L[otz], W. "Die Aubette in Strassburg." *Die Form* 4 (1929): 44–48.

Lotz, W. "Theo van Doesburg anno 1968." *Museumjournaal* 13 (1968): 291–297.

Martin, H. "De Middenstandswoningen." *Dragster Courant*, October 11, 1921. [Photocopy in Museum It Bleekerhûs, Drachten.]

Martin, H. "Moderne kunst." *Dragster Courant*, October 21, October 28, November 4, November 11, 1921. [Photocopies in Museum It Bleekerhûs, Drachten.]

Oud, J. J. P. "Glas-in-lood van Theo van Doesburg." *Bouwkundig Weekblad* 39 (1918): 199–202.

"Ouverture de l'Aubette." [Clipping in Van Doesburg Archive, Dienst Verspreide Rijkskollekties, The Hague.]

Paris: Centre National d'Art et de Culture Georges Pompidou. Musée National d'Art Moderne. *Théo van Doesburg: Projets pour L'Aubette.* October 12–December 12, 1977.

Polano, Sergio, ed. *Theo van Doesburg: Scritti di arte di architettura.* Rome: Officina, 1979.

Prisma der Kunsten 1 [special van Doesburg number] (1936).

Schippers, H. K. "Theo van Doesburg en Kurt Schwitters." *De Strikel* 6 (1963): 162–166.

Schwitters, Kurt. "Theo van Doesburg and Dada." 1932. Translated in *Dada Painters and Poets*, edited by Robert Motherwell (New York: Wittenborn, Schultz, 1951), pp. 275–276.

Seuphor, Michel. "L'Aubette de Strasbourg." *Art d'Aujourd'hui* IV, 8 (1953): 10–13.

Shand, P. Morton. "An Essay in the Adroit: At the Villa of the Vicomte de Noailles." *Architectural Review* 45 (1929): 174–176.

Trotwaer 9–10 [Special "Dada in Drachten" number] (1971).

Troy, Nancy J. "Theo van Doesburg: From Music into Space." *Arts Magazine* LVI, 6 (1982): 92–101.

Welsh, Robert. "Theo van Doesburg and Geometric Abstraction." In *Nijhoff, Van Ostaijen, "De Stijl": Modernism in the Netherlands and Belgium in the First Quarter of the 20th Century*, edited by Francis Bulhof (The Hague: Martinus Nijhoff, 1976), pp. 76–94.

Wils, Jan. "In Memoriam Theo van Doesburg." *Bouwbedrijf* 8 (1931): 105.

Wolters, Théo. "L'Aubette de Strasbourg (1928): Monument disparu d'Art Concret." *L'Information d'Histoire de l'Art* 13 (1968): 143–149.

4. Cesar Domela

Clairet, Alain. *Domela*. Paris: Galerie Marguerite Lami, n.d.

Clairet, Alain. *Domela: Catalogue raisonné de l'oeuvre de César Domela-Nieuwenhuis (peintures, reliefs, sculptures)*. Paris: Carmen Martinez, 1978.

Dusseldorf: Kunstverein für die Rheinlande und Westfalen. *Cesar Domela: Werke 1922–1972*. October 12–December 3, 1972.

Garrel, Betty van. "Cesar Domela, de laatste overlevende van de Stijl-groep: 'Kunst is artistocratisch.' " *Haagse Post*, April 21, 1973: 57–58. [Clipping in Rijksbureau voor Kunsthistorische Documentatie, The Hague.]

The Hague: Gemeentemuseum. *Domela: Schilderijen, reliëfs, beelden, grafiek, typographie, foto's*. September 6–October 26, 1980.

5. Cornelis van Eesteren

Blijstra, Reinder. *C. van Eesteren*. Tr. Roy Edwards. Amsterdam: Meulenhoff, 1971.

Jaffé, Hans L. C. "Prof. C. van Eesteren 4 juli 70 jaar." *Bouwkundig Weekblad* 85 (1967): 213–219. Abridged and translated: *Architectural Design* 37 (1967): 514.

6. Robert van 't Hoff

Eindhoven: Stedelijk Van Abbemuseum. *Van 't Hoff*. March 17–April 23, 1967.

Jonker, Gert. "Een Poging tot reconstructie: De Werken van R. van 't Hoff." *Bouw* 13 (1979): 17–23.

Jonker, Gert. "Robert van 't Hoff maker van het kleinst denkbare oeuvre." *Bouw* 12 (1979): 6–8.

Tummers, Nicolaas H. A. "Rob van 't Hoff en het werk van Wright." *Cobouw* June 16, 1967: 25. [Clipping in Rijksbureau voor Kunsthistorische Documentatie, The Hague.]

7. Vilmos Huszar

Badovici, Jean. "Entretiens sur l'architecture vivante: Intérieur par V. Huszar." *L'Architecture Vivante* (autumn and winter 1924): 14–15.

Brouwer, Willem C. "Een Praatje naar aanleiding van de 'Aesthetische Beschouwingen door V. Huszar.' " *Levende Kunst* 1 (1918): 102–104.

Bruynzeel's fabrieken, Zaandam: Gedenkboek. Privately printed, n.d. [1931].

Doesburg, Theo van. "Huszar's beeldend tooneel." *Het Vaderland*, February 23, 1923: 2. [Clipping in Rijksbureau voor Kunsthistorische Documentatie, The Hague.]

Ex, Sjarel. "Vilmos Huszar en de toegepaste kunsten." *Bijvoorbeeld* XIII, 4 (1981): 29–32.

Huszar, Vilmos. "Aesthetische beschouwingen." *De Stijl* I, 2 (1917): 20–23 (I: 29–35); I, [3] (1918): 33–35 (I: 49–53); I, 5 (1918): 54–57 (I: 82–87); I, 7 (1918): 79–84 (I: 121–126); I, 12 (1918): 147–150 (I: 219–222); II, 1 (1918): 7–10 (I: 241–244); II, 3 (1919): 27–31 (I: 273–279).

Huszar, Vilmos. "Beschouwingen over kunst." *Blad Voor Kunst*, March, 1922. [Clipping in Rijksbureau voor Kunsthistorische Documentatie, The Hague.]

Huszar, Vilmos. "Over de moderne toegepaste kunsten." *Bouwkundig Weekblad* 43 (1922): 59–63, 72–77.

Huszar, Vilmos. "Over de organisatie in de ambachts-kunst." *Bouwkundig Weekblad* 41 (1920): 182–184.

Huszar, Vilmos. "Ruimte-kleur-compositie voor een eetkamer." *De Stijl* V, 1 (1922): 7–8 (II: 162).

Huszar, Vilmos. "Das Staatliche Bauhaus in Weimar." *De Stijl* V, 9 (1922): 135–138 (II: 266–267).

Huszar, Vilmos. "Le Théâtre plastique mécanique olandese." *Noi* II serie, anno 1, 6–9 (1924), 19, 43.

"Op twintig minuten lopen. . . ." *Provinciale Overijsselsche Courant*, February 18, 1955. [Clipping in Rijksbureau voor Kunsthistorische Documentatie, The Hague.]

Oven, Ro van. "Moderne glasschilderkunst in Holland. I: Vilmos Huszar." *Levende Kunst* 2 (1919): 48–57.

Scheffer, H. J. *Portret van een fotograaf: Henri Berssenbrugge, 1873–1959.* Leiden: A. W. Sijthoff, 1967.

Tussenbroek, Otto van. *Speelgoed, marionetten, maskers en schimmenspelen.* Rotterdam: W. J. & J. Brusse, 1925.

V., H. "V. Huszar bij d'Autretsch, Den Haag." *Elsevier's Geïllustreerd Maandschrift* 58 (1919): 67.

W., L. "De Tooneelmaand: V. Huszar." *Het Vaderland*, February 17, 1923: 3. [Clipping in Rijksbureau voor Kunsthistorische Documentatie, The Hague.]

8. Bart van der Leck

Amsterdam: Stedelijk Museum. *Bart van der Leck.* March 9–April 6, 1959.

Amsterdam: Stedelijk Museum. *Overzicht van het levenswerk van Bart van der Leck.* February 11–April 4, 1949.

Deventer, S. van. *Kröller-Müller: De Geschiedenis van een cultureel levenswerk.* Haarlem: Tjeenk Willink, 1956.

Feltkamp, W. C. B. A. *van der Leck: Leven en werken.* Leiden: Spruyt, Van Mantem & De Does, 1956.

Gans, L. "Bart van der Lecks beelding in ruimtelijke vlakheid." *Museumjournaal* 5 (1960): 168–174.

Joosten, Ellen. *The Kröller-Müller Museum.* New York: Shorewood, 1965.

Leck, Bart van der. "Klaarhamer's meubelen." *Onze Kunst* 3 (1904): 73–78.

Otterlo: Rijksmuseum Kröller-Müller. *Bart van der Leck, 1876–1958.* July 18–September 5, 1976.

Oxenaar, Rudolf Willem Daan. Bart van der Leck tot 1920: Een Primitief van de nieuwe tijd. Ph.D. diss., Rijksuniversiteit te Utrecht, 1976.

Oxenaar, Rudolf Willem Daan. "The Birth of De Stijl, Part Two: Bart van der Leck." *Artforum* XI, 10 (1973): 36–43.

Paris: Institut Néerlandais. *Bart van der Leck 1876–1958: A la recherche de l'image des temps modernes.* February 7–March 23, 1980.

Seuphor, Michel. "Le Peintre Bart van der Leck." *Werk* 38 (1951): 357–360.

Veth, C. "Werken van Van der Leck bij Walrecht, Den Haag." *Elsevier's Geïllustreerd Maandschrift* 46 (1913): 319–320.

9. Piet Mondrian

Amersfoort: Zonnehof. *Piet Mondriaan: Een Documentatie.* March 9–May 13, 1973.

Amsterdam: Stedelijk Museum. *Piet Mondriaan herdenkingstentoonstelling.* November–December, 1946.

Banham, Reyner. "Mondrian and the Philosophy of Modern Design." *Architectural Review* 122 (1957): 227–229.

Bendien, Jacob. "Piet Mondriaan zestig jaar." In Paul Citroen, *Jacob Bendien 1890–1933: Een Herinneringsboek* (Rotterdam: W. L. & J. Brusse, 1940), pp. 73–80.

"Een Bezoek bij Piet Mondriaan." *Het Vaderland*, July 9, 1920. [Clipping in Documentation Archive, Gemeentemuseum, The Hague.]

"Bij Piet Mondriaan." *Nieuwe Rotterdamse Courant*, March 23, 1922. [Clipping in Rijksbureau voor Kunsthistorische Documentatie, The Hague.]

"Bij Piet Mondriaan." *De Telegraaf*, September 12, 1926. [Clipping in Documentation Archive, Gemeentemuseum, The Hague.]

"Bij Piet Mondriaan." *Het Vaderland*, June 15, 1935. [Clipping, courtesy Joop Joosten, Stedelijk Museum, Amsterdam.]

Blok, Cor. *Piet Mondriaan: Een Catalogus van zijn werk in Nederlands openbaar bezit.* Amsterdam: Meulenhoff, 1974.

Blotkamp, Carel. "Mondriaan als literator." *Maatstaf* XXVI, 4 (1978): 1–23.

Blotkamp, Carel. "Mondriaan—Architectuur." *Wonen TABK* 4–5 (1982): 12–51.

Boime, Albert, "A Visit to Mondrianland: 'Salon de Madame B. . . , à Dresden' at the Pace Gallery." *Arts Magazine* XLIV, 8 (1970): 28–30.

Bois, Yve-Alain. "Mondrian et la théorie de l'architecture." *Revue de l'Art* 53 (1981): 39–52.

C., J. "Mondrian, Créateur de l'ambiance moderne." *Demain* II, 66 (1957): 16.

Domselaer-Middelkoop, M. van. "Herinneringen aan Piet Mondriaan." *Maatstaf* 7 (1959): 269–293.

Geest, Jan van. "Schilder Wim Schumacher over kunst en liefde." *Vrij Nederland* XXXVI, 2 (1975): 22.

Grohmann, Will. "Dresdener Ausstellungen: Kühl & Kühn, P. Mondrian, Man Ray." *Der Cicerone* 17 (1925): 1007–1008.

Grohmann, Will. *Die Sammlung Ida Bienert, Dresden.* Potsdam: Müller & I. Kiepenheuer, 1933.

The Hague: Gemeentemuseum. *Mondriaan in de collectie van het Haags Gemeentemuseum.* 1968.

Harrison, Charles, et al. "Mondrian in London." *Studio International* CLXXII, 884 (1966): 285–292.

Henkels, Herbert, ed. *Seuphor.* The Hague: Gemeentemuseum; Antwerp: Mercator Fonds, 1976.

Joosten, Joop P. "Abstraction and Compositional Innovation." *Artforum* XI, 8 (1973): 55–59.

Joosten, Joop P. "Grenzen van Mondriaan." *Openbaar Kunstbezit* (1977): 182–188.

L., H. v. "Parijsche Brief: Piet Mondriaan." *Hollandsch Weekblad* V, 35 (1937): 17–22.

Lampe, G. G. "Piet Mondriaan: Schilderen met de ruimte." *Vrij Nederland*, February 26, 1955. [Clipping in Rijksbureau voor Kunsthistorische Documentatie, The Hague.]

Löffler, Fritz. "Ida Bienert und ihre Sammlung." *Literatur und Kunst der Gegenwart*, Jahresring 71–72 (1971): 187–198. [Photocopy courtesy of Fritz Löffler, Dresden.]

London, Marlborough Fine Art Ltd. *Art in Britain 1930–40 centered around Axis, Circle, Unit One.* March–April, 1965.

Loon, H. van. "Mondriaan, de mensch, de kunstenaar." *Maandblad voor Beeldende Kunsten*, 4 (1927): 195–199.

Loon, Maud van. "Mondriaan zooals hij leefde te Parijs." *De Groene*, December 7, 1946. [Clipping, courtesy Joop Joosten, Stedelijk Museum, Amsterdam.]

Mondrian, Piet. "L'Architecture future Néo-Plasticienne." *L'Architecture Vivante* (autumn and winter 1925): 11–13.

■ 236

Mondrian, Piet. "*Art* puréte + abstraction." *Vouloir* 19 (1926).

Mondrian, Piet. "Les Arts et la beauté de notre ambiance tangible." *Manomètre* 6 (1924): 107–108.

Mondrian, Piet. "De Jazz en de Neo-Plastiek." *i10* 1 (1927): 421–427.

Mondrian, Piet. "Moet de schilderkunst minderwaardig zijn aan de bouwkunst?" *De Stijl* VI, 5 (1923): 62–74 (II: 375–376).

Mondrian, Piet. *Le Néo-Plasticisme: Principe général de l'équivalence plastique.* Paris: Editions de l'Effort Moderne, 1920.

Mondrian, Piet. "Le Néo-Plasticisme, sa réalization dans la musique et le théâtre future." *La Vie des Lettres et des Arts* (1922).

"Het Neo-Plasticisme in schilderkunst, bouwkunst, muziek, litteratuur." *Het Vaderland*, October 17, 1924. [Clipping in Rijksbureau voor Kunsthistorische Documentatie, The Hague.]

New York: Museum of Modern Art. *A. Kertesz, Photographer.* 1964.

New York: Pace Gallery. *Mondrian: The Process Works.* April 11–May 16, 1970.

New York: Solomon R. Guggenheim Museum. *Piet Mondrian 1872–1944 Centennial Exhibition.* 1971.

O'Doherty, Brian. "Inside the White Cube, Part III: Context as Content." *Artforum* XV, 3 (1976): 38–44.

Oud, J. J. P., and L. J. F. Wijsenbeek. *Mondriaan.* Zeist and Antwerp: W. de Haan, 1962.

Roth, Alfred. *Begegnung mit Pionieren: Le Corbusier, Piet Mondrian, Adolf Loos, Josef Hofmann, August Perret, Henry van de Velde.* Basel and Stuttgart: Birkhauser, 1973.

Saalborn, Louis. "Herinnering aan Mondriaan." *De Telegraaf*, March 17, 1955. Reprinted in *Nieuws van de Dag*, April 6, 1955. [Clippings in Rijksbureau voor Kunsthistorische Documentatie, The Hague.]

Saalborn, Louis. " 'Mondriaan zag in mij de schilder.' " *De Telegraaf*, March 12, 1955. [Clipping, courtesy Joop Joosten, Stedelijk Museum, Amsterdam.]

Seuphor, Michel. *Piet Mondrian: Life and Work.* New York: Harry N. Abrams, 1956.

Stuttgart: Staatsgalerie. *Mondrian: Zeichnungen, Aquarelle, New York Bilder.* December 6, 1980–February 15, 1981.

Toronto: Art Gallery of Toronto. *Piet Mondrian 1872–1944.* February 12–March 20, 1966.

Troy, Nancy J. "Mondrian's Designs for the *Salon de Madame B. . . , à Dresden.*" *Art Bulletin* 62 (1980): 640–647.

Troy, Nancy J. "Piet Mondrian's Atelier." *Arts Magazine* LIII, 4 (1978): 82–87.

Welsh, Robert P. "The Birth of De Stijl, Part I: Piet Mondrian. The Subject Matter of Abstraction." *Artforum* XI, 8 (1973): 50–53.

Washington, D. C.: National Gallery of Art. *Mondrian: The Diamond Compositions.* July 15–September 16, 1979.

10. Jacobus Johannes Pieter Oud

Badovici, Jean. "Entretiens sur l'architecture vivante: Les Possibilités architectoniques de demain." *L'Architecture Vivante* (spring and summer 1924): 29–32.

Baljeu, Joost. "De Stijl toen en J. J. P. Oud nu." *Forum* 15 (1961): 285–288.

Colenbrander, Bernard. "Nawoord." In J. J. P. Oud, *Nieuwe Bouwkunst in Holland en Europa (1935).* Amsterdam: Van Gennep, 1981.

Doesburg, Theo van. "De Architect J. J. P. Oud 'voorganger' der 'kubisten' in de bouwkunst?" *De Bouwwereld* XXI, 30 (1922):1.

Form V, 5–6 [special Oud number] (1951).

Gratama, Jan. "Vacantiehuis te Noordwijkerhout." *Klei* 12 (1920): 13–19.

The Hague: Gemeentemuseum. *Herdenkingstentoonstelling J. J. P. Oud.* February 11–March 8, 1964.

Hitchcock, Henry-Russell. *J. J. P. Oud.* Paris: Editions "Cahiers d'art," 1931.

London: Architectural Association. *The Original Drawings of J. J. P. Oud 1890–1963.* n.d. [1978]

Munich: Die Neue Sammlung. *J. J. P. Oud: Bauten 1906–1963.* July 12–August 22, 1965.

Oud, J. J. P. "Bouwkunst en kubisme." *De Bouwwereld* 21 (1922): 245.

Oud, J. J. P. "Bouwkunst en normalisatie bij den massabouw." *De Stijl* I, 7 (1918) (I: 77–79). Translation: *Lotus International* 16 (1977): 53–54.

Oud, J. J. P. "Een Café aan het Caland-plein te Rotterdam." *Bouwkundig Weekblad* 46 (1925): 397–400.

Oud, J. J. P. "Gemeentelijke Volks-woningen, Polder 'Spangen', Rotterdam." *Bouwkundig Weekblad* 41 (1920): 219–222.

Oud, J. J. P. *Holländische Architektur.* 1926. Reprinted: Mainz: Florian Kupferberg, 1976.

Oud, J. J. P. *Mein Weg in "De Stijl".* Tr. Kees and Erica de Wit. The Hague: Nijgh & Van Ditmar, 1961.

Oud, J. J. P. "Over Cubisme, Futurisme, moderne bouwkunst, enz." *Bouwkundig Weekblad* 37 (1916): 156–157.

Oud, J. J. P. "Over de toekomstige bouwkunst en hare architectonische moge-lijkheden." *Bouwkundig Weekblad* 42 (1921): 147–160.

Oud, J. J. P. *Ter Wille van een levende bouwkunst.* The Hague and Rotterdam: Nijgh & van Ditmar, n.d.

Oud, J. J. P. "Uitweiding bij eenige afbeel-dingen." *Bouwkundig Weekblad* 43 (1922): 418–424.

Oud, J. J. P. "Verbouwing huize 'Alle-gonda' Katwijk aan Zee." *Bouwkundig Weekblad* 39 (1918): 29–30.

Polano, Sergio. "Notes on Oud: Re-reading the Documents." *Lotus International* 16 (1977): 42–54.

Rotterdam: Museum Boymans. *J. J. P. Oud Architect.* February 1951.

Stamm, Gunther. "Het Jeugdwerk van de architect J. J. P. Oud 1906–1917." *Muse-umjournaal* 22 (1977): 260–266.

Tallahassee: Florida State University Art Gallery. *The Architecture of J. J. P. Oud 1906–1963.* May 4–25, 1978.

Wiekart, K. *J. J. P. Oud.* Tr. C. de Dood. Amsterdam: J. M. Meulenhoff, 1965.

11. Gerrit Rietveld

Amsterdam: Stedelijk Museum. *G. Rietveld, Architect.* November 20, 1971–January 9, 1972.

Badovici, Jean. "Entretiens sur l'architecture vivante: Maison à Utrecht (Pays-Bas) par T. Schräder et G. Rietveld." *L'Architecture Vivante* (autumn and winter 1925): 28–29.

Baroni, Daniele. *Gerrit Thomas Rietveld Furniture.* London: Academy Editions, 1978.

Bless, Frits. *Rietveld 1888–1964: Een Bio-grafie.* Amsterdam: Bert Bakker; Baarn: Erven Thomas Rap, 1982.

Boeken, A. "Bij een paar afbeeldingen van werk van G. Rietveld." *Bouwkundig Weekblad* 45 (1924): 381–382.

Boeken, A. "Eenige opmerkingen over de winkelverbouwing Kalverstraat 107 te Amsterdam; arch. G. Rietveld." *Bouwkundig Weekblad* 43 (1922): 476–478.

Boeken, A. "De winkelpui Kalverstraat 107 te Amsterdam; arch. G. Rietveld." *Bouwkundig Weekblad* 45 (1923): 455.

Brown, Theodore M. *The Work of G. Rietveld, Architect.* Utrecht: A. W. Bruna & Zoon, 1958.

Brown, Theodore M. "Rietveld's Egocentric Vision." *Journal of the Society of Architectural Historians* 24 (1965): 292–296.

Buffinga, A. *G. Th. Rietveld.* Tr. Ina Rike. Amsterdam: Meulenhoff, 1971.

D[oesburg], T[heo] v[an]. "Aanteekening bij een leunstoel van Rietveld." *De Stijl* II, 11 (1919) (I: 439).

Kroon, Ben. "De Geboorte van het Riet-veld Schröder Huis." *De Tijd*, November 29, 1974: 24–26. [Clipping in Rijksbureau voor Kunsthistorische Documentatie, The Hague.]

Mulder, Bertus, and Gerrit Jan de Rook, eds. *Rietveld Schröder Huis 1925–1975*. Utrecht and Antwerp: A. W. Bruna & Zoon, 1975.

Rietveld, Gerrit. "In Memoriam Architect P. J. Klaarhamer." *Bouwkundig Weekblad 72* (1954):101.

Rietveld, Gerrit. *Rietveld, 1924: Schröder Huis*. Amsterdam: De Jong, 1963.

Rooy, Max van. "Rietveld Schröder Huis." *De Vorm: Maandblad voor Vormgeving* 3, June–July, 1975. [Clipping in Rijksbureau voor Kunsthistorische Documentatie, The Hague.]

12. Georges Vantongerloo

Bilcke, Maurits. "Pionier zonder weerklank in Vlaanderen: Georges Vantongerloo is eenzaam begraven." *De Standaard*, October 19, 1965: 8. [Clipping in Rijksbureau voor Kunsthistorische Documentatie, The Hague.]

Cologne: Galerie Gmurzynska. *De Boeck, Joostens, Servranckx, Vantongerloo: Pioniere der abstrakten Kunst Belgien, 1915–60.* November 11, 1976–February, 1977.

Staber, Margit. "Georges Vantongerloo." *Art International* X, 2 (1966): 13–15.

Staber, Margit. "Georges Vantongerloo: Mathematics, Nature and Art." *Studio International* CLXXXVII, 965 (1974): 181–184.

Vantongerloo, Georges. *L'Art et son avenir*. Antwerp: De Sikkel; Santpoort: C. A. Mees, 1924.

Vantongerloo, Georges. "L'Art plastique $[L^2] = [s]$ Néo-Plasticisme." *Vouloir* 22 (1926).

Vantongerloo, Georges. *Paintings, Sculptures, Reflections*. New York: Wittenborn, Schultz, 1948.

Washington, D.C. : Corcoran Gallery of Art. *Georges Vantongerloo*. April 22–June 17, 1980.

13. Jan Wils

B[randes], C[o]. "Eenige gedachten over de komende architectuur, in verband met het werk van Jan Wils." *Levende Kunst* I (1918): 129–139.

Dongen, F. van. "Jan Wils en de Stijl-groep: 'De Stijl was Katalysator.' " *Cobouw*, June 16, 1967, 27–28. [Clipping in Rijksbureau voor Kunsthistorische Documentatie, The Hague.]

H[off], [Rob] V[an] 't. "Het Hotel café-restaurant 'De Dubbele Sleutel' (eerste gedeeltelijke verbouwing) te Woerden, Bijlage

10: Architect Jan Wils." *De Stijl* II, 5 (1918): 58–59 (I: 318–321).

Wils, Jan. *Jan Wils*. Genf: Verlag "Meister der Baukunst," 1930.

Wils, Jan. "De Nieuwe bouwkunst." *De Stijl* I, 4 (1918): 31–33 (I: 47–49).

Wils, Jan. "De Nieuwe bouwkunst. Bij het werk van Frank Lloyd Wright." *Levende Kunst* I (1918): 209–219.

Wils, Jan. *De Sierende elementen van de bouwkunst*. Rotterdam: W. L. & J. Brusse, 1923.

E. Piet Zwart

Bool, Flip. "Naar aanleiding van de tentoonstelling van Piet Zwart." *Museumjournaal* 18 (1973): 97–101.

Brandes, Co. "Meubelen en kunsthandwerk van den heer en mevr. Zwart." *Levende Kunst* I (1918): 14.

Broos, Kees. "Piet Zwart." *Studio International* CLXXXV, 954 (1973): 176–180.

The Hague: Gemeentemuseum. *Piet Zwart*. 1973.

Müller, Fridolin, ed. *Piet Zwart*. London: Alec Tiranti, 1968.

Zwart, Piet. "Kunst op de Jaarbeurs." *Elsevier's Geïllustreerd Maandschrift* 29 (1919): 316–320.

VI. Belgium

A. General Works

Antwerp: Hessenhuis. *De Eerste abstrakten in Belgie: Hulde aan de pioniers.* October 10–November 8, 1959.

Delahaut, Jo. "Les premiers abstraits belges." *Bulletin des Musées Royaux des Beaux-Arts de Belgique, Bruxelles* 8 (1959): 231–250.

Goyens de Heusch, Serge. *"7 Arts" Bruxelles 1922–1929: Un front de jeunesse pour la révolution artistique.* Ministère de la culture française de Belgique, 1976.

Mertens, Phil. " 'Het Overzicht' en de plaats van de vlaamse kunst in het Europa van de jaren twintig." *Bulletin des Musées Royaux des Beaux-Arts de Belgique, Bruxelles* 13 (1963): 67–82.

B. Jozef Peeters

Antwerp: Galerij Jeanne Buytaert. *Hulde aan Jozef Peeters.* October 7–November 10, 1972.

Antwerp: Internationaal Cultureel Centrum. *Jozef Peeters (1895–1960).* July 1–September 3, 1978.

Devoghelaere, Edmond. "Abstrakt Jozef Peeters schilderde in eigen huis: Antwerpen onbewust in bezit van kunstschatten." *Gazet van Antwerpen,* July 15, 1970: 10. [Clipping in Rijksbureau voor Kunsthistorische Documentatie, The Hague.]

C. Henry van de Velde

Brussels: Palais des Beaux-Arts. *Henry van de Velde: 1863–1957.* December 13–29, 1963.

Hagen: Karl-Ernst-Osthaus Museum. *Der junge Van de Velde und sein Kreis, 1883–1893.* October 18–November 22, 1959.

Hammacher, Abraham M. *Le Monde de Henry van de Velde.* Tr. Claudine Lemaire. Paris: Hachette, 1967.

Joosten, Joop. "Henry van de Velde en Nederland, 1892–1902: De Belgische Art Nouveau en de Nederlandse Nieuwe Kunst." *Cahiers Henry van de Velde* 12–13 (1974): 6–48.

Sembach, Klaus Jürgen. "Van de Velde's nalatenschap." *Museumjournaal* 8 (1962): 8–14.

van de Velde, Henry. "Henry van de Velde: Extracts from his Memoirs, 1891–1901." Tr. P. Morton Shand. *Architectural Review* CXII, 669 (1952): 143–155.

van de Velde, Henry. *Formules d'une esthétique moderne.* Brussels: L'Equerre, 1923.

van de Velde, Henry. *Geschichte meines Lebens.* Munich: R. Piper, 1962.

VII. France

A. General Works

Gee, Malcolm. "The Avant-Garde, Order and the Art Market, 1916–23." *Art History* II, 1 (1979): 95–106.

Miner, Laura. Abstract Art in Paris. M. A. report, Courtauld Institute of Art, University of London, 1971.

Mourey, Gabriel. *Essai sur l'art décoratif français moderne.* Paris: Librarie Ollendorf, 1921.

Rob Mallet-Stevens, architecte. Brussels: Editions des Archives d'Architecture Moderne, 1980.

B. The Maison Cubiste

Cabanne, Pierre. *The Brothers Duchamp: Jacques Villon, Raymond Duchamp-Villon, Marcel Duchamp.* Tr. Helga and Dinah Harrison. Boston: New York Graphic Society, 1975.

Hamilton, George Heard, and William Agee. *Raymond Duchamp-Villon 1876–1918.* New York: Walker, 1967.

Kahn, Gustave. "La Réalisation d'un ensemble d'architecture et de décoration." *L'Art Décoratif* 29 (1913): 89–102.

Malone, Margaret M. André Mare and the 1912 Maison Cubiste. M.A. thesis, University of Texas, Austin, 1980.

■ *239*

Pach, Walter. *Raymond Duchamp-Villon, sculpteur (1876–1918)*. Paris: Povolozky, 1924.

Pach, Walter. *A Sculptor's Architecture*. New York: Association of American Painters and Sculptors, 1913.

Pradel, Marie-Noëlle. "La Maison cubiste en 1912." *Art de France* 1 (1961): 177–186.

Roches, Fernand. "Le Salon d'Automne de 1912." *L'Art Décoratif* 28 (1912): 281–328.

Vera, André. "Le Nouveau style." *L'Art Décoratif* 22 (1912): 21–32.

C. Félix Del Marle

Bresle, Valentin. *Del Marle peintre*. Paris: Mercure Universel, 1933.

Del Marle, Félix. "L'Art d'aujourd'hui." *Vouloir* 18 (1926).

Del Marle, Félix. "La Couleur dans l'espace." *Art d'Aujourd'hui* II, 5 (1951):11–13.

Del Marle, Félix. "Enquête sur l'architecture: Comment concevez-vous l'aménagement d'un hôtel particulier dans une grande ville?" *Bulletin de l'Effort Moderne* 35 (1927): 12–13.

Del Marle, Félix. "Esprit collectif—culture prolétarienne." *Vouloir* 23 (1926).

Del Marle, Félix. "Métal." *Bulletin de l'Effort Moderne* 39 (1927): 14.

Del Marle, Félix. "Le Suprématisme—le Néoplasticisme—le Constructivisme." *Art d'Aujourd'hui* II, 3 (1951): 8–11.

Del Marle, Félix. "Vers un art prolétarien," *Vouloir* 22 (1926).

Gindertael, R. V. "Del Marle." *Art d'Aujourd'hui* III, 1 (1951): 6.

Milan: Galleria Milano. *Félix Del Marle: Disegni dal 1912 al 1949*. April 7–May 14, 1976.

Paris: Galerie Jean Chauvelin. *Félix del Marle*. June 6–July 15, 1973.

Reviol, P. "Félix Del Marle 1889–1952: La Couleur au service de l'homme." *Art d'Aujourd'hui* IV, 1 (1953): opposite 1–2.

D. Jean Gorin

Amsterdam: Stedelijk Museum. *Jean Gorin: Schilderijen, reliëfs en ruimtelijke constructies*. September 30–November 5, 1967.

Bois, Yve-Alain, ed. "Lettres à Jean Gorin." *Macula* 2 (1977): 117–139.

Gorin, Jean. "Plastique constructive de l'espace-temps architecture." *Leonardo* 2 (1969): 231–238.

Gorin, Jean. "La Fonction plastique dans l'architecture future." *Revue Cercle et Carré* (1930). Reprinted: Paris: Jean-Michel Place, 1977.

Gorin, Jean. "Is a Synthesis of the Plastic Arts Possible?" *The Structurist* 2 (1961): 32–33.

Nantes: Musée des Beaux-Arts. *Jean Gorin*. February 27–March 30, 1965.

Paris: Centre National d'Art Contemporain. *Jean Gorin: Peintures, reliefs, constructions dans l'espace, documents, 1922–1968*. 1969.

Paris: Centre National d'Art et de Culture Georges Pompidou. Musée National d'Art Moderne. *Dessins de Jean Gorin*. October 12–December 12, 1977.

Sartoris, Alberto. *Jean Gorin*. Venice: Alfieri, 1975.

E. Le Corbusier

Boesiger, W., and O. Stonorov, eds. *Le Corbusier et Pierre Jeanneret: Oeuvre complète de 1910–1929*. Fourth edition. Zurich: Erlenbach, 1946.

Boudon, Philippe. *Lived-in Architecture: Le Corbusier's Pessac Revisited.* Tr. Gerald Onn. Cambridge, Mass.: MIT Press, 1972.

Gabetti, Roberto and Carlo Olmo. *Le Corbusier e "l'Esprit Nouveau".* Turin: Giulio Einaudi, 1975.

Jeanneret, Ch.-E. *Étude sur le mouvement d'art décoratif en Allemagne.* 1912. Reprinted: New York: Da Capo, 1968.

Jencks, Charles. *Le Corbusier and the Tragic View of Architecture.* Cambridge, Mass.: Harvard University Press, 1973.

Le Corbusier. "L'Exposition de l'École Spéciale d'Architecture." *L'Esprit Nouveau* 23 (1924).

Le Corbusier. "Pessac." *L'Architecture Vivante* (autumn and winter 1927): 29–30.

Le Corbusier. *Towards a New Architecture.* Tr. Frederick T. Etchells. London, 1923. Reprinted: New York: Praeger, 1960.

Moos, Stanislaus von. *Le Corbusier: Elements of a Synthesis.* Cambridge, Mass.: MIT Press, 1979.

Stewart, David Butler. Le Corbusier's Theory of Architecture and 'L'Esprit Nouveau.' " Ph.D. diss. Courtauld Institute of Art, University of London, 1972.

Taylor, Brian Brace. *Le Corbusier et Pessac, 1914–1918.* Two volumes. Paris: Fondation Le Corbusier, 1972.

F. Fernand Léger

Green, Christopher. *Léger and the Avant-Garde.* New Haven: Yale University Press, 1976.

Green, Christopher. "Painting for the Corbusian Home: Fernand Léger's Architectural Paintings, 1924–26." *Studio International* CXC, 977 (1975): 103–107.

Léger, Fernand. "L'Architecture polychrome." *L'Architecture Vivante* (autumn and winter 1924): 21–22.

Léger, Fernand. *Functions of Painting.* Translated by Alexandra Anderson; edited by Edward F. Fry. New York: Viking, 1973.

Robinson, Duncan. "Fernand Léger and the International Style." *Form* 1 (1966): 16–18.

A. General Works

Adriani, Gotz, ed. *Hannah Höch.* Cologne: DuMont, 1980.

Anderson, David Christian. Architecture as a Means for Social Change in Germany 1918–1933. Ph.D. diss., University of Minnesota, 1968.

Behne, Adolf. "Kroniek van de Duitsche bouwkunst, sedert het einde van de oorlog." *Bouwkundig Weekblad* 44 (1923): 29–34, 193–196, 211–212.

Berlin: Akademie der Kunste. *Herman Muthesius 1861–1927.* December 11, 1977–January 22, 1978.

Berlin: Europa Center. *Erich Buchholz.* December 1966.

Berlin: Galerie Daedalus. *Erich Buchholz.* May 15–June 20, 1971.

Blaser, Werner. *Mies van der Rohe,* revised edition. New York: Praeger, 1972.

Bletter, Rosemarie Haag. Bruno Taut and Paul Scheerbart's Vision: Utopian Aspects of German Expressionist Architecture. Ph.D. diss. Columbia University, 1973.

Campbell, Joan. *The German Werkbund: The Politics of Reform in the Applied Arts.* Princeton University Press, 1978.

■ *242*

Deutsche Werkbund. *Bau und Wohnung: Die Bauten der Weissenhof Siedlung in Stuttgart errichtet 1927 nach Vorslagen des Deutschen Werkbundes im Auftrag der Stadt Stuttgart und im Rahmen der Werkbund Ausstellung "Die Wohnung"*. Stuttgart: F. Wedekind, 1927.

Graeff, Werner. "Concerning the So-Called G. Group." *Art Journal* 23 (1964): 280–282.

Joedicke, Jürgen, and Christian Plath. *Die Weissenhofsiedlung*. Stuttgart: Karl Krämer, 1977.

Junghanns, Kurt. *Bruno Taut, 1880–1938*. Berlin: Henschelverlag Kunst und Gesellschaft, 1971.

Kliemann, Helga. *Die Novembergruppe*. Berlin: Gebr. Mann, 1969.

Lindahl, Göran. "Von der Zukunftskathedrale bis zur Wohnmaschine: Deutsche Architektur und Architekturdebatte nach dem ersten Weltkriege." In *Idea and Form* (Figura: Uppsala Studies in the History of Art, New Series, volume I, 1959), pp. 226–282.

Ohff, Heinz. *Hannah Höch*. Berlin: Gebr. Mann, 1968.

Posener, Julius. *Anfange des Funktionalismus: Von Arts and Crafts zum Deutschen Werkbund*. Berlin: Ullstein, 1964.

Posener, Julius. "Herman Muthesius." *Architects' Year Book* 10 (1962): 45–61.

B. The Bauhaus

Atlanta: High Museum of Art. *Bauhaus Color*. January 31–March 14, 1976.

Bayer, Herbert, Walter Gropius, and Ise Gropius. *Bauhaus 1919–1928*. Teufen: Arthur Niggli und Willi Verkauf, 1955.

Behne, Adolf. "Bauhaus-Resume." *Bouwkundig Weekblad* 44 (1923): 446–448.

Gilbert, Basil. "The Reflected Light Compositions of Ludwig Hirschfeld-Mack." *Form* 2 (1966):10–14.

Humblet, Claudine. *Le Bauhaus*. Lausanne: L'Age d'Homme, 1980.

Naylor, Gillian. *The Bauhaus*. New York: Dutton, 1968.

Neumann, Eckhard, ed. *Bauhaus and Bauhaus People*. New York: Van Nostrand Reinhold, 1970.

Röhl, Peter. "Die Ausmalung des Residenz-Theaters in Weimar." *De Stijl* IV, 9 (1921): 143–144 (II: 114).

Röhl, Peter. "Der Beginn und die Entwicklung des Stil's 1921 in Weimar." *De Stijl* VII, 79–84 (1927): 103–105 (II: 580–581).

Schreyer, Lothar. *Erinnerungen an Sturm und Bauhaus*. Munich: Albert Langen-Georg Mueller, 1956.

Wingler, Hans M. *Bauhaus: Weimar, Dessau, Berlin, Chicago*. Cambridge, Mass.: MIT Press, 1969.

C. Walter Gropius

Fitch, James Martin. *Walter Gropius*. New York: G. Braziller, 1960.

Franciscono, Marcel. *Walter Gropius and the Creation of the Bauhaus in Weimar: The Ideals and Artistic Theories of its Founding Years*. Urbana: University of Illinois Press, 1971.

Gropius, Walter. *The New Architecture and the Bauhaus*. Tr. P. Morton Shand. New York: Museum of Modern Art, 1937.

D. Adolf Loos

Banham, Reyner. "Ornament and Crime: The Decisive Contribution of Adolf Loos." *Architectural Review* CXXI, 721 (1957): 85–88.

Münz, Ludwig, and Gustav Künstler. *Adolf Loos: Pioneer of Modern Architecture.* Tr. Harold Meek. New York: Praeger, 1966.

Rykwert, Joseph. "Adolf Loos: The New Vision." *Studio International* CLXXXVI, 957 (1973):17–21.

E. Sophie Taeuber-Arp

New York: Museum of Modern Art. *Sophie Taeuber-Arp.* September 16–November 29, 1981.

Paris: Musée National d'Art Moderne. *Sophie Taeuber-Arp.* April 24–June 22, 1964.

Schmidt, Georg, ed. *Sophie Taeuber-Arp.* Basel: Holbein, 1948.

Staber, Margit. *Sophie Taeuber-Arp.* Tr. Eric Schaer. Lausanne: Rencontre, 1970.

Winterthur: Kunstmuseum. *Sophie Taeuber-Arp.* January 23–March 6, 1977.

Wolters, Théo. "Décorations d'intérieurs créées et realisées à Strasbourg par Sophie Täuber et Jean Arp." *L'Information de l'Histoire de l'Art* 15 (1970): 73–81.

A. General Works

Birnholz, Alan D. "Forms, Angles, and Corners: On Meaning in Russian Avant-Garde Art." *Art International* LI, 6 (1977): 101–109.

Boeken, A. "Iets over de Constructivisten op de Eerste Russische Kunsttentoonstelling." *Bouwkundig Weekblad* 44 (1923): 213–214.

Bowlt, John. "Concepts of Color and the Soviet Avant-Garde." *The Structurist* 13–14 (1973–1974): 21–29.

Bowlt, John. *Russian Art of the Avant-Garde.* New York: Viking, 1976.

Cologne: Galerie Gmurzynska-Bargera. *Von der Fläche zum Raum: Russland 1916–24.* September 18–November 1974.

Gray, Camilla. *The Great Experiment: Russian Art, 1863–1922.* New York: Harry N. Abrams, 1962.

Paris: Galerie Jean Chauvelin. *Suprématisme.* October 25–December 25, 1977.

Steneberg, Eberhard. *Russische Kunst Berlin 1919–1932.* Berlin: Gebr. Mann, 1969.

Stockholm: Moderna Museet. *Tatlin.* July–September, 1968.

B. El Lissitzky

Birnholz, Alan C. *El Lissitzky.* Ph.D. diss., Yale University, 1973.

Birnholz, Alan C. "El Lissitzky and the Jewish Tradition." *Studio International* CLXXXVI, 959 (1973): 130–136.

Birnholz, Alan C. "El Lissitzky, The Avant-Garde and the Russian Revolution." *Artforum* XI, 1 (1972): 70–76.

Birnholz, Alan C. "El Lissitzky's Writings on Art." *Studio International* CLXXXIII, 942 (1972): 90–92.

Birnholz, Alan C. "For the New in Art: El Lissitzky's Prouns." *Artforum* VIII, 2 (1969): 65–70; 3 (1969): 68–73.

Birnholz, Alan C. "Time and Space in the Art and Thought of El Lissitzky." *The Structurist* 15–16 (1975–1976): 89–96.

Cologne: Galerie Gmurzynska. *El Lissitzky.* April 9–June, 1976.

Dorner, Alexander. "Die neue Raumvorstellung in der bildenden Kunst." *Museum der Gegenwart* 2 (1931–1932): 30–37.

Eindhoven: Stedelijk Van Abbemuseum. *El Lissitzky.* December 3, 1965–January 16, 1966.

Frampton, Kenneth. "The Work and Influence of El Lissitzky." *Architects' Year Book* 12 (1968): 253–268.

Helms, Dietrich. "The 1920s in Hanover." Tr. Lydia Dorner. *Art Journal* 22 (1963): 140–145.

Kallai, E. "El Lissitzky." *Der Cicerone* 16 (1924): 1058–1063.

Lissitzky, El. "Proun." *De Stijl* V, 6 (1922): 81–85 (II: 223–225).

Lissitzky, El. "Prounen Raum." *G* 1 (1923).

Lissitzky, El. *Russia: An Architecture for World Revolution*. Tr. Eric Dluhosch. Cambridge, Mass.: MIT Press, 1970.

Lissitzky, El, and Hans Arp. *Die Kunstismen 1914–1924*. Rentsch: Erlenbach, 1925.

Lissitzky-Küppers, Sophie. *El Lissitzky: Life, Letters, Texts*. Tr. Helene Aldwinckle and Mary Whittall. Greenwich, Conn.: New York Graphic Society, 1968.

Lissitzky-Küppers, Sophie. "Die ersten Jahre." In *Wegbereiter zur modernen Kunst—50 Jahre Kestner-Gesellschaft*, edited by Wieland Schmied (Hanover: Schmidt-Kuster-Gundt, 1967).

Lissitzky-Küppers, Sophie, and Jen Lissitzky, eds. *El Lissitzky, Proun und Wolkenbugel: Schriften, Briefe, Dokumente*. Dresden: V. E. B., 1977.

List of Figures

16 Vilmos Huszar, *Color Applications, Bedroom of Bruynzeel House, Voorburg,* 1918–19. Photograph: Nederlands Documentatiecentrum voor de Bouwkunst, Amsterdam. *42*

17 Vilmos Huszar, *Color Applications, Bedroom of Bruynzeel House, Voorburg,* 1918–19. Photograph: Nederlands Documentatiecentrum voor de Bouwkunst, Amsterdam. *42*

18 Theo van Doesburg, *Example of Coloristic Composition in an Interior,* 1919. Illustrated in *De Stijl* III, 12 (1920), plate XIV. *44*

19 Vilmos Huszar, *Spatial Color Composition for Bedroom of Bruynzeel House, Voorburg,* 1918. Illustrated in *Levende Kunst* 2 (1919): 59. *45*

20 Vilmos Huszar, *Spatial Color Composition in Gray, Brugman House, The Hague,* 1924. Photograph: Department of Applied Arts, Stedelijk Museum, Amsterdam. *48*

21 Music/Sitting Room, Brugman House, The Hague, before 1924. Photograph: Department of Applied Arts, Stedelijk Museum, Amsterdam. *48*

22 Vilmos Huszar, *Design for Spatial Color Composition in Gray,* 1924. Photograph: Department of Applied Arts, Stedelijk Museum, Amsterdam. *49*

23 Piet Zwart, *First Design for Celluloid Manufacturer's Stand, Annual Industrial Fair, Utrecht,* 1921, pencil and watercolor on paper, 23 × 28.5 cm. Gemeentemuseum, The Hague. *52*

24 Piet Zwart and Vilmos Huszar, *Design for Chair,* 1920, ink and watercolor on paper, 51.3 × 34 cm. Gemeentemuseum, The Hague. *53*

25 Piet Zwart, *Second Design for Celluloid Manufacturer's Stand, Annual Industrial Fair, Utrecht,* 1921, pencil and crayon on paper, 21.5 × 33.4 cm. Gemeentemuseum, The Hague. *54*

26 Piet Zwart, *Design for an Interior,* 1913, ink, watercolor and conté crayon on paper, 31.9 × 30.9 cm. Gemeentemuseum, The Hague. *55*

27 P. J. C. Klaarhamer and Bart van der Leck, *Bruynzeel Stand, Annual Industrial Fair, Utrecht,* 1919. Illustrated in *Elsevier's Geïllustreerd Maandschrift* 29 (1919): 317. *57*

28 Piet Zwart, *Design for Interior, Cramer House, The Hague,* 1921, pencil and colored pencil on paper, 23.2 × 31 cm. Gemeentemuseum, The Hague. *57*

29 Piet Zwart, *Design for Interior, Dans Instituut Gaillard-Jorissen, The Hague,* 1921, pencil and watercolor on paper, 18.5 × 47.2 cm. Nederlands Documentatiecentrum voor de Bouwkunst, Amsterdam. *58*

30 Piet Zwart, *Definitive Design for Celluloid Manufacturer's Stand, Annual Industrial Fair, Utrecht,* 1921, pencil and watercolor on paper, 45.7 × 64.7 cm. Gemeentemuseum, The Hague. *59, 88*

31 Theo van Doesburg, *Color Design for Flower Room, de Noailles Villa, Hyères,* 1924–25, ink, pencil, and gouache on paper, edges 54 × 61 cm. Stedelijk Van Abbemuseum, Eindhoven. *61*

32 Courtyard, 26 rue du Départ, Paris. Photograph: Rijksbureau voor Kunsthistorische Documentatie, The Hague. *67*

33 Piet Mondrian in his studio, Paris. *De Stijl* VI, 6–7 (1924): 86. *69*

34 Theo van Doesburg, *Color Design for Ground-Floor Interiors, Spangen Housing Blocks IV and V (detail),* 1920, pencil and gouache on paper, 26.5 × 100 cm. Collection of Mrs. Annie Oud-Dinaux, Wassenaar. *74*

35 Léonce Rosenberg, *Sketch for Private Villa, Ground Floor,* 1921, ink on paper, 22 × 17.3 cm. Fondation Custodia, Institut Néerlandais, Paris. *78*

36 Léonce Rosenberg, *Sketch for Private Villa, First and Second Floors (recto),* 1921, ink on paper, 22 × 17.3 cm. Fondation Custodia, Institut Néerlandais, Paris. *79*

37 Léonce Rosenberg, *Sketch for Private Villa, Third Floor and Basement (verso)*, 1921, ink on paper, 22 × 17.3 cm. Fondation Custodia, Institut Néerlandais, Paris. *79*

38 Theo van Doesburg, *Color Design, Facade on Potgieterstraat, Spangen Housing Block VIII, Rotterdam*, 1921, ink and watercolor on paper, 15.7 × 25.5 cm. Fondation Custodia, Institut Néerlandais, Paris. *84, 89*

39 Theo van Doesburg, *Color Design, Spangen Housing Block VIII, Rotterdam*, 1921, ink and watercolor on paper, 35.5 × 53.2 cm. Fondation Custodia, Institut Néerlandais, Paris. *84, 89*

40 Theo van Doesburg, *Diagram of Color Scheme, Spangen Housing Block VIII, Rotterdam*, 1921, ink and watercolor on paper, 29 × 32.3 cm. Fondation Custodia, Institut Néerlandais, Paris. *85, 90*

41 Theo van Doesburg, *Color Design for Exterior of Middle-Class Housing, Drachten*, 1921, ink, pencil and gouache on paper, 30.2 × 70.5 cm. Collection of D. Rinsema, Meppel. *94, 155*

42 Theo van Doesburg, *Color Design for Exterior of Agricultural School, Drachten*, 1921, ink and watercolor on paper, 27.9 × 112.5 cm. Museum It Bleekerhûs, Drachten. *95, 156*

43 Theo van Doesburg, *Diagram of Color Scheme, Agricultural School, Drachten*, 1921, ink and watercolor on paper, 27.8 × 93 cm. Museum It Bleekerhûs, Drachten. *95, 156*

44 Cornelis van Eesteren, *Ground Plan of Amsterdam University Hall and Connecting Buildings*, 1922, pencil, ink and chalk on paper, 149 × 99 cm. Van Eesteren-Fluck & van Lohuizen Foundation, Amsterdam. *98*

45 Theo van Doesburg, *Study for a Composition*, 1923, gouache on paper mounted on board, 17 × 17 cm. Mc-Crory Corporation, New York. *100*

46 Theo van Doesburg, *Color Design for Amsterdam University Hall*, 1923, ink, tempera, and collage on paper, 63 × 145.5 cm. Van Eesteren-Fluck & van Lohuizen Foundation, Amsterdam. *101, 157*

47 Theo van Doesburg, *Color Design for Floor, Amsterdam University Hall*, 1923. Illustrated in *L'Architecture Vivante* (autumn 1925), plate 12. *102*

48 Theo van Doesburg, *Window for House at Maasdam*, 1917. Photograph: Van Doesburg Archive, Dienst Verspreide Rijkskollekties, The Hague. *102*

49 Theo van Doesburg, *Color Design for Amsterdam University Hall*, 1923, pencil, ink, and gouache on paper, 16.5 × 25 cm. Inv. no. AB5110, Dienst Verspreide Rijkskollekties, The Hague; Schenking van Moorsel. *104*

50 Theo van Doesburg, *Color Design for Amsterdam University Hall*, 1923, ink and gouache on paper mounted on cardboard, 7 × 32.5 cm. Inv. no. AB5112, Dienst Verspreide Rijkskollekties, The Hague, Schenking van Moorsel. *105, 157*

51 Cornelis van Eesteren (with Theo van Doesburg and Gerrit Rietveld), *Model, Private Villa, Paris*, 1923. Photograph: Van Doesburg Archive, Dienst Verspreide Rijkskollekties, The Hague. *107*

52 Theo van Doesburg, *Analysis of Architecture, Private House*, 1923, ink on paper, 55.7 × 59 cm. Van Eesteren-Fluck & van Lohuizen Foundation, Amsterdam. *108*

53 Theo van Doesburg, *Color Construction: Project for a Private House*, 1923, gouache and ink on paper, 57 × 57 cm. Museum of Modern Art, New York; Edgar Kaufmann, Jr., Fund. *109*

54 Cornelis van Eesteren and Theo van Doesburg, *Model, Private House*, 1923. Photograph: Van Doesburg Archive, Dienst Verspreide Rijkskollekties, The Hague. *111*

55 Cornelis van Eesteren and Theo van Doesburg, *Model, House of an Artist*, 1923. Photograph: Van Doesburg Archive, Dienst Verspreide Rijkskollekties, The Hague. *113*

56 Gerrit Rietveld, *Schröder House, Utrecht*, 1924. Photograph: collection of Mrs. Truus Schröder, Utrecht. *118*

■ *250*

82 Hans Arp, *Caveau-Dancing, Café Aubette, Strasbourg*, 1926–28. Photograph: Documentation Archive, Musées Municipaux, Strasbourg. *170*

83 Sophie Taeuber-Arp, *Tea Room, Café Aubette, Strasbourg*, 1926–28. Photograph: Documentation Archive, Musées Municipaux, Strasbourg. *171*

84 Theo van Doesburg, *Cinema-Dance Hall, Café Aubette, Strasbourg*, 1926–28. Photograph: Documentation Archive, Musées Municipaux, Strasbourg. *172*

85 Le Corbusier, *Pavillon de l'Esprit Nouveau, Paris*, 1925. Illustrated in W. Boesiger and O. Stonorov, *Le Corbusier et Pierre Jeanneret: Oeuvre complète. 1910–1929* (1974), p. 101. *177*

86 Georg Muche, *Haus am Horn, Weimar*, 1923. Photograph: Bauhaus-Archiv, Berlin. *179*

87 J. J. P. Oud, *Housing Block, Weissenhof Colony, Stuttgart*, 1927. Photograph: Nederlands Documentatiecentrum voor de Bouwkunst, Amsterdam. *181*

88 Piet Mondrian, *Studio of the Artist, New York*, 1944. Photograph: collection of Harry Holtzman, Lyme, Connecticut. *190*

Certain photographs and permissions were obtained from sources not indicated in the above list. These sources follow.

Annely Juda Fine Art, London: figure 11

Architectural Publishers Artemis, Zurich: figure 85

Beeldrecht, Amsterdam/VAGA, New York, copyright 1982: figures 61–63, 67

Fogg Art Museum, Cambridge, Massachusetts: figure 78

B. Frequin, Voorburg: figures 7, 24, 26, 28, 62

Gemeentemuseum, The Hague: figures 41, 70–72, 79

Frank den Oudsten, Amsterdam: figures 3–5, 15–17, 27, 29, 42, 43, 56, 81

Pace Gallery, New York: figures 68, 69

Prentenkabinet, Kunsthistorisch Instituut der Rijksuniversiteit, Leiden: figures 12, 19

Stedelijk Museum, Amsterdam: figures 18, 33, 47, 58

F. Tas, Antwerp: figure 77

N. Troy, Baltimore: figures 34, 59–60

Walker Art Center, Minneapolis: figure 64

Index

DATE DUE

SEP 4 '83			
JAN 24 '84			
FEB 6 '84			
GAYLORD			PRINTED IN U.S.A.